IN THE LAND OF KING ABDULAZIZ

IN THE LAND OF KING ABDULAZIZ

THE SIRDAR IKBAL ALI SHAH

The Scheherazade Foundation

The Scheherazade Foundation CIC
85 Great Portland Street
London
W1W 7LT
United Kingdom
www.SF.Charity
info@SF.Charity

First published, by The Scheherazade Foundation CIC, 2023

IN THE LAND OF KING ABDULAZIZ

The various authors listed above assert the right to be identified as the Authors of the Work in accordance with the Copyright, Designs and Patents Act 1988. A CIP catalogue record for this title is available from the British Library.

ISBN 978-1-915311-14-6

All rights reserved. No part of this publication may be reproduced, stored in a retrieval system, or transmitted, in any form or by any means, electronic, mechanical, photocopying, recording or otherwise, without the prior written permission of the publisher.

This book is sold subject to the condition that it shall not, by way of trade or otherwise, be lent, re-sold, hired out or otherwise circulated without the publisher's prior consent in any form of binding or cover other than that in which it is published and without a similar condition including this condition being imposed on the subsequent purchaser.

Editor's Note

THE MANUSCRIPT OF this anthology was prepared by The Sirdar Ikbal Ali Shah in the months before his death, at Tangier, Morocco, in the winter of 1969.

A collection of the most extraordinary journeys, which took place over a period of forty years – it is a time-capsule of culture and lore: a reflection of remarkable people, places and encounters.

Although compiled more than fifty years ago, the manuscript has only been made ready for publication now – in the hope that its contents will be informative on the faith and culture of Arabia, and on the traditions and the reign of His Majesty King Abdulaziz.

Contents

Introduction	1
His Majesty King Abdulaziz	7
Pre-Islamic Arabia	38
The Holy City	59
The Land & the People	74
The Building of The Kaaba	79
Mecca & Beyond	87
Government of Pre-Islamic Mecca	108
Perils of Man-Smuggling	128
The Birth of The Prophet	145
Merchant & Citizen	160
The Golden Caravan	168
In the Veiled Mecca	174
The First Voice of Truth	179
The Quraish	187
The Persecution & Ascension	196
The Flight	209
Entry Into Medina	227
The Establishment of Other Islamic Injunctions	238
The Battle of Badr	242
Battle of Ohud	249
The Expansion of Islam	256
Journey To Mecca	265
A Fight to The Finish	271

The Conquest of Mecca	277
The Battle of Hunain & Beyond	282
The Life of The Prophet	290
The Prophet: The Last Phase	300
The Cardinal Practices of Islam	305
The Qur'an	315
The Spirit of Islamic Ideals	322
Mecca Revisited	330

Foreword

ONE OF THE greatest sorrows of my life is that I never got to know my paternal grandfather, The Sirdar Ikbal Ali Shah.

In November 1969, he was knocked down in Tangier, by a reversing Coca-Cola truck. The end of his life came outside Mimi Calpe, the villa in which he lived, perched as it was on rue de la Plage, a steep lane running down to the port.

Three years before that, I had been born, and was brought to visit by my doting parents in the summer before the accident. I may have only been a toddler then, but I can clearly remember the fragrant scent of orange blossom in the garden, and the outline of my grandfather silhouetted by the afternoon sun, pipe in hand.

The 'motor accident', as it was referred to in The London Times, robbed me not only of a grandfather, but of the most intoxicating people imaginable – a man of mystery and of myth... the kind of character anyone with a lust for adventure would have wished to know.

Hailing from another time, in which courtesies were de rigueur, my grandfather insisted that at least one of his various hereditary titles was employed when addressing him.

Indeed, it was with amusement that, while reading a collection of George Orwell's letters, I stumbled upon a caution to staff at the wartime BBC, not to fail in using his title, as it infuriated him.

In childhood, I once plucked up courage to admonish my father for being so serious with us. Regarding me with a look of pure consternation, he rose up over me like a stormcloud and yelled:

'You think I'm serious! You think I'm serious! You have no idea! I wasn't permitted to sit down in the presence of *my* father!'

I've always been fascinated by the man who carried our name two generations before. Within the family, everyone referred to him as 'Chiefie', a sobriquet born during his travels in South America – and one that evidently pleased him.

In the decades I have trod this earth, I've done all I could to piece together the riddles and the mysteries of the enigmatic, inimitable Sirdar Ikbal Ali Shah.

Almost everyone who knew him first-hand has now left us. Yet, such was my obsession, that I made sure to hunt down everyone who had encountered him face-to-face before they departed.

They included doddering old colonial officials living in the home counties, and old university dons, fellow adventurers and writers, army men, and even spies.

Some of them revealed a great wealth of information about his preoccupations and eccentricities, while others proffered no more than a fleeting detail, or two.

I've written elsewhere of my grandfather's greatest friend, a Foreign Office agent ordered to follow him for years in a game of international cat and mouse. His name

FOREWORD

was Laurence Fredric Rushbrook Williams, and he was as unusual a gentleman as one could ever hope discover.

My grandfather was a man who walked with all men – equally comfortable in both Occident and Orient, just as he was at a desert caravanserai or in a palace. Through the blood in his veins, he was linked to the royal families of Arabia, and had known their leading members all his life.

One winter evening, while clustered around the log fire in the drawing room of our home in England, my father was poking the embers, his memories stirred no doubt by the blaze of flames.

All of a sudden, he said:

'No one ever impressed him like King Abdulaziz.'

'No one ever impressed *who*, Baba?'

My father frowned, as if realizing he'd given voice to inner thoughts.

'No one ever impressed Chiefie, like King Abdulaziz.'

I sat there, the fire's glow warming me, waiting for the next line of conversation, or for an anecdote to begin.

But, it didn't.

Instead, my father, laid the poker down, and strode purposefully out of the room. I continued to sit there, staring into the fire. I'd all but forgotten the random mention of King Abdulaziz, when my father returned. In his hand was a 'misbah', a string of ninety-nine green glass beads.

'These were presented to my father by King Abdulaziz', he said, 'when they first met back in 1926. He gave them to me when I was about your age, and now I'm giving them to you.'

As I write this, misbah sits before me on my desk.

I know it by sight as well as I know anything in the world, but it's the sound the little glass beads make when clattering together that touches me most.

When I run them through my fingers, the little glass beads sound as they have always done – like the sound of the waves crashing on rocks.

My grandfather had known King Abdulaziz even before the Kingdom of Saudi Arabia had been formed. Both men were descended directly from The Prophet's line, each was pious, courteous, and utterly sensible to the needs of others.

When I first discovered the manuscript of this book in my grandfather's papers, I was affected by the respect 'Chiefie' held for the great desert King. It was though he understood in that the right man was ruling in the right place, and at the right time.

Almost a century has elapsed since they both sat together for the first time.

And, in that span of years, Saudi Arabia has developed from a fledgling state to a vibrant, modern nation – one built on the rock-solid foundation stone hewn by King Abdulaziz Ibn Saud.

Tahir Shah
Riyadh, 2023

Introduction

HINDSIGHT CAN BE the finest teacher and the dearest friend.

To take full advantage of it, one of course requires certain tools. In my case, these are a pot of sweet mint tea, a deep leather armchair, and a pair of bedroom slippers that may appear rather tattered to others, but are much-cherished by the feet that wear them.

Casting my mind back through many decades, and over so many journeys in the Land of His Majesty King Abdulaziz, I can only feel blessed.

Blessed at having experienced a realm touched by dreamlike wonder, and the values our Muslim Faith calls for us to live by – tolerance, honour, chivalry, selflessness, and charity.

And, blessed, too, at having encountered a great deal of unusual people and places on my travels between the Red Sea and the Persian Gulf. People and places that not only inspire, but also elevate by their association the humblest pilgrim.

As I sit here in my favourite armchair, pouring a second cup of tea, I am reminded by perhaps the finest and most illuminating conversation of my life.

To make a conversation great, it must contain three things:

The first is a tranquil setting.

The second is a sagacious interlocutor.

The third, and most important, is a subject of extraordinary interest.

The conversation of which I speak took place in the summer of 1951, while I was visiting Saudi Arabia on a private sojourn, to perform the Haj, and to visit various acquaintances. No stranger to the royal courts of the Arab world, I had been honoured to meet His Majesty King Abdulaziz on several occasions, even before he had founded the Kingdom that now bears his family's name.

The King received me in the Majlis of the Murabba Palace in Riyadh, the adobe walls of the elegant structure a reminder of the simplicity by which he lives. Although we are both more ripened by adventure since we sat together the first time, back in 1926, His Majesty was as sharp-minded as I had ever seen him.

When one is in the company of a truly great man, one finds oneself overcome with a sense of formidable fortune. In the years that had slipped by since our first rendezvous, His Majesty had forged a nation, and had brought together a great many warring tribes. Such an achievement would have been regarded as a magnificent contribution to human society by any other – but to King Abdulaziz, the greatest Arab Statesman of his time, it was only the beginning.

The monarch of Saudi Arabia appears to have glimpsed the future – a time when peace is not the rare delight, but

INTRODUCTION

rather a normality ... a time in which every man, woman, and child within the Kingdom has food in their bellies, and lives beneath a sky tempered by a lasting and benevolent peace.

Once I had presented my credentials, and greeted the King, kissing his hand, and honouring him as a servant, I renewed the pledge that I had made as a younger man:

Namely that throughout my life I would stand as a defender of Saudi Arabia, a protector and champion to the realm which His Majesty King Abdulaziz had shaped from ancient conurbations, caravanserais, and desert sands.

As we sat together in the Majlis, two pious men of the same unerring Faith – yet one a King and the other a humble professor – we spoke of the march of progress, of existing challenges, and of days to come.

His Majesty explained how the search for water had in recent years led to the discovery of what some had termed 'black gold' – oil, and yet more oil. 'It has brought change', he told me, the words uttered with grave reflection.

'The wealth has made it possible to improve facilities for pilgrims at the Holy Shrine, as well as modernising a great many other things.'

Pausing, His Majesty seemed to stare into space, his eyes weakened by life and adventure.

'In order for our nation to move towards its destiny', he said at length, 'we would be wise to learn from the treasuries of tales passed on by travellers beneath the desert stars.'

As folklore has always been a great interest of mine, I begged His Majesty to elucidate.

'The tales that we heard spoken and respoken in our youth, and which lie dormant within us, have the capacity to show us the way forwards. They hold lessons and they contain wisdom. Tell and retell stories, like "Antar wa Abla", and we may be reminded of how to be.'

It was at this point, following another lengthy pause, I spoke the name of 'Alf Layla wa Layla', the greatest treasury if tales ever compiled – 'The Thousand and One Nights'.

The King peered in my direction, a smile roaming over his lips.

'They call it 'The *Arabian* Nights', he said.

Awkwardly, I offered the following:

'But, Your Majesty, as I understand it, many of the tales did not actually come from Arabia.'

King Abdulaziz, a man more sage than any I have ever encountered, responded:

'Stories do not merely contain wisdom', he said. 'They *are* wisdom. Who is to say where they come from? Tales found in one place surely come from another – as, with time, and the right conditions, they will venture beyond the most distant horizon.'

An official approached the chair in which the King was seated, with a document for him to sign. When he was gone, I prepared to beg my leave, for I sensed that my audience was nearing an end.

But, His Majesty uttered something that will live with me until my dying day:

'The stories of which we speak – the kind spoken daily across this Kingdom and across the world', he said, 'are what is needed for wisdom to be passed on. They are the

INTRODUCTION

way by which future generations will learn and prosper, and will not forget where they came from.'

An hour later, I was sitting in a small café in Riyadh, a tiny porcelain cup of coffee perched on upturned fingertips. Despite the relentless summer heat, I had become accustomed to the temperature from decades spent in Oriental climes.

As I savoured the delicate flavour of cardamom, the waiter sashayed up.

'I surmise from your accent that you are not from our Kingdom', he said.

'Indeed, my brother', I responded. 'The blood in my veins is Afghan, yet beyond that I am a modest servant of God.'

The waiter dabbed the side of his face with a rag clutched in his hand.

'And, when you return to your own land', he said, 'what will you tell of what you found here?'

I thought for a moment, and replied:

'My dear brother, when I leave the hallowed realm of Arabia, I shall tell others of the precious moments passed in the Holy City, and I shall tell, too, of the wisdom of King Abdulaziz.'

Written by my hand in the course of forty years or more, the pieces presented in this manuscript are a reflection of the course of my life, just as they are an echo of the Arabian Peninsula.

Perhaps one day in the future, the collection will be submitted for publication – but I shall leave it for others to attend to. As I sit here in my favourite leather armchair, a pot of sweet mint tea within easy reach, and a tattered old pair of slippers on my feet, my first interest is to entertain myself with memories that, by the grace of Allah, I have been privileged to experience.

Ikbal Ali Shah
Tangier, 1968

His Majesty King Abdulaziz

IN THE EAST, life leapfrogs.

One cannot just say of a man, as one can of so many prominent figures of the Occident, he did this and that; he started with a bicycle and now pounds metal into motorcars, so many to the hour; or that he ran away before the mast and ended as a belted earl.

Life there is much more complex. One is an individual, yet one is of a family; one of a clan; one of a tribe. To understand why 'A' suddenly goes berserk and shoots 'B', one has probably to go back two generations; to understand why 'C', obviously a poor man, is one to whom respect and veneration is shown by those with many of this world's goods, one has to trace back to his grandfather or great-grandfather, who was probably the paramount sheikh of the district.

The East does not forget.

Tomorrow is tomorrow only when it comes, and Qur'an is not of much consequence. It is yesterday and the day before that which really matters, because then that happened; before then, that happened, and it gives one so much to talk about. With the past one need never be at a loss for material.

There, in them, are to be found good stories and much laughter, or, if the mood so takes one, ample material for a quarrel or a fight. There is plenty for argument, much for philosophy, and even more for moralizing. The past is magnificent, for it feeds the present, and every man's mind dwells in the past out in the desert and in the barren hills of Arabia.

This clan has a feud with that, and this tribe with that. Men must know each other and each other's business. There is not that sense of privacy which obtains in the West, and the knowing of each other's business is second cousin to meddling in it. Consequently, it frequently happens, when one sets out to tell the story of an individual, many other personages have necessarily to intrude if the tale is to have full measure. It is for this reason, and this reason alone, that so much Oriental history is fatiguing to Western readers, who become confused with the many figures darting on and off the printed page.

In order to tell of Feisal, Hussein, Sharif of Mecca, crept on to the canvas. This was not unnatural, as Hussein was his father. General Allenby also intruded, and here he had right, for Feisal and Allenby were partners in a wonderful cause. The ubiquitous Hussein must also appear in the story of Ibn Saud, if only because Hussein ruled Mecca before Mecca and Arabia became Saudi by force of arms. No story of the Aga Khan would be complete without some historical background, and the same can be said of most of us, the Orientals.

In the case of Ibn Saud, one must necessarily hark back a little, because when Ibn Saud took the Hejaz, he merely reclaimed it for his clan. His forebears had been there before as rulers, and when he took Mecca, he was merely completing a cycle.

Hussein, Sharif of Mecca through the efforts of the valiant Feisal, became paramount, and King of the Hejaz. When Sultan Vahededdin, the Caliph, fled from his Constantinople palace by a side door and boarded the British warship *Malaya*, he sent out a cry for protection and assistance to Hussein in Mecca. The cry went unheeded, and Vahededdin was first to find asylum in Malta and later in San Remo, where he shortly died. Hussein, King of the Hejaz, now a much older man, and his soul still bleeding because his son's efforts and not his own had added to his lustre, had reason in ignoring the departing and deposed Caliph. He saw himself, firmly entrenched as he was in Mecca, as the leader of the Muslim world. He wanted to have himself proclaimed Caliph, but the Muslims of Egypt, India and elsewhere were far from willing to endorse his candidature.

Hussein was not only old and senile, but he had now grown querulous, and though having sons who could have relieved him of much responsibility, he preferred to retain every administrative string in his hands. This did not make for efficiency or goodwill, for Hussein had completely failed to grasp the change in Arabia's outlook.

As Caliph, it was necessary for him to be orthodox, and a Sunni before everything else, but his misty mind wavered between Sunni and Shia, and in such a manner that he found the respect or support of neither. He was a pathetic old man, groping in the shadows for the indefinable, and that which he sought had only the substance of a blacker shadow.

In this, he was unconsciously preparing the way for the Wahhabis, of whom Ibn Saud is the head – puritanical, almost fanatical, Sunnis, who place the most rigid interpretation upon the teachings of The Prophet, and allow no elasticity. Abdulaziz Ibn Saud relieved Hussein of his charge in good time and secured the Hejaz.

Prior to his seizing the Hijaz, he had been living in comparative poverty, and he had had his fill of adventures. He was a fully-fledged warrior before he came to try conclusions with Hussein, for his life had been spent in fighting, either against the Turks or against his own near relations.

The story of Abdulaziz Ibn Saud is one of almost continual conflict, and, like so many others, has its genesis in the bygone generations.

His Majesty King Abdulaziz Ibn Saud is the fifth direct descendant of the famous Emir Mohmed ibn Saud, the founder of the Al Saud dynasty, and a most powerful supporter of the teachings of Sheikh Mohamed Ibn Abdul Wahhab. Emir Mohamed Ibn Saud can be said to be the first of the great Wahhabis, and the one who really gave form and name to the sect.

The Al Saud of those days had their seat at Diriyya, and though they sat firmly in the saddle, around them was a chaotic jumble of warring emirates, and their borders saw continuous disorder and bitter fighting. The pious Sheikh Mohamed ibn Abdul Wahhab arrived in Diriyya in 1736, preaching as he went a great religious revival which would exorcise from misrepresented Islam much that savoured of excess and licence.

He preached austerity of outlook and rugged simplicity. He imbued the Emir Mohamed ibn Saud with his fiery ideals, and the great religious revival was launched. From that moment Ibn Saud increased his sphere of influence. Forty years later, his grandson, yet another Ibn Saud, was also to complete what his grandfather had begun by establishing himself as the ruler of a vast kingdom which spread from the borders of Syria m the north to a point near Saana in the south, and from the shore of Oman to the Red Sea.

The Al Saud dynasty was now a power, and with the new order peace and tranquillity replaced the disorder of former days, justice and the principle of equality being firmly established. Islam became the law of the country, and everyone bowed to the law.

The Al Saud were too successful. This new kingdom stood out as a beacon amidst the floundering mismanagement of the Ottomans, and the Sultan in Constantinople took umbrage. He had reason for his regal displeasure, for his Viceroy, Mohamed Ali, in Egypt was speedily forgetting that he was a vassal of the Porte and was becoming embarrassingly regal.

In the vast solitude of the Yeldiz Kiosk, the Sultan conceived a scheme which would dispose of both upstarts. He sent his ambassadors with his own particular brand of vitriolic scandal, and these whispered into the ears of Mohamed Ali in Egypt and Ibn Saud in Arabia. Soon there was dissension, and speedily a war, which progressed with varying fortune for five years.

Then the Egyptian Khedive had Ibn Saud prisoner, and he razed Diriyya to the ground. Even the date palms were hewn down, and the Wahhabis were scattered. This was in 1815. The Turks resumed their political sway over Arabia, and disorder and chaos returned, the Porte maintaining its hold by exercising the same tactics which had set Arabia and Egypt at war. Every family of note had a feud with its neighbour, and the Turkish governors were deemed to have been lacking in enterprise if there was not turmoil between families. The members of Al Saud did not escape, and their quarrels were many and serious. In 1818, the head of the clan settled in Riyadh, but in 1831 he was assassinated by one of his cousins.

The murderer did not live long, as Feisal – not our Feisal, but grandfather of he who is now Ibn Saud – avenged the death of his father in true Arab style and declared himself Emir. This was in 1832. He had to fight hard to preserve his title, and he was still embroiled in war when Khorshid Pasha, the famous Egyptian general of the time, arrived on the scene and carried him off as prisoner to Egypt, placing one of Feisal's cousins in the Emirate.

Seven years Feisal remained as prisoner in Cairo, and then he escaped. He travelled back to Nejd and declared war. He was eminently successful, and he succeeded in large measure in restoring the ancient glories of the Al Saud. The Hejaz, however, proved too much for him, and he was unable to add it to his domains. To this day, his reign is remembered in the Arabian Peninsula for its prosperity, affluence, and general justice.

On the death of Feisal, disputes broke out between his two sons, and the Ottoman Government seized the opportunity once more to intervene, and by 1888 Nejd had once again been completely reconquered. The father of Abdulaziz Ibn Saud found life in Riyadh under the tutelage of a Turkish governor completely insupportable, and as the Sultan refused to elevate him to a governorship, he retired, with many members of his family, to Kuwait.

This was in 1889, and a desperate effort was made by the clan to exist on the sixty pounds a month allowed by the Turkish Government. Some months the money arrived, but more often its glitter attracted the attention of some Turkish official en route, and the Al Saud were compelled to restrain their appetites with true Arab fortitude.

King Abdulaziz Ibn Saud was then nine years of age, and his principal memories were of privation and suffering. Misfortune hung at the heels of his father, but the fire and youthful ardour of Ibn Saud could not be repressed.

In 1895, when Ibn Saud was fifteen years of age, one Sheikh Mobarak al Sabah rose to eminence in Kuwait, and the inevitable dispute arose between this new ruler and the Porte. War followed, and it wafted into the nostrils of young Ibn Saud. Despite his years, he proclaimed himself an ally of the Sheikh against the Porte, found men to follow him, and took Riyadh. However, he and his few desperadoes could not hold it.

Two years later – in 1901 – he was to make a dramatic entry into the town. He had forty men of the Al Saud, and a motley gathering of Bedouins, and he pitted this negligible force against the might of the Ottoman Empire.

He decided to make his attempt upon Riyadh from the south. Not unnaturally, the Porte heard of his activities, and a much-tried Sultan stopped the allowance which had been made to his clan, and also forbade any of the neighbouring tribesmen, whom through he had to pass, to furnish him with provisions. Learning of this, the Bedouins in Ibn Saud's train incontinently departed, and he was left with his forty Al Saud stalwarts who were pledged to follow him to the death.

Ibn Saud's father and other notables did their utmost to dissuade Ibn Saud from his mad quest, for how, they asked, could he hope to overcome the might of the Turkish Empire? Ibn Saud held on, but the situation was desperate. He bethought himself of a desperate plan.

Fired by his resolve, twenty more men of Al Saud joined his party, bringing his total forces up to sixty, and he and his men arrived at the outskirts of Riyadh soon after dusk. In the groves around the town, and carefully concealed, he left thirty-three of his men under the command of his brother Mohamed.

He selected a palm tree and cut it down, leaning it against the wall of the town he hoped to conquer. Leaving twenty men to guard his way, he, with the remaining six, shinned up the palm and into Riyadh.

So far, and so good, but seven men grouped inside a town's wall do not necessarily indicate that the town has fallen. Actually, Ibn Saud's six stalwarts looked around them in the darkness and felt rather ridiculous; but they had not reckoned with Ibn Saud. They saw him make his way up the street and stop at the house next door to that occupied by the Turkish Governor, Emir Ajlan. He went to the door and knocked, and a woman's voice answered querulously, 'Who's there?'

'Servants of Emir Ajlan, the Governor, come to summon your husband', remarked Ibn Saud with due meekness.

'Begone, wretch!' screamed the woman. 'You must be robber, or you would not knock at doors at this time of night.'

'My good woman', returned Ibn Saud, 'I assure you that my intentions are not evil, and I am bound to advise you that unless your husband appears before the Governor without delay nothing will save him from death in the morning.'

Hearing this unwelcome news, the husband himself came to the door to inquire the meaning of the din. The husband was an old servant of the Sauds, and Ibn Saud was aware of this when he knocked. As soon as he appeared at the doorway, Ibn Saud whispered in the man's ear, bidding him be quiet. Pushing him over the threshold, he followed him within. There he was recognized, the woman crying: 'Our master, Abdulaziz Ibn Saud!'

Ibn Saud was surely master, for he gathered the women together, locked them in an adjoining room, and bade them preserve silence. Remarkably enough, they obeyed him. With the husband, he climbed the garden wall and into the governor's house, where, coming upon two sentries asleep on their bedding, he rolled them up in their rugs and, tied and helpless, locked them also in a room. This done, he summoned all who had been left outside the walls and began to search the rooms of the governor's house, one by one.

In the course of his search, he came across a bed which he was certain contained the elusive governor. He shone a lantern in the face of the sleeper, and it was the governor's wife! She recognized him and smiled.

'What do you want?' she whispered.

'Ajlan!' he said shortly and undiplomatically.

The woman became the counsellor and the mother. 'My son', she urged, do not gamble with your life. Flee while the night is still young, or you are dead.'

'I have not come for advice', returned Ibn Saud, with that grim pertinacity of the Wahhabi, 'but to learn when Ajlan emerges from the inner palace.'

'An hour after sunrise', Ajlan's wife replied, equally shortly, for she was a woman with a grievance against her husband, and she, too, suffered from a sense of disappointment.

Not to be taken by surprise, Ibn Saud collected the rest of the women and shut them in with Ajlan's wife and took final counsel with his men. Except for their quiet whisperings, absolute silence reigned over Riyadh on this memorable night.

At last came the impatiently awaited false dawn, and then the magnificent sun of the Arabian day.

Slowly the doors of the inner palace were forced outward, and slaves emerged, leading horses, the favourite charges of Ajlan the governor. Shortly afterwards Ajlan himself appeared, and he fondled the horses as was his wont. Secreted behind a wall were Ibn Saud and ten men. They rushed at Ajlan and his guards first: then they started firing.

The governor's slaves and guards had been taken by surprise, but now they recovered their senses and fired upon these interlopers. Excited heads appeared at the palace windows, and a heavy fusillade was let loose, which killed two of Ibn Saud's men, severely wounded four, and compelled the rest to break cover and retreat.

The Governor, meanwhile, whose wound was a flesh one, and of little consequence, was gradually overpowering the youthful Ibn Saud, but his cousin Abdullah rushed to the rescue, and with a shot fired at close quarters, laid Ajlan lifeless.

Observing this, the remainder of the Wahhabis opened a heavy fire, and believing that it was engaged by a large and superior force, the garrison capitulated on condition that lives were spared.

By noon, Ibn Saud had been proclaimed ruler of Riyadh, and he had accomplished his object with sixty men – twenty of whom were never called up.

He had sufficient good sense to realize that he could not hold the town, for the Porte was beating up strong forces against him, so after imposing his will upon the inhabitants and organizing a garrison of sorts, he left Riyadh with a relative in charge as Governor. Wherever he went he proclaimed himself ruler, but he never remained in one place long enough to be overtaken by the Ottoman army now pursuing him. He took al Kharj, and eventually all the south of Nejd. He set his face northward and dominated the north of Nejd. Then, deeming himself strong enough, in 1905 he turned on the Sultan's still faintly pursuing army and effectively disposed of it.

Ibn Saud was now a force and was too near Mecca for the peace of mind of Hussein, and, in 1907, Ibn Saud found himself attacked on three sides. His cousins in al Hariq in the south still cherished the blood feud and marched against him. The Turks attacked him in Kassim, and Hussein, Sharif of Mecca, joined in. Ibn Saud refused to be daunted. He attacked the Turks first and routed them. He returned their camels, on condition that they marched either toward Baghdad or Medina, and kept on marching. Having disposed of the Turks, he turned his attention to his cousins and, having trounced them in their turn, forgave them, and his treatment was both generous and indulgent. There remained Hussein, but having heard of the defeat of the Turks and the cousins, Mecca's Sharif made off and was well within the security of the Hejaz before he could be attacked.

Ibn Saud was pious, but he was also an opportunist. In 1913, when the Turks had sustained yet another reverse in the Balkan War, he took advantage of the chaotic conditions which obtained and annexed el Hasa and el Katif. He took the Turkish garrisons prisoner, but he refused to emulate the tactics of the Porte. There was no throat-slitting, and the garrisons were allowed to return to Turkey by sea with their guns and ammunition.

In 1921 he captured Hayil, the seat of the powerful al Rashid, and put finish to the rule of this famous house in Nejd. The members of the al Rashid family were conveyed to Riyadh, where they remain to this day in honourable and comfortable retirement.

In 1924 Ibn Saud opened his campaign for the conquest of Hejaz. In a year, he was master of the country, and in 1927 he proclaimed himself King of the Hejaz and of Nejd. Thus, it was that modern Saudi Arabia came into being.

For a quarter of a century, Abdulaziz Ibn Saud had devoted himself to war. During the first ten years of this deadly strife, he himself lived the life of a soldier on active service – an Arab soldier on active service, that is, which is something far different to that expected of the private in a Western army.

The Western soldier has to be fed at regular intervals. Long years of regularity in the West have evolved an eating and drinking complex. In many cases, the stomach acts as does a clock. It registers turbulence at certain hours and has to be quietened with sustenance. But that is not real hunger. The Arab soldier eats his fill when he can get it, and drinks at the same time. In the prime of his manhood, he eats less than that accorded a Westerner of advanced years, and his gastronomic occasions are extraordinary.

For ten years Ibn Saud dwelled in tents, moving from place to place, often as a fugitive, and frequently with a price on his head, sometimes eating, and more often going hungry. He flitted across the desert fastnesses, sometimes hunting, sometimes hunted. The soft downiness of beds knew him not. A hole scratched in the sand for his hip, and he had to be content, and was content, for in that position the sword comes readily to hand, and the soft drowsiness of sleep does not linger upon bruised and aching flesh.

The Ottoman Government was never enamoured of Al Saud, whom it strove to misrepresent in the eyes of the Muslim world, accusing the clan of introducing into Muslim thought matters that were outside The Qur'an. It made mischief between the clan and the Egyptians, split the community into warring factions, and did everything which a wily and subtle Porte could to bring about its extinction.

The gradual rise to power of the youthful descendant of the great Wahhabi Emir caused the Porte not a little uneasiness, and in Nejd the powerful al Rashid was constantly reinforced against Al Saud. The Sultan dreaded more than anything else the rise of a powerful Arab kingdom, for in this he saw the death-knell of his position as Caliph.

The conquest of el Hasa in 1913 brought Ibn Saud to the Persian Gulf, and it was here, discovering that he had many interests with the British, that he first established relations with them. Shortly after his conquest of Hejaz, he concluded a treaty of friendship with them, whereby he strengthened and consolidated the old ties, and further enhanced their purpose by establishing the first Saudi Arabian legation in London.

The dispute between Ibn Saud and the Sharif of Mecca dated back, as I have indicated, to the time when the religious programme of Sheikh Mohamed ibn Abdul Wahhab was launched under the auspices of the first Ibn Saud, whose influence thereby received a sudden impetus, and spread rapidly through Nejd. At that time, the influence of the Meccan Sharifs dominated the Hejaz, the Porte maintaining only nominal suzerainty. Alarmed at the rapid forward march of the Wahhabis, the Sharifs leagued themselves with other Emirs in Nejd, but this was not sufficient to hold the Wahhabis who, in 1803, were able to occupy Mecca.

During the Great War, Ibn Saud remained strictly neutral, but not so neutral that he was unable to prevent al Rashid rising to the assistance of the Turks against Hussein in Mecca. Ibn Saud was in full sympathy with the Arab revolt, and to a very large extent with Hussein himself. It is probable, if Hussein had been worthy of the position which Feisal won for him, and which he appropriated, Ibn Saud would never have marched against him. Letters exchanged between Ibn Saud and Hussein during the conduct of the Arab revolt show quite clearly that Al Saud was well disposed toward Mecca and entertained the liveliest feelings of respect and loyalty toward the House of The Prophet. Hussein, however, did not live up to expectations.

He had spent seventeen years in Constantinople as the Sultan's 'guest' before being appointed to the Sharifate, and the Arabs expected great things of him. He was fully cognizant of the sinister aims of Turkish policy toward the Arabs, and the Arabs looked to him to utilize his Constantinople experience and devote himself to a policy of unification. Turkish policy was always to split the Arabs and to turn tribe against tribe. With Hussein at Mecca, every Arab looked toward an era of peace and prosperity.

Hussein, however, had hardly settled in the saddle at Mecca before he began playing the old Turkish game. On the slightest pretext, or without pretext, he made war on his neighbours. It was open for Hussein, with his great experience, and with the undoubted gifts which were his in his earlier years, to make for himself a great Arab kingdom, for the Arabs were willing and, indeed, impatient.

In the dispute which rose between Ibn Saud and Hussein – a dispute which eventually meant war – the position of Great Britain was rendered especially delicate. She did her utmost to induce either side to compose its differences, and she worked hard for an understanding. If anyone was prepared to concede it was the 'fanatical' Wahhabi, and the aged Hussein it was who remained uncompromisingly hostile. Great Britain evolved many opportunities for a settlement of differences and throughout,

Ibn Saud displayed a willingness both to listen and be persuaded. At the last of the conferences – that arranged at Kuwait in 1923 – Hussein so forgot his Arabian courtesy as to neglect to send representatives.

With the almost inevitable disappearance of Hussein, and the rise of Ibn Saud, a new impetus was given to the idea of Arab nationality. Sufficient time has now passed for it to be evident that the old enmities and animosities of the desert are disappearing, and that a new order has come.

Perhaps the first real evidence of this was vouchsafed in the meeting between King Feisal of Iraq and Ibn Saud, when they amicably settled the disputes which were outstanding between them and concluded agreements which put an end to the old causes of friction. Since that historic meeting, one has been encouraged by other events in the hope that this new policy will prevail in all the new Arab kingdoms, replacing the old feuds, animosities, and dissension. Other instances of Ibn Saud's peace-loving endeavours can be cited by noting that he made friendly treaties with Transjordan, and even with Imam Yahya of Yemen – whose more than half of the territory was recently conquered by the Wahhabis, but given back – and a treaty of Islamic Brotherhood was signed; the sincerity of the spirit of which the Christian West might well copy.

Unity, co-operation and friendship is becoming increasingly the keynote of the relations between the Arabic-speaking States. Here again one is encouraged, because behind this movement there is no coercion. There is no central force dragooning the States into a common weal. The force which is there is mutual attraction, and the realization that in unity and peace amongst Arabs, of whatever nation, can best devote themselves to the uplift of Arabia and to regaining that place among the nations to which the ancient civilization and culture of the East entitles them.

Ibn Saud has a distaste for the stupidly ostentatious. His tastes are simple, and his ways are frugal. Notwithstanding his staunch Wahhabi upbringing, and the rigid Wahhabi code which colours his every action, Ibn Saud is a man of charm and of endearing personality. To find a Western counterpart, one has to look to the stern old Quakers under whose immense hats and unsmiling exterior was a force at once kindly, helpful and tolerant.

His is a personality which retains friendships. Although a Wahhabi, and one who places the strictest possible interpretation upon the Muslim code, he is sufficiently modern to allow electric lights and power into Mecca. He sees no reason why the Faithful should be denied light, or electric fans to cool their bodies after the rigours of the pilgrimage.

He is not an Eastern prince who looks upon the Infidel with distaste and suspicion. For both Sir Percy Cox and the late General Clayton, Ibn Saud cherishes the warmest affection and the most pleasant memories.

Tall and muscular, this man who now dominates Holy Mecca stands well over six feet and has broad shoulders to carry off his height. His favourite pastimes are hunting and riding – pastimes in which he indulges whenever his State duties will permit. This Napoleon of the Desert – Feisal was never that; he is an accomplished marksman and swordsman, yet he is no tyrant. In war there were no half-way measures, but prisoners were prisoners and human, and not cattle to be led to the charnel house. In war a thruster and essentially a cavalryman, in peace he is unassuming. His manner is mild, and his address kindly. He has a lively sense of humour, and a great love of society and of men's companionship.

This Wahhabi warrior king rises an hour before dawn and reads The Qur'an until the Muezzin gives the call for the dawn prayer. After praying, he returns home to recite more verses from The Qur'an, as well as some of the traditions of the Holy Prophet. Then, after attending to urgent matters of state, he retires to his quarters to rest for a while, rising later to bathe, dress and break his fast.

Thereafter, he attends his Privy Council where important matters of state are discussed and instructions issued to the sheikhs and officials. Then he receives the sheikhs of the desert and tribal chiefs in private interview, listens to their plaints and their grievances, and discusses with them important questions of the moment.

These private interviews over, Ibn Saud repairs to his General Council, where anyone who desires word with the king has already preceded him. Then there is lunch, and a short siesta, and the observance of the noon prayer.

Again, the Privy Council meets, when matters discussed in the morning come again under review. This Council is terminated when the king leaves for the afternoon prayer, after the recitation of which Ibn Saud is free to receive his brothers and his other relatives, who join in a homely family circle.

In the cool of the evening, he drives or rides, and after dinner once again holds a General Council where it is usual for someone to read for an hour and a half from one of the many books on the traditions of The Prophet, or Islamic literature.

When in Riyadh, Ibn Saud was wont to conclude his day with a special visit to his father and his other relatives, and only when he had concluded these ceremonial visits, did he retire to bed.

Every Friday Ibn Saud visits the graveyards of his family, and he never journeys to Medina without visiting the Holy Mausoleum over the grave of The Prophet, and those of The Prophet's Family.

In Mecca, he still upholds the customary evening visit to such relatives as may be in the Holy City.

Ibn Saud has diverse views on money and its value. In peace he is extremely generous, being wont to aver that money is only a means to an end and should be utilised for the benefit of humanity. 'What we sow, we shall reap', he exclaims as he gives freely, 'and if we sow in the days of peace and affluence, we shall reap the fruit of that good in the days of war and adversity.'

In war, Ibn Saud proved himself the reverse of generous and earned for himself the reputation of being more than economical. One of his maxims in war was: 'If you are generous to a Bedouin during war, he at once suspects you of weakness.'

In the Western conception the Arab, or the desert dweller, is so concerned with war, tribal feuds and vendettas that he has little time or inclination for the softer passions. Actually, of course, the Arab has a heart as have other humans, and Arab history abounds in instances of the dominating influence of women.

Ibn Saud's wife died in 1919, and he makes no secret of the sorrow which this occasioned him, or of the fact that he still mourns her passing. He treasures small articles which he has kept as souvenirs of a beautiful love – a love that is now reflected in Ibn Saud's affection for his late wife's two sons, Mohamed and Khalid.

Ibn Saud has confessed that his wife was the most charming, the wisest and the sweetest woman in Nejd. Even now he can scarcely restrain the tears which spring to his eyes when he speaks of her qualities.

In his dress, diet, and mode of living, Ibn Saud is obviously Wahhabi. He is a plain and simple man, who can scarcely be distinguished by his attire from any of his subjects. To his people he is not Ibn Saud, the king, but plain, unadorned Abdulaziz whom they can approach at all times to claim their rights and voice their grievances in language shorn of the ceremonial. It is to Abdulaziz that they appeal, and not to 'Sire' or 'Majesty.' At his table, the humblest Bedouin is as welcome as the son of the great sheikh or the sheikh himself.

An incident which occurred in 1928 comes to my memory. Ibn Saud was sitting at a window, and a Bedouin came and stood before it. The king asked him to move away.

The Bedouin turned and asked: 'O, Abdul Azeez, can you sit there and see me starve?'

'Come in and tell me how it is that you are starving', rejoined Ibn Saud.

The Bedouin accepted the invitation and explained to the king how he had arrived in Mecca at nine o'clock the night before, only to be informed when he called at the guesthouse that he was too late for dinner. He had replied that he would be content with any food that was at hand, but officialdom only repeated that the appointed hour for dinner had passed, and he was forced to go empty away.

Ibn Saud sprang to his feet as if stung by a puff adder on hearing these words and ordered the superintendent and the assistant superintendent of the guest house immediately to be brought before him. When they arrived, he demanded to know why it was that the man before him had not been given food, and they replied, taking refuge in their regulations, that the man had presented himself too late.

Ibn Saud demanded to be told why the man had not been furnished with dates or other such food if the cooked repast had been ended, and the officials fell silent.

Quivering with rage, for these servants had 'blacked' his face in outraging the laws of hospitality, Ibn Saud ordered them a beating, the first instalment of which he administered with his own cane. In addition, he suspended them from their duties for a fortnight, and only allowed them to resume their duties on their promise that in future no man should be refused food, no matter what hour of the day or night he made his request.

Ibn Saud brings the same simplicity into the political sphere, where he remains the practical man and without delusions, and one who bases his judgment on a true understanding of the realities of life. He has suffered himself and has lived the life of an ordinary man of the desert. There is no need, therefore, for the introspective. A wise statesman, and a capable leader, he abhors flattery and hypocrisy.

The men of Al Saud were the first to rise against the ineptness and the tyrannies of the Ottoman Empire. They were the first to draw their swords for an Arabian Arabia, and if one examines the tactics of Ibn Saud in his many engagements with the Turks, one can see this policy emerge time and again. He desired the removal of the Turks from the land of the Arabs; he did not want their death.

When he captured them, it was his invariable custom to bundle them off back to Turkey with a polite intimation to a furious Sultan that they were no longer *persona grata*. It was upon the fabric built by the clan of Al Saud that Hussein of Mecca erected his pyramid of hope when the Arab revolt proper broke out, but it required Ibn Saud himself to complete the work of a bungler. It was Ibn Saud who reached the ideal. It was Ibn Saud who first achieved an Arab State completely independent of any other State or Power. When the Saudi Legation was opened in London, the Arab nation, for the first time in modern history, had achieved real diplomatic representation.

Also, it was the lone hand of Ibn Saud which played the greatest part in the building of modern Arabia outside of Iraq. He took from modern progress and modern thought as much as was compatible and consistent with his strict Islamic principles, the interests of his Faith, and those of the country which he had welded together from many diverse fragments.

This great task of blending the ancient and modern was by no means easy of accomplishment, and, indeed, it is impossible for anyone who has not a deep insight into Arab mentality and Arab conservatism, to realise the immense difficulties which Ibn Saud encountered. Always did he lay himself open to the criticism that he was departing from the ways of his fathers, and it was his upholding of the ancient tradition that constituted his principal hold upon a people always ready to be noisy and turbulent once their conservatism was menaced or attacked.

The abolition of the customary annual celebrations of Ibn Saud's anniversary of accession provides an illuminating case in point.

The religious luminaries of Nejd, and with them those of the Hejaz, passed a resolution in which they declared these annual celebrations to be an unnecessary function, adding that true Muslims knew only two festivals in their calendar. The annual celebration of the King's accession they characterised as a European custom and not an Arabic or Muslim one. Accordingly, they wrote to Ibn Saud, and on these grounds asked him to discontinue the practice.

Ibn Saud might very easily have replied that the religious luminaries were stepping beyond their province and were impinging upon his preserves as the ruler. Instead, he gave one an insight into his greatness, for he saw that the celebrations did not affect anyone but himself, and he bowed to the decision.

In reply, he gave the following quotation from The Qur'an:

'Oh, Lord, I have sinned against myself, and if thou forgivest me not, and hast not mercy on me, I shall surely be among the losers.'

He proceeded:

'Whatever good I have done is surely due to God's guidance, and whatever bad I have done is surely my own fault and Satan's influence. I do not exculpate myself; one is being perpetually prompted to evil.'

A very different stand he took when these same religious luminaries opposed the installation of wireless telegraphy and the introduction of the modern sciences into Mecca. There he met their opposition with a stern refusal, and plainly told them that there is nothing in the religion of Islam that could justify their attitude of antagonism to improvement in communications or to scientific advance.

Thirty-five years ago, Arabia was nominally divided between three ruling families – the Sharifs ruling the Hejaz, al Rashid over most of Nejd, and the greater part of the Arabian Peninsula, and al Sabah over the remainder. There was perpetual disorder, and chaos was the one static rule. The tribesmen warred one against the other, exploiting the jealousies of the Emirs, and persuading each in turn that excesses and misdeeds had been committed in their service and to embarrass one of a rival ruling house. All commerce and all caravans were completely at the mercy of the Bedouins, who knew no law but that of rapine and plunder. The Bedouin would spare no one, not even the Arabs they plundered, the Turks or their soldiers, or even the Emirs and their men, who were often held to ransom.

Ibn Saud conquered one Emirate after another, and in the space of thirty years extended his beneficent rule over the whole of Nejd, el Hasa, al Katif, Assir and the Hejaz. His very success provided him with problems, and it is not uninteresting to see how he faced them.

The first to engage his attention was the age-old one of the Bedouin population of the deserts. Here, a large proportion had led a predatory life, moving constantly from one place to another, their direction dictated by pasturage and the presence of water. This element had no stake in the country. It had no interest in the static. Raids, plunder and highway robbery were its beginning and end. Here was a large section of the population whose activities, far from being productive to the State, and far from making for the common weal and common prosperity, was a constant deterrent to advance, and a black smudge on the deficit side of the ledger.

From a constructive point of view, an administrator had to regard it as a complete loss. Even from the military standpoint it was of little value, for the old Emirs had found it necessary to recruit their armies almost exclusively from the town dwellers. The desert Bedouin was a good fighter while the battle lasted and went well, but the battle won, the commander could only sit back impotent while the Bedouins pillaged the captured and the fallen. The Bedouin would only fight for material and immediate gain and would fight those who stood in his way or sought to deter him, with as much fiery enthusiasm as he had fought the enemy.

This lawless people had to be reclaimed to the State and taught the corporate sense. Others, in the past, had failed most abysmally in the task. He conceived the idea of erecting villages where water existed, and in these he 'planted' Bedouins, trusting to the ease with which they could secure water and the greater comfort of home life for them gradually to wear down the roving propensities. He appointed men of learning to teach the Bedouins their religion, of which they were woefully ignorant, and instruct them in their duties to God, their king, and their fellow men.

This policy has borne unexpected fruit, and it is hardly possible to recognise in the prosperous agriculturists of The Qur'an the predatory Bedouin of yesterday.

To a degree little short of extraordinary, these pillagers and cut-throats have become imbued with the principles of self-esteem, determination and courage, and they recognise the greatness of the Arab State in which they are an enthusiastic part of the whole. Land ownership and prosperity has brought out that national complex, and they are now as fearless of death in defending their own as they were in the robbing of others in the past. A Bedouin wife or mother, when bidding good-bye to the menfolk on their departure for war, says: 'May God unite us in Paradise.' These warriors now chant as they attack: 'The perfume of Paradise is in the air; hasten to it, all you who long for it!'

Uplifted by this spirit, they have become a force which cannot be denied. Tribes which from time immemorial had been in a condition of watchful hostility, are now united in brotherly love, so much so that they have earned the name of 'Ikhwan' or 'The Brethren.' Now they recall their former state with shame and disgust, calling it 'Aljahiliyya', or 'the state of ignorance', thus comparing it with the ancient 'Jahiliyya', preceding the mission of Mohamed The Prophet.

Another reform initiated by Ibn Saud was in the sphere of medicine, and to him belongs the credit of introducing modern medical treatment for the first time into Nejd. Against a terrific opposition, he imposed his will, and insisted upon vaccination as a protection against the ravages of smallpox. He insisted upon great changes in the sanitation of the towns and villages, and he instituted veterinary hospitals, hospitals for the people, dispensaries and clinics.

Neither did he neglect the intellectual welfare of his people, and to Ibn Saud is due the credit of introducing, again in the face of much opposition, modern scientific education side by side with religious education in the schools. In addition to increasing the number of the schools, and enlarging their scope and importing competent teachers from sister countries such as Egypt and Syria, it was found necessary in order to maintain a steady state of progress in this sphere, to send a number of youths to study abroad, in the hope that they might become proficient in modern science and art, and return to spread the light in their own country. There are now educational missions in Egypt, and the students are displaying an intelligent receptiveness.

Quite apart from settling the Bedouins at oases and at known wells, Ibn Saud initiated a careful survey of this country in order the more fully to tap its water supplies, his object being to bring as great an area as possible under cultivation. He realises that the old conception of wealth has gone. No longer can a man be judged by the number of camels he owns, for slowly but surely the ship of the desert is having to give way to the motor. The motor cannot go as long as a camel without liquid, but it can traverse distances which make the camel uneconomic. Discarded tyres are now taking the place of bleached camel bones along the pilgrims' way from Jeddah to Mecca.

Investigations have also been set on foot to ascertain the exact extent of the mineral wealth of the country, and the best means of developing it. Gold has already been found, and the presence of oil is more than suspected.

Ibn Saud's stern opposition to unyielding conservatism where that conservatism stood in the way of progress led to difficulties at first, but when the processes of modern science were to be observed in practice, much of the futility of the old was realised, and the forwardists carried the others in their enthusiastic urge. An example of this can be found in Ibn Saud's introduction of modern machinery for irrigation purposes. Almost with malice aforethought did he instal his imported machinery where the old-fashioned was doing its inefficient best, and the comparison was there for all to see and to convince. The cry for modern irrigation machinery went up all over Nejd and the Hejaz, and its use is spreading.

Similarly in respect to transport: it required a brave man to introduce the motorcar, but Ibn Saud put them on the road to Mecca. The streams of pilgrims, more accustomed to the speed and luxury of the motor than they were to the slow-moving camel, left no doubt as to their preference. Those who could secure the cars were wafted to the Holy City in hours, and soon the camel drivers were clamouring to be introduced to the mystery of the petrol engine. Now a fleet of motors is at the service of the pilgrims who proceed to the Hejaz from all parts of the Muslim world.

In order more rapidly to knit the various parts of the country together, Ibn Saud installed wireless stations in all outlying parts. Even Mecca itself possesses a powerful plant, though this was not accomplished without a stern struggle.

As with the first introduction of the motorcar, the people believed wireless to be the work of ungodly hands and to be closely associated with witchcraft. Faintly they could understand a voice being conveyed by wires, but wireless was beyond their comprehension. I do not altogether blame them, for with a mind profoundly unmechanical, it is beyond mine. Ibn Saud had to break down this prejudice in much the same manner that he overcame fear of the petrol engine.

I call to mind an interesting incident which attended the first introduction of motorcars. Ibn Saud left Riyadh with some of his retinue for a pleasure drive into the desert, where engine trouble developed, and the king was delayed. When Ibn Saud failed to return at his appointed time, the rumour went round that the infidel had sold the king a bewitched vehicle which had flown him away to the lands of the ungodly and delivered him a prisoner into their hands. In a short space of time, a large number of persons had armed themselves and left the town in the direction taken by the king, but they had not proceeded far when they saw Ibn Saud returning triumphantly in his chariot.

This incident reminds me rather forcibly of the Knights of Charlemagne who, filled with alarm when they saw Arab horsemen emerge from the interior of the magnificent clock of exquisite workmanship which Haroun al-Raschid at the zenith of Arab civilisation had presented to Charlemagne, believed that they were confronted with magic. They suspected the clock of evil influences and would have destroyed it. In the centuries which have passed, the West has become the custodian of 'magic', and the East that to be affrighted.

Great as these reforms have been, they are really as nothing when compared with the law, order and security which Ibn Saud has evolved throughout the length and breadth of his dominions. The wisdom of Ibn Saud lies in the fact that he was alive from the very beginning to the fundamental truth that until law and order were established, no reforms were possible.

Not only did Ibn Saud transform the Bedouins into citizens, God-fearing and law-abiding, but he hastened the process by establishing a strong government capable of meting out exemplary punishment to those who dared disturb the peace. Until the Bedouin women had become house-proud and to demand comforts as their right, the stick had to be there to keep the Bedouin within his newly acquired door. Often, of course, he hungered for his tent and for the excitements of the chase, and when hunger got the better of his judgment, the stick, in the guise of the motorcar, which proved invaluable for patrolling the desert; the aeroplane, which could pick up his movements from afar; and the wireless, which told of his peccadilloes in unheard cadences. Against such a combination, if only it could be applied with prudence and patience, the Bedouin had really no chance, and it was not long before the Bedouin women displayed a marked reluctance to allow their men to forsake the plough and the greater comforts to be found beneath a firm roof.

In this manner, a vast terrain which had previously bowed only to force and to the law of the rifle and the knife, was subjected to direct control, and peace, order and security gradually came.

Now, instead of a knife-thrust, one can expect a welcome from the desert.

Let another century roll on, and who can tell?

FROM: THE CONTROLLING MINDS OF ASIA

Pre-Islamic Arabia

YOU MAY KNOW of Imra ul-Qais, or on the other hand you may not.

Suffice to add here that few ranked higher than he in the Dark Ages of Arabia, both as a poet and as a warrior-prince.

Recollecting the desert escapades and song of that Pre-Islamic Singer, The Prophet Mohamed himself had described him as 'their leader to Hellfire.' For it is from what is related of him, and others; in the scenes of battles, poetical contests, gala fairs and revelry, that you can correctly comprehend as to what extent the hedonistic state of society had reached, before and during the early period when the Muslim drama was cast upon the stage of humanity.

The day was hotter than other days in the parched valleys of Arabia of which I speak as related, when Imra raced on and onward through the stunted thorny bushes. His heart was sinking with fear, for although he loved his father as little as was his father's affection for him; withal the murder or burning at the stake of his parent by the rival tribe, meant an inter-clan war, a war perchance to last for generations: especially at that time of the year, it was most inconvenient to him, for the day of annual fair was nigh and the gallant lads of the clans had many allurements there amidst song, wine and dancing.

Presently, a rider climbed the edge of a sand dune, 'Ya' Imra ul-Qais!' he called to the racing poet, 'what hastens thy steps; and where thy train of retainers?' Imra, however, was too wroth to reply. He continued his journey towards where they were reported to have slain his father. But the camel rider questioned again, for prince though that hastening man was, the desert scouts must know the reason, for raiders were many in Arabia, and the safety of the tribes was their first consideration.

'My father wasted my youth', he tarried to reply, 'and now that I am old, he has laid upon me the burden of blood-revenge.' And he tore his way through the thorny bushes. The scout, alighting from his mount, sat chewing some dried berries. In his narrowed eyes lurked the suspicion of the desert, as he saw the swiftly disappearing figure of the poet dip and rise between the sand dunes afar off.

For long he sat thus scanning the horizon, then his gaze floated northward. Little clouds of dust were now seen arising in the distance, gradually they became larger; white-clad riders were kicking the bellies of their she-camels.

The scout had no doubt that the best part of valour was now to get out of the way of Imra's hordes; he leapt to his saddle and was swathed by that mysterious vastness, where sand seems to stretch to the other end of the world.

Imra in the meantime, so says the narrative, was nearing the gully where his father was reported to have been ambushed. At the distance he could hear, now faint, now slightly louder, those plaintive notes which only the reed flutes can make. Their notes beat and rose through the gullies. A sinister meaning there was to that flute playing. And he rode on towards them with the fury of a maddened man.

The warmth of the afternoon sun was disappearing with the waning sunshine; before he could reach another five hundred yards, the twilight had come and had gone. A blood-red glow lit the little pocket of the rocky defile, as he reached the opening which led to the pass.

He thought that he was seeing the blaze of a giant bonfire, and hearing boughs crackling like muffled drums as flames went up and down. Presently, he was standing beside his father's mutilated form. Those who had killed him had celebrated the event by a feast, and had gone. Free, lawless sons of Arabia, had a grudge against Imra's father and his class.

That he was a harmless wayfarer did not matter. Had not more than five of them jagged their arms and collected their blood in one common bowl, and then dipping their fingers in it before their clan, sworn to kill at least one man from Imra's tribe? For the sheer devilry of it, in order to prove that the savagery of the desert can always conquer.

'Bah', they drank the date wine, saying; 'whosoever heard of taming the desert-born.' Every man was a law unto himself.

Upon the arrival of Imra's men on the scene of the outrage, a war council was held. Revenge burnt in their hearts. Was there going to be another Forty Years' War of tribal revenge as raged between Bakr and Taghlib? Are they to accept so many camels or coins as Diya (blood-money) and warriors like them suffer the jeering of tribes by owning 'that they preferred milk of she-camels to blood.'

'With the sword will I wash my shame away,
Let God's doom bring on me what it may!'

'Aye, aye!' the chorus rose, as a hundred spear heads shot up in the air, 'we shall fight.'

But valiant though Imra was, at any other time but just then he would have ridden ahead of his men, and slain 'even the children of the rival tribe.' At that time, however, it did not suit him. It meant his taking an oath not to touch wine till the murder was avenged; it meant also non-participation in the gala fair 'where merry makers will see paradise on earth at gambling tables', it meant his not seeing the whirling dancers of Greece and Rome and not hearing the lilting lays that gladden the heart of youth wedded to incarnate love. 'Could the taking of revenge not tarry a while', asked Imra? 'Besides, would it not be all the greater punishment to the offenders to know that they will be slain by our hands, yes slain, even their wives and children!'

Those of sensual mind amongst his men appear to be weakening, even at a time when an Arab should banish everything from his heart and proceed to the business of killing as a point of honour. The affair, after all, in the first instance concerned Imra; and if he is prepared to swallow the insult; they were surely not going to urge him. There was, of course, the fair, the merry making, the gambling tables, and the women: but of this they said nothing to Imra.

But one, bolder than the rest, eyed his companions darkly, 'Nay, nay', his voice rose: mine ears have heard the hooting of Nama (owl), perched as it was on the tomb of my relation, whose blood revenge I had delayed in taking. Even now, by the spirits of the four winds can I tell that the soul of my murdered kinsman had entered that owl. Thou shalt hear the spirit of thy father', he pointed to Imra, 'and hear the bird cry and hoot for water to drink.'

And although nothing was dearer to the mind of Imra than to postpone going on the warpath at that time, yet he was over careful not to give a definite order to his clansmen, lest he may lose control over his blood thirsty followers. At last, one of the younger men, reading what was in the mind of their Chief, reminded them that at a moment of grave importance, when significant issues were involved and opinions were divided, the only plan to adopt is to beg guidance from their idol.

To the valley of Tabala, north of Najran, they hied forth, as an idol by the name of Dhul Khalasa stood there. That oracle will give the answer. Three arrows marked, the 'Commanding', 'Forbidding', and the 'Waiting' lay in a case. In the usual manner of seeking the answer, he drew an arrow. The reply was the second arrow, 'Forbidding.' Inwardly, Imra rejoiced, but to show his faith in bloodthirstiness, he assumed a wrathful attitude to show his men. Breaking the arrow in two, he threw the parts before the idol exclaiming in apparent anger to the deity: 'If thy father had been slain, thou would'st not have hindered me.'

Some further particulars about this prince-poet, which I give below, are calculated to show how even the best specimen of Arab rulers, as he was of his time, inclined towards pleasure, superstition and savagery of the most sordid type; and how the rendezvous of unspeakable vice at the fair of Ukaz, near Mecca, fascinated 'the best princes of their line.'

The ebb and flow of that society can be gauged by knowing what great importance Imra ul-Qais possesses. This is my only excuse of giving any account of him here. When his father, Hajr, was assassinated, Imra shouldered the task of punishing Banu Asad, the rebels, aided by Mudhir. But he failed. He then went to the court of Justinian at Constantinople, from where he received a high appointment and was to be installed as Phylarch of Palestine, but before reaching his destination he died at Angora, 'by putting on a poisoned shirt – a gift from Justinian.'

The Ukaz fair, however, rivalled the scenes of Rome's greatest glory in gaiety, and all that enthroned debauchery and licentiousness. Warriors of all tribes, sworn blood enemies for generations, sat in open-air cafes, in taverns wine goblets were filled and emptied with alarming rapidity.

Hundreds had set out in a gay cavalcade of mules, camels or on foot. Ribbons flirted from their hair, bells tinkled in their toes as dancing, prancing women and girls walked alongside their menfolk. Gay Lotharios rode back and forth, round and about on their prize mares, proud of their horsemanship. Every heart beat with the joy of amusement unrestrained 'where shame had left the eyes of women.'

As caravan after caravan of merry makers flocked to the fair, from every corner of the desert, the plain of Ukaz was filled to overflowing; it stretched to Mecca and beyond'. The streets of Mecca, too, were a surging sea of humanity. In the heart of the city lay the Shrine of Idols: Lat, Minat and Uza, the stone representation of the three daughters of their god.

Sword-dancers twirled and twisted to the music of the flute. Girls clad in scanty dresses danced and hopped in the street. Storytellers and soothsayers rubbed shoulders with beggars displaying their sores and, last of all, the poets were seen hastening to the poetical contests. Singers of renown assembled before the shrine of Mecca, each poet recited his poem, and the most celebrated ones – at least those which appealed to the sensual side of a debased society, or excited revenge and warfare, or extolled the vain glories of tribal rivalry – were suspended at the door of the Kaaba.

But the places where people thronged most were the wine-bibbing booths, converted into a sort of gambling dens. Beside the many murderous-looking nomads of the desert who had come 'to drink the purest wine of date and millet', play dice and watch the dancing girls, lay a kind of low divan; on which the woman proprietress of the tavern displayed her charm by inviting first one, then other, man from amongst her customers to share the wine with her. In the centre of the gathering, the hired dancer whirled and danced to the amusement of rival tribesmen. Other girls sat around with men they had never seen before.

One of the girls of a particular tribe is now pushed on the floor to perform an intricate dance. Her performance is loudly applauded, they rise and take her forcibly into their arms. Another girl of a rival clan jumps now on the floor, and the taunting and jeering of the rival men is only drowned by the drawling and drunken voices of newly arriving men of the desert.

Wine having gone to their heads, men and women, quite strangers to each other, throw the dice upon the floor; the whole gathering shouts, roars, even pass unseeming remarks about the comeliness of one and another, one more sober than the rest rising to her feet, taut as a bowstring, and quivering like a thrown dagger, dances amidst the hilarity of men reeling in the dust with the strong date wine.

The dance gets wilder and wilder, they clap hands, they extol her beauty, the music wells up loud and confident, the dancer whirls, throws her dagger high into the air, and then catches it in her teeth. The savage passions of the spectators are let loose, they run to clasp her in their arms; she may be a chief's daughter, but what matters in that night of revelry, the three daughters whose idols are even then watching them from the Kaaba have sanctioned it all, for they owed no allegiance to a god which prohibited the full play of their animal appetites. They hungered to satisfy nothing but lust.

Raids and blood feuds having been prohibited during those four months of feasting and riotous orgies, clan after clan gathered, not at their places of worship – idol adoration though it was – but betook themselves from tavern to tavern, drinking, singing, dancing and making beasts of themselves generally: for whether men of the desert or the town, love of gambling, the pleasure of romantic song was all they cared for: beyond that lay the grave, as the following in Hamasa shows:

Roast meat and wine: the swinging ride
On a camel sure and tried,
Which her master speeds amain

O'er low dale and level plain:
Women marble – white and fair
Trailing gold-fringed raiment rare:
Opulence, luxurious ease,
With the lute's soft melodies –
Such delights hath their brief span;
Time is Change, Time's fool is Man.
Wealth or want, great store or small,
All is one since Death's are all.

Occasionally, however, young and old gathered at the steps of the shrine of Kaaba to hear the poems of the great singers. Long robed, or almost naked, they encircled the Kaaba, the former being the Quraish, the custodians of the shrine, and those who circumvented without any clothes at all were non-Quraish tribes. Then human sacrifice was offered to the idols, cases were decided when, according to their accepted traditions, one's widowed stepmother was forthwith wedded to one, even real sisters were given in marriage to brothers, so says Nomani. There was no limit to the number of wives that a man might have; and the custom of polyandry was celebrated at such gatherings.

It was at meetings like these, at the shrine too, when Imra ul-Qais, aforementioned, read his Qasida, a poem before a crowded audience with gusto, and described in the most obscene language his adulterous behaviour towards his cousin. The relish with which he paused after each stanza of that notorious poem thrilled his hearers, but even in the most debauched society of the world The Qur'an its recitation could not be tolerated. Withal the poem was so highly commended by those who heard it, that they immediately voted for the excellence of this creation of the poet-prince. It was forthwith exalted to the rank of Muallaqat, was written on finest Egyptian linen with gold, and suspended at the door of the shrine as the choicest gem of poetical work; so true was it to the mind of men and women of Arabia of that period.

A little too outspoken, though such poetical compositions of the Pre-Islamic Arabs may be to us, or obnoxious as they certainly were to The Prophet Mohamed – who, as will be shown later, rigorously stamped out licentiousness – it must be admitted that the art of poesy in the desert regions was much coveted. A poet was as great a personality as a conquering hero of many battles. The popularity of such singers, as can be judged, was due to the fact that they produced none other than those compositions which appealed to the people of their age. They let people have what people wanted: consequently, you may find an Arab woman pray that she may be blessed with a son who should become a poet, and a she-camel to feed such a renowned poet, whose Qasida might hang over the door of the holy Kaaba.

Such being the case, it is permissible to conclude, that those giants of Pre-Islamic poetical literature, whose works flirted over the shrine, and included in Muallaqat were symptomatic in their time of a period which we Muslims call the Dark Ages of Arabia: so that when we quote from the life and work of any of these poets, we are fairly close to a correct data to judge of the society in Arabia before the advent of Islam. At that period, we know that pleasure reigned supreme; and whosoever spoke of it in a fashion as to draw people near any aspect of that pleasure was a favourite bard and singer.

And whereas I quote from Lyall's Ten Ancient Arabic Poems, in testimony of what is stated above, the following extract from Asha's works should not be confused with the outpouring of later singers, like Omar Khayyam or Moulana Rumi, whose mystic meaning couched in terms of wine and flowers and beauty has no counterpart in Asha's pure and unadulterated reference to naked vice, with no trace of illusion of the Divine, but mere carnal love and depravity of manners.

In the description of gatherings of wine-bibbers, Asha has no rival. The following lines from his most celebrated poems are interesting, especially when it is added that his devotion to earth's good things was so great that when midnight wine drinking orgies took place at his tomb, as a tribute to his genius, it was the custom to pour the unconsumed wine over his grave. Here is what he says in 'Asha and Alqama':

> Many a time I hastened early to the tavern – while there ran
> At my heels a ready cook, a nimble, active serving-man –
> 'Midst a gallant troop, like Indian scimitars, of mettle high;
> Well they know that every mortal, shod and bare alike, must die.
> Propped at ease I greet them gaily, then with myrtle-boughs I greet,

Pass amongst them wine that gushes from the jar's mouth bittersweet.
Emptying goblet after goblet – but the source may no man drain –
Never cease they from carousing save to cry, 'Fill up again!'
Briskly runs the page to serve them: on his ears hang pearls: below,
Tight the girdle draws his doublet as he bustles to and fro.
'Twas the harp, thou mightest fancy, waked the lute's responsive note.
Here and there among the party, damsels fair superbly glide:
Each her long white skirt lets trail and swings a wineskin at her side.

Considering the state of society in which the poet lived, and the many ceremonies which were held in Arabia over his grave, it is impossible to escape the conclusion that Asha meant literally every word that he wrote. There were no allusions, nothing whatever of gorgeous imagery which characterised the later mystics of Islam. In Asha's poems dwelt no deep significance of hidden instructions, which he who seeks may find – shall find, if he be eager enough, ardent enough. It was a plain tale of riotous living; no more, no less.

Asha's or Imra's wine, for example, did not signify devotion; sleep, meditation of the Divine perfection; perfume, the hope of the Divine afflatus.

IN THE LAND OF KING ABDULAZIZ

In the songs of these spokesmen of Pre-Islamic Arabia zephyrs did not signify the gift of godly grace and kisses the transports of devotion and piety. The keeper of the tavern was no hierophant with them. Compare these materialistic poems with what was sung in the Musnawi centuries afterwards, the song is there, the flute and all the elements of passion, but cast in a different mould. The Moulana sings:

> Oh! hear the flute's sad tale again:
> Of Separation I complain:
> E'er since it was my fate to be
> Thus cut off from my parent tree,
> Sweet moan I've made with pensive sigh,
> While men and women join my cry.
>
> Man's life is like this hollow rod;
> One end is in the lips of God,
> And from the other sweet notes fall
> That to the mind the spirit call,
> And join us with the All in All.

Whatever disparity may exist between these two classes of poets, no one can deny that each class was a mouthpiece of its epoch; and it is my purpose to show how the poet's art in both cases brings the contrast vividly before us as a result of the preaching of Islam. Here again we have Omar Khayyam singing:

> And lately by the Tavern Door agape,
> Came stealing through the Dusk an Angle Shape

Bearing a Vessel on his Shoulder; and
He bid me taste of it; and 'twas – the Grape!

The Grape that can with Logic absolute
The Two-and-Seventy jarring Sects confute:
The Subtle Alchemist that in a trice
Life's leaden metal into Gold transmute:

In this, like Rumi's work you have the imagery par excellence, for these men acquired the state of self-initiation. The term beauty is used to denote the perfection of God, and lovelocks and the tresses the infinitude of His Glory. Down on the cheeks is symbolic of the multitudinous spirits which serve Him. Inebriation and dalliance typify that abstraction of soul which shows contempt of mundane affairs.

The reason of it is, as I have said before, to be found in self-initiation, which the authors of Muallaqat sadly lacked, even though their poems were hung at the shrine in Mecca. The moral glow and warmth which you find in Islamic poets was not due entirely to their devotion to the rites and ceremonies of the religion, it was on account of attuning to a State of Spirituality as well.

Ritual of itself is naught compared with this spiritual knowledge. They no doubt symbolise the process and lend dignity to it, but that is all: for rite and symbols, apart from high intentions and spiritual significance, can even be degrading if performed for show, yet they express much more than mere words, that is, they are efficacious as supplementing the imperfect medium of human speech in the conveyance of subliminal ideas.

And whereas it is entirely in virtue of self-initiation which exalts the Islamic poets above those of the Dark Ages, yet initiation itself can never reveal the truth in its entirety. The degree of truth unveiled is in ratio of the seeker's own potentialities. Of such potentialities, those who sang at Mecca before their idols, were singularly barren. Their Society, vitiated as it was, did not demand anything other than what they were. Here, however, we must see how that self-initiation worked in the mind of men which characterises their Islamic poetry.

The nature of the doctrine revealed to their initiates is assuredly capable of expression in one formula. It is the entrance into a new life, or, rather, the return to an old and real one, that is, to that 'paradise' from which man fell, to that divine communion from which he, by his own acts, has been excluded. Initiation is the instinctive as well as intellectual aspiration of the higher man towards restoration to the divine communion, unity with, or absorption in the divine. The initiate is equipped with the knowledge of how he came into the material world, and how he must re-ascend.

The several grades of initiation, although they differ considerably in respect of the various orders which have existed in the history of mankind, may actually be reduced to three, or perhaps four: the nascent grade, or 'rebirth' not in the Hindu or Buddhist sense, however, the stationary, or that of spiritual 'hovering', or juvenility, the third, the new life proper, and, lastly, and more occasionally, its sequel, symbolical of the experience of the new condition. It is only when material life is left behind and 'supernatural rebirth' is achieved that initiation has taken place. The three great degrees may roughly be described as purification, consecration, and illumination.

Does initiation in itself suffice for actual illumination? That actual spiritual knowledge was passed on to the epopts we cannot doubt. Even so, it must have been insufficient of itself without a spiritual transformation in the soul of the neophyte. Indeed, the genuine neophyte is himself the true hierophant, nor can the official hierophant be other than a demonstrator, adviser and inspiring force. He cannot by any word or act transform the neophyte into the perfected initiate unless there be already in the heart of the latter a supreme intention and responsive desire. Initiation is, indeed, an inward act of the soul, a supernatural act of the psychic entity in man, free, unfettered, determined, responsive, yet wholly self-inspired in the ultimate.

But it may well be said that, having accomplished initiation, it is impossible for the epopt to convey its full significance to those outside of the portals even if he would. Words and forms he can reveal if he be so minded, but these would hold no meaning for the uninitiated, simply because he would be confronted with matters unterrestrial and outwith the scope and vocabulary of mundane knowledge and apprehension. Indeed, such secrets as are unveiled to him are, and were, conveyed to his spirit through the voiceless message of symbols and not through words. And they are actually apprehended as often as not through subsequent reflection and contemplation rather than through immediate illumination.

There is, to be sure, nothing in the Mysteries which the born mystic may not excogitate for himself by dint of his own genius, just as the born poet invariably discovers for himself those fundamental truths regarding his inspirational art which appear almost as of a semi-supernatural order to workaday men. He will shortly find, for example, that of itself the human soul is imperfect, that, lacking the quality of receptivity, the spirit is powerless – and other and equally cogent illuminations will rapidly present themselves to the veridical mystic. It follows that self-initiation is perfectly possible, has been attained in hundreds of instances by not only the exceptional.

The descent of the soul into matter is one of the most profound mysteries of human existence, as is its converse, the ascent of the spirit into the realms immaterial. These twain constitute symbolic death and 'rebirth', and were bodied forth in the Mysteries. It is a legend of ages untold, embraced by all the mystical orders. It is, indeed, the intellectual and psychic discernment of the divine, when the soul, making not a mythos for herself, but through sheer sleight of awakened and instinctive spirituality, arrives at a knowledge of the truth concerning her actual origin and the 'realities' of her existence. It is a novel, or rather, a re-awakened sense of perception, and initiation is merely its drama, the symbolic gesture of its aroused consciousness of the need for reunion with divinity.

By initiation nothing can be gained but that which has to be gained. The seeming crudity of such a statement includes a truth so obvious, yet so deep as to appear as needless as profundity frequently appears to persons of material tendency, for there is but one way which God opens into the temple which was founded before the beginning of the world. The way is well trodden, the stones are deeply worn. There are no unessentials of power, of mere romantic potentialities won for the adept – wealth, charm, long life, the ability to wield occult powers. These are, indeed, the insignia of the slight and fatuous soul dallying in the purlieus of the temple, vain and degenerate in essence. The true secrets are those of grace, understanding, perfect apprehension and joy in the knowledge of the abounding life unrolled before the spirit, rhythmic delight, the sovereign poise of certainty.

The core of the revelation in the Greater Mysteries lay in intellection, in which the archetypal image of universal nature was revealed. The contemplation and union with the Highest supervened. Thus it will be seen that the ritual and drama had little to do with the higher stages, which were almost purely of a supernormal and spiritual character. But to express this adequately mere language fails. These things are apprehended, neither seen nor heard.

What is there to learn in this apprenticeship of life other than the essential poise necessary to the approach to Otherwhere? This world is, indeed, an aerodrome, in which man is building, fitting and testing those winged pinnaces which shall bear him to immortality. If he fails in his 'prentice task then must he assuredly lose and suffer accordingly. It is merely the self-discipline of the Divine endeavouring at great distances to justify itself by various experiments in the depths of time and space, sending out its colonist particles to replenish the spheres and to triumph ere they return to the Fatherland to gain new strength from the sources of the Ultimate, and answer for what they have done.

So that it becomes essential to cultivate toward this end a particular psychic state through steady contemplation of the divine, the afar, that distance, that wonder of aloofness which is the heart of Paradise. Intellection, inspection, the reduction of the mental and psychical chaos, the worldly confusion of the heart, mind, and soul, to the orderly through rapt comprehension of the one simple truth and necessity – 'union with God.'

Moreover, the true significance of the divine union is too frequently misapprehended, especially by those who dread it as being peradventure of the nature of individual psychic extinction. In one sense the human soul is never entirely out of communication with the divine, indeed its native character renders it more easy to aspire than to grovel, the doctrine of its native wickedness notwithstanding. The wretched and truly damnable doctrine that the heart of man is 'desperately wicked' has, I contend, wrought mischief untold, and has probably wrecked more lives than it has helped to ways of grace. It is a dark saying of hierophantic superiority, based on a degenerate assumption of universal and widespread human depravity, which could only have been engendered in some hypersensitive and cloistered mentality unused to human converse and aloof from the true nobility and divineness of the common mind which shows visibly in the neighbourhood of each and every one of us.

The soul of man is tired of being told it is wicked, when, on the whole, it is good, and is essaying most admirably to find its way through the fogs of sin to the sun. And who can blame it if it is equally tired of religions, in which the truth that eternal life must inevitably not end in spiritual ecstasy (if its laws be adequately fulfilled), and is somewhat occluded by a ministry which, with all its virtues, which is prone to lay stress on the gloomy side of things, and is certainly unvisited by the spirit of rapture in things divine, devoting all its song and poem to love of this world as did the authors of intellectual outpouring in Pre-Islamic Arabia?

The consciousness of fellowship with God is the first significant token that the process of union with the divine has commenced. But of this I am very sure, that it does not imply the full achievement of unity. It is, I believe, an expression prior and preparatory to initiation, for union with God grows and advances as comprehension and expression and intuition grow through successive acts of the spirit. The wings strengthen and the flight grows longer. The lamp is constantly burning, and it behoves man to make use of the light.

The neophyte, however, understands that the Mysteries, as we know them, must assuredly be described as the Mysteries of Earth. Their whole intent is a stepping from this mortality to immortality, consequently they cannot in any way be related to the Mysteries of the divine, of which man has rumours, but cannot even conceive the nature or the felicity thereof. The Prophets alone have that honour. Mystery, in short, reveals on its unveiling, fresh mystery, and so must the progression proceed far past the human ken.

The peculiarly insensible attitude of the greater part of the Pre-Islamic Arabs toward the deeper mysteries of spiritual existence constituted a grave danger to humanity. Avidly seizing upon the husks of the material, it had permitted itself to forget the inestimable treasures of the spirit; its attitude of impatience with affairs spiritual and of the utmost importance to its own racial and individual welfare ought undoubtedly to have aroused the gravest unrest in men and women of serious and exalted character.

A country, like Pre-Islamic Arabia, which could not afford to examine and to grapple with the great problems of psychic existence, which was wrapped up in things material and pleasurable, which was not established on the rock of indubitable truth, whose people believed all wisdom to be based on material fact, which had, in short, no strain or desire towards spiritual ascension, was indeed in a perilous position. Just as I am well assured that no individual can lead a life of psychic security without at least a minimum of contemplation upon things hidden and divine, so am I equally persuaded that no nation which in the main ignores them can be secure in justice and in loftiness of ideal, if it lived only on a passion-exhausting programme of life, as did the people of Arabia, before the advent of The Prophet Mohamed.

FROM: MOHAMED: THE PROPHET

The Holy City

IN A FIERCE midday heat, enveloped in clouds of choking dust, sweating and with jaded face, I was among a heterogeneous mass of Muslim pilgrims, as we lumbered on our way to the Bombay harbour in western India.

Afghans, Persians, Javanese, Indians and Uzbeks, all staring at one another and endeavouring to follow diverse languages we had never heard of before. On the arrival of the medical officer, the babel of tongues died away, as all sat on the floor of the shed and were vaccinated.

But as soon as a medical certificate was granted and the pilgrim was free to move, you could see him hurrying along the passage with his left shirt arm folded. A moment later you noticed him behind the shed, washing the wound inflicted by the vaccinator. Many think that the lymph is 'an impurity of cow' and hence not fit to be absorbed by the skin of a Faithful bound for sacred Mecca, the mystic city of Arabia where only the Muslims can go.

Close by the quay platform lay the pilgrim boat to Jeddah on the Red Sea, and when the final word of 'depart' was given by the medical authorities, there was a rush to the gangway. Stalwart Pathans of the frontier, weak and ill-fed Bengalis, sleepy-eyed men of Bokhara, veiled women bearing children in their arms, made one dash. They carried their valuables along with them, in sacks, crudely made tin boxes, or bulging baskets insecurely tied with ropes.

The sacks, however, were in predominance as items of 'portable luggage' intended for 'cabin only.' All the passengers were excited, and the noise and smell of the East blended with the sanctified air of the pilgrim boat. They rushed the gangway, people pushing into the sacks and bundles, and baskets pushing into the people.

A water receptacle peeping out of a sack, now pushed up by the jolting crowd and, then slipping out of the hands of its owner into the sea. Thus, the narrow pathway led the Faithful to the deck and away down to enormous and utterly cavernous depths.

Three shrill blasts, a thud of the engines, and slowly we moved away from the Indian shores amid the cries of 'Allahu-Akbar! Allahu-Akbar! God is Great! God is Great!'

As a pious Muslim, I had a craving to visit the Holy City of my faith. Taking, therefore, little or no account of the future, believing that what is written is written, relying on the philosophy of my forefathers, I resolved to face the discomforts and perils inseparable from a pilgrimage to Mecca as stoically as possible.

Existence on the pilgrim ship, to one used to the ordinary comforts of life was, to say the least of it, harassing. And although much has recently been done by the Wahabi Government to provide liveable conditions, the devotees were packed like pilchards in a tin.

The worst phase of the voyage began on the third day after we had left Karachi for Jeddah, because practically every pilgrim was in the throes of *mal-de-mer*; and one of them, who only the day before had told me he could not be seasick, was prostrated, praying loudly for death to release him.

The shouting and harrying scenes had come to a standstill, for the sky was now grey, the wind swept the vessel, and the waves beat of the sides with more than ordinary force. Corpse-like men lay on the deck, on their charcoal sacks, on coiled ropes, everywhere, uttering not a word, hardly interested in existence and readily denying food and drink.

They thought an evil spirit had come upon the boat. But it takes more than a rough sea to hide life altogether, for as soon as the waves subsided, the corpse-like ones rolled up their beddings, sat up, cooked their food, the Persians made tea, the Bengalis skinned fish, the Pathans were busy with their palau rice of the most excellent flavour.

During the spell of the seasickness the pilgrims had lost all clear idea of their purpose; but on recovering they soon remembered the solemn idea that induced them to journey to the city of their childhood dreams and lifelong prayers.

The air on the boat was 'thick with religion', prayer carpets were spread, recitations of the Qur'an were chanted, doctors of theology were busy reading to the devotees those chapters of the Holy Book of Islam which related to that part of the journey of the pilgrimage.

In the afternoons, religious discussions took place, even political, and both used to end where they began. And thus, the life of the pious on a pilgrim ship was spent, till one day, soon after dawn, the captain appeared on the deck and pointed out to us in the haze of distance a dark blue line, the Holy Land of Islam! The Arabian Coast! The port of Jeddah!

We could hardly speak for excitement.

Little by little it became clearer, as we stood watching it in our *ahram* – our regulation pilgrim costume – till the white city of minarets and domes of Jeddah lay as cut in marble when the boat dropped anchor some two miles from the shore. From that point no ship could go near, as the reefs are very numerous and many traversed that portion in tiny sail boats tossing like cockle shells on the crests of the waves.

The first sight of Jeddah gripped me.

I gazed at it as a Muslim with pleasure mingled with awe and reverence.

Beyond that city, at the distance of fifty miles or more, lay Mecca, the goal of my hopes.

The Holy of Holies of every Muslim.

Life's dream, I thought, had at last been realized. The pallor of my face and those tears that dimmed my eyes were indications of my emotions. The scene was strangely familiar, for had I not faced the Holy City five times every day of my life in prayer? Absorbed in these thoughts, I remained in Jeddah for the night, and next day in a motor car started towards Mecca, the Cradle of Islam.

Those of us who had more money than sense were bundled into a large motor car, and were told that by this means we were to travel the fifty miles to Mecca. We had not proceeded far when a halt was made at the reputed tomb of Eve. Curious as to the grave of my great ancestress, I alighted to examine it. She must have been a lady of formidable proportions, for the original grave, I was told, was some eight feet long.

It was perhaps as well, therefore, that she had not survived to welcome us in the flesh, for although it is rumoured that we Muslims have an eye for ladies of heroic proportions, we draw the line at the titanic. But I was told that the grave had mysteriously extended itself, by the time I arrived, to the altogether gigantic dimensions. On payment of a fee, I learned, one could receive an oracular message from the buried progenitress of suffering humanity. This was, of course, supplied by a confederate in an underground crypt, who, for a shilling or two, droned out a 'prophecy'. Fortunately, the evil practice is now stopped since the advent of the Wahabis.

As we trundled over the sandy tract, we felt the grilling heat of the desert overpoweringly on our skin. I was dressed in the traditional *ahram*, which consists of two sheets, one for the upper part of the body, another for the lower, knotted together, as pins or sewing are frowned on by Muslim law. In accordance with immemorial custom, too, my head was shaved and unprotected from the merciless sun.

To make matters worse, no water was to be had.

At last, after twenty-five miles of torture, with parched lips and baking limbs, we drew up at the post of Bahra, where, we were told, there was a well, and, thanks to the Wahabi

King, we found not only water, but even cool drinks; a God-sent thing in the scorching heat of the desert.

Hardly had we journeyed three miles beyond the well, when the rear wheels of our car sunk deep in a sand heap. We alighted, and strove to move the venerable vehicle, but to no purpose, and much to the contemptuous amusement of a passing Bedouin, who, from the back of his swift-trotting camel, jeered at us unmercifully.

'It serves you right for bringing that creation of Satan into the sacred land', he yelled. 'Why can't you travel on camel-back like other folks?

'See, I can make my camel stop when I want and go when I wish him to. Take that iron contraption back to the devil who made it!'

By this time, I was well in the grip of fever, and it was with pounding head and swaying legs that I made the seven-fold circumambulations of the sacred Kaaba, that Holy of Holies, believed to have been built by Adam, which contains the sacred black stone set in silver. The Haram, or sacred enclosure in which it is situated, is surrounded on all sides by graceful colonnades, surmounted by white domes, forming Mecca's sacred mosque.

On the day in question, it was crowded by thousands of pilgrims from all parts of the East, eager to kiss the holy relic.

From the moment pilgrims enter Mecca to the time of their departure they are kept in a state of excitement and pious frenzy. Ceremony after ceremony claims their constant and unfaltering attention. They are for hours wedged in swaying and seething crowds.

THE HOLY CITY

One of the most arduous rites is the passing seven times between the space of Safa and Marwa, the alleged tombs of Hagar and Ishmael, a distance of perhaps three hundred yards, which is known as the Sai Ceremony, and from which one may acquire much merit.

The road is not narrow but is constantly crowded with pilgrims. Add to this prayers five times a day, and one has not much time to see the sights of Mecca. Not that there is really much to see. Moreover, King Ibn Saud has rightly banned all diabolical amusements. Mecca is exceptionally dry in every regard, and to light a cigarette is to call down anathemas from pious Muslims.

The most striking picture in Mecca is that provided by the vivid and colourful life of its wonderful bazaars. The most celebrated of these is the Soayga, which occupies one side of the Haram, and which has a great reputation throughout the East for its fine silks, its wonderful beadwork, and its rich and choice perfumes.

The latter are a necessity of life in Mecca, where the sanitation of the rest-houses till lately was most execrable. Indeed, scented woods had constantly to be burned in these houses to keep down the effluvia of overcrowded humanity which is constantly rising.

But purchasing an article in Mecca is scarcely the same sort of business as in a European city. Goods in the bazaars are unticketed and if you fancy anything the merchant will ask six or eight times its value. Of course, the turbaned gentleman well knows that you will at once depreciate it, which you proceed to do, if you are skilful, with a flow of rhetoric which bamboozles him.

But when he has recovered, he comes back at you with an eloquence of praise for his goods worthy of a Hafiz.

So, it goes on until one or the other is exhausted.

On one occasion I bought a melon, which, the merchant assured me, was 'sweeter than the honeycombs on the hills of Paradise.' On finding the inside blacker than Eblis, I returned it to the seller, 'who looked at me pityingly.

'Oh, my unwise brother', he chanted, 'the melon was made by Allah. Why not complain to him about it?!'

One might describe Mecca under Wahabi rule as a 'Calvinist' city, the metropolis of the Muslim purists. It has no lighter side to its austerities. Indeed, Mecca should be nothing else. Yet the very colourfulness of its crowded and enthusiastic life, and the sight of thousands of devotees massed together from all the lands of the East, cannot fail to rouse a lasting sense of the picturesque and the devout, never to be effaced; and the security it offers has been possible only since the Wahabi regime.

After much prayer and meditation in the Holy City of Islam, I resolved to trek northward, not as a scientific explorer, but as a wanderer, without knowing that the raiding season of recalcitrant Bedouins begins in the desert at the termination of the pilgrimage.

Caravans for Basra and Mecca were now constantly passing across the desert to and fro from the Muslim Holy City, on the termination of the world-wide pilgrim season there. Those who pay tribute to the Bedouins are immune. If they do not – well, sand leaves no traces, even of green turbans. It was during this season that I fell into the hands of the bandits.

The only way to get out of their clutches was to play the brigand and then, watching an opportunity, make good one's escape.

Three ruffians stood before me with loaded rifles. 'I shall shed no blood', I protested, 'if you insist upon my becoming one of you.' After that there was nothing for it but to 'savvy', and I fell into the line. I must explain that the Government of Iraq at the time had about as much authority in its southwestern outposts as the London police have in the Scilly Isles.

A couple of days after I had unwillingly joined up for safety's sake, a rumour ran through the camp that a caravan from Kuwait was crossing the desert to Medina, and that it would hold by that part of the frontier where we were situated before striking south for the sacred places. Naturally the news aroused the wildest enthusiasm among the eighty-odd blackguards who composed the band.

Life in the camp had been somnolent enough before, a matter of occasional scouting, interspersed with coffee-drinking and smoking dried tobacco slightly mixed with hashish. Now vedettes were sent out all over the horizon and an extraordinary feverish activity prevailed. Even so, it was another three days before we got reliable news of the whereabouts of the caravan, and this necessitated a camel ride of more than thirty miles.

It was in the evening that we got our first sight of it: a thin black streak on the pale face of the limitless sands, a moving thread of life among the far hills of the desert. Down we swooped with a wild whooping. I cannot help laughing as I remember that in my nervousness of the ugly chieftain, I gave vent to some of the most blood-curdling yells ever heard out of transpontine drama. If the talkies ever want anyone to shriek in a peculiarly ghastly manner, I offer my services as an invisible ghoul. Yes, indeed, it was great!

The caravan came to a dead halt, and the ends drew back on the centre. Not a shot was fired, for the payment of the tribute was the usual custom.

Shortly we came up with our victims, who were obviously demoralized. The leader of the train rode out and explained to us that it was composed of exceptionally poor pilgrims, who were unable to pay anything in the way of blackmail. In the name of all that is holy, would the chief not allow them to pass?

But the chief had heard that story before. 'We shall investigate their poverty', he said sternly, and then the fun began. Fat Hadjis and portly merchants were manhandled and forced to part with their personal jewellery, money and other belongings. Bales of costly merchandise were unwrapped and hypothecated.

Camels of pedigree and valuable dromedaries were impounded. Fine Arab horses were selected. And those who complained or resisted were badly beaten up and mauled. Cries of fear and indignation, curses and malediction, resounded on all sides.

I felt the chief's eye on the man standing next to me. He strode up to a little wizened fellow who was making more uproar than half a dozen others. The chief presented his Arab blade near the old man's head.

'Pay up', he yelled, 'or by the beard of the holy priest, I shall scratch your neck in a fashion of my own.'

'Brother', he shrieked, 'I have nothing, nothing, but the holy memory of my aunt, which I carry to the shrines; let the angels hear me.'

'Off with your turban', growled the Arab menacingly, 'or the devils will hear you quick.'

Weeping, protesting, he drew off his headgear. Within its folds was a handful of choice turquoises from Persia. On these the brigand chief swooped like a hawk, giving him a look of commendation.

It was a sorry train that was left in the desert after we rode back.

But now came my opportunity.

That night as the raiders sat in the moonlight dividing their loot, and much too busy to notice me, I quietly mounted my camel and made off. By morning I was well on my way to where I thought lay the track to Basra in Iraq, and, endeavouring to avoid all Black Tent dwellers of the desert, rode on till dusk had swallowed the shimmering sand dunes, and I lay down utterly exhausted beside my camel.

I had been asleep and woke to find the sharp end of a jezail rifle rammed so hard into my neck as to be near breaking the skin. I struggled into a sitting posture and saw a lean dark face peering through the opening of the tent curtains into mine.

'Hello', I spoke. 'What about it? Take that shooting iron away from my jugular, will you?'

'Peace be with you!' said my visitor devoutly. 'I thought for a moment that you were an infidel.'

'There's another thing coming to you', I told him; 'but what's it all about?'

'Truly you are a man of strange words', replied my new Arab friend, 'Don't you know that in the country of the Bedouins sleeping men are apt to be rudely awakened?' I assured him that I had gathered the idea previously but had resolved to ignore it. And as the trusting son of Shaitan laughed consumedly, I raised my heavily sandalled foot and kicked him so hard on the knock-out area of the chin that he began to dream of the planets at once. As nearly painless as might be.

So, I roped him up, and knowing that some of his crowd would be along soon, took his camel and left him mine. His was a fleet one of the desert, one of the best, I saw at a glance. The camel, however, is a froward beast. He will obey his master grudgingly, but being lawless at heart, he is only too prone to rebel against others. And before I had well mounted him, this demon of the desert made off like the tempest towards the place of sunrise, bumping me at every stride till I felt like the makings of an omelette.

Great Scott, and then some! How that brute did career over the burning desert. And then, just like a donkey, he stopped dead, and I went over his long neck, ploughing my way down, down, through seeming oceans of hot sand.

When I came to the surface again, blaspheming in an argot of six languages, and shaking the burning particles from my eyes, ears and hair, I was amazed to hear a woman's voice greeting me. Now women unsponsored in the desert are about as rare as larks in December, and I gazed through my watering eyes in amazement, until I saw by her dress and lack of veil that this was what is known as one of the 'Free Women' of Arabia, a caste of ladies who for some reason or another have always been regarded with especial reverence by the Arabs, and who are not subject to their rather wearing social laws.

'And what can I do for you?' I asked weakly.

'Your *beri* has gone', she replied smilingly, 'and unless I give you a lift on mine, you'll have to remain here, as far as I can see.'

'Very kind of you', I assured her. 'Come, let us be moving, for there are certain people in this vicinity who are looking for my heart's blood, and I haven't a drop to spare at the moment.'

'I will help you on one condition', she said very firmly, 'and that is that you take me to wife.'

'But I thought you Free Women never married.'

'That's just it', she remarked pettishly, 'and I am tired of the single state.'

Now I didn't want to trice up with this lady, and I knew it would be suicide to tell her I had a wife at home, so I merely nodded gravely.

She made her camel kneel, I mounted behind her and off we went.

'Where do we go from here, Bulbul?' I asked.

'We go to Kuwait', she said, 'for I want to see the pictures. And my name's not Bulbul, but Khawala; so please remember.'

The pictures! A traitorous thought leaped into my mind.

Five hours of clop-clopping through the sand, and we were in Kuwait. It must be the pictures at once, hungry and thirsty as I was. Night had fallen, as we entered the picture house, and the interior was as dark as the cave of Eblis.

So far, so good!

The film on the screen was one of those sob-stuff torments which turn most women into perfectly good understudies of Niobe for about six reels or so. My prophetic hopes, I found, were correct. Khawala was no exception to the rule. At the first sad caption she began to sniff, and when the Italian heroine writhed on a marble seat on reading the telegram that told of her lover's accident, she reached for my hand. At last, when the said lover returned on crutches, she broke down entirely and laid her head on my shoulder.

'You are overcome', I whispered; 'let me get you some coffee. A cup will just put you right.'

The cup of coffee is to the Arab woman what the cup of tea is to her European sister, a never-failing solace. Khawala peered up at me through the gloom.

'You are so good', she murmured. 'Yes, I think I should like a cup. But you won't be long, will you, dear?' Assuring her that I would not, I crept from the picture house and at greyhound speed made for the docks. A felucca was in the act of weighing out for Basra. The lateen sails were going up and the anchor was on the deck.

'Hi, hi!' I shouted to the skipper; 'take me with you and I'll split a gold piece with you when we get to Basra.'

'Jump, then', he cried, 'and save your neck if you can. I can't put back.'

I closed my eyes and jumped. A broken neck seemed a mild way out compared with what waited for me at the picture house yonder. For I should have told you that

THE HOLY CITY

Khawala was forty-five if she was a day, and that she had quite three teeth in the upper gum and a smile like that on the visage of the proverbial tiger.

Pressed by circumstances, I may go 'back to Alabam', as a popular song assures us its hero declares he will do. But come weal, come woe, I shall not return to Kuwait. There are other and less exciting ways of facing Azrael, the Angel of Death.

The Land & the People

It now behoves us to know something of the geographical and tribal history and distribution of the country where early Arabian drama was enacted. The country of Arabia usually styled as Jazirah, or the island, is bounded on the east by the Persian Gulf, in the south by the Arabian Sea and the Gulf of Aden, and on the west the Red Sea separates it from Egypt, whilst on the north an imaginary line, drawn across the Syrian desert from Basra to Jerusalem, marked its extent and separated it from the warring hordes of Chosroes and Cassars.

This vast region, which embraces an area twice the size of France is, geographically speaking, a plateau. Down practically the entire western border of it runs a wall of mountains from north to south as I have described it in one of my earlier works on Arabia. All along the Red Sea, from ten to fifteen miles eastward of the shore, one finds it rising to varying heights of several thousand feet above sea level. Gradually, however, the wall of these mountains merges into the plateau and these slope eastwards in the direction of the central areas of the sandy desert.

The plains, whether on the western, southern or eastern shores, are scarcely broader than thirty miles. The western face of the mountain attains its highest point at its southern extremity, where an altitude of ten thousand feet is reached. The slopes of the plateau too, show a difference as they plunge into the central and northern Arabian sandy wastes, for there are two of these slopes, the one dropping away north-eastwards into the sandy tracts of the Syrian desert, and the other south-eastwards into the Arabian no-man's land of Rubi-el-Khali.

In the peninsula itself we find three distinct regions. There is a middle portion of hard, boulder-strewn sand with a very considerable number of oases, which maintain a large population. Around this hard sand, in both the south and the north, lie hundreds of miles of mere waste tracts of the desert, where there is almost complete absence of life. The plateau or highlands of Nejd are mostly composed of areas as described in the first of the three above-mentioned divisions, Rubi-el-Khali, is an area of the second type, and the mountain regions of Asir and Yemen fall in the third category.

Nejd and Yemen are separated by a mountainous province known as Yamama which figures very prominently in the Islamic history. North-east of Nejd lie the deserts of Iraq bordering on the fertile regions of the Chaldasans, more easterly again is Al-Ahsa. It is, however, in the barrier-land on the eastern shores of the Red Sea that the Hijaz lies, in whose lap repose the holy cities of Mecca and Medina, and around which Islam battled with paganism. Mecca has the honour of being the birthplace of The Prophet Mohamed, and it was to Yathrab or Medina he was forced to flee from his people when they menaced him on his proclaiming himself the Messenger carrying Allah's word.

The climatic conditions vary too in Arabia with the characteristic geographical change of the land. In Nejd the temperature is hardly ever below 102° in shade, and in Mecca a degree of 133° has been recorded: and yet at night keen frost is experienced in the desert. The central portion of the country has probably the healthiest climate. Dry conditions of heat or cold are to be met there. So refreshing is the morning breeze of Nejd that the fame of its zephyrs, or Nasim, has passed into poetry. It is then the coastal regions of Arabia which have given a bad name to the country so far as its climate is concerned. There is no bracing atmosphere, there is a closeness near the coast, the air is humid and damp heat is most oppressive. The Red Sea coast is notorious for its unhealthiness for this reason.

The province of Yemen in the southernmost corner of the peninsula receives more rain because of its mountains than other regions, as much as sixteen inches of rain in one year are said to have fallen in Yemen, and in Aden, for instance, which adjoins it, has received only a degree less than Hodada. At Oman on the eastern coast not only a good rainfall is registered but also snowfalls have been experienced, the rest is arid and at times very severe on human endurance especially during the daytime.

The interplay of events which followed the advent of The Prophet Mohamed cannot be followed without an adequate knowledge of that historical background which alone can show the transformation the ministry of the Great Arabian wrought in the minds of an ancient people. For this we will have to go to the original sources of Arab historians.

THE LAND & THE PEOPLE

The Arabs divide the people who inhabited their country as early as can be comprehended into three classes. The first the Arab ul Baidah, traces of whom vanished almost completely before Islam, although the Hamitic colonies which came slightly prior to the Semites were included amongst this section. The section subdivision were termed as Arab ul Aariba, the original Arabs believed themselves to be descended from Kohtan, and are supposed to have extirpated or absorbed the native elements of astra-worshippers. A third, the so-called Arab ul-Mustaariba or the naturalised Arabs, the Abrahamitic Semites, however, were the most important.

From the fold of the second section, namely Arab ul Aariba, rose four powerful clans of Bani Aad, the Amalika, the Bani Thamud and Bani Jadis. The first named covered the whole of Central Arabia with their settlements, and by dint of desert hardiness and colonisation skill these people soon grew in power and set up principalities. One of their kings, Shaddad, is spoken of in The Qur'an, and is believed to have carried his victorious armies up to the borders of India on one side and to Egypt and beyond on the other. Whether this Arab invasion of Babylonia more than two thousand years before Christ is the same as that with which Shaddad is credited may remain a moot point, but at least regarding his march towards Egypt and the check placed there in the way of the Eastern invaders by the princes of Thebaid in alliance with the Ethiopians admits of a measure of credence.

The second clan, that of Banu-Amalika, entering Arabia by way of Yemen, spread all along the coast right up to the confines of Syria thus embracing modern Yemen, Asir, the

Hijaz and Palestine. There is evidence to show that several Egyptian Pharaohs originally belonged to this clan; but were overthrown by a branch of Banu Kohtun who had settled in the south of Arabia. These were called Banu-Jurhum.

The third section, the Banu Thamud, populated the country between the Hijaz and Syria. These people were cave dwellers, but as they lay on the trade routes, and provided both shelter and guards for the passing caravans, their prosperity increased enormously, but were rooted out by Khozar al Ahmar, the Elamite conqueror. The Qur'an also made an allusion to the terrible fate which befell these troglodytes. One fact of interest to note here, is that when the southern hordes of Banu-Jurhum – who, as we have seen above, exterminated Amalika – settled down and consolidated their position in Yemen, they showed tolerance towards the Ishmaelites and allowed them to live in peace amongst them. These Ishmaelites were destined to play a great part in Islamic history, as the foundation of Mecca, attests Amir Ali, was apparently coeval with the establishment of the Abrahamite Arabs in the peninsula; for according to the Arab traditions a Jurhumite chief named Meghass-ibn-Amr, whose daughter was married to the progenitor of the 'naturalised Arabs', Ismail or Ishmael, was the founder of the city. It was, too, Abraham who erected the Temple of Kaaba; and it was the line of descent from which The Prophet Mohamed's ancestry is traced. We will now examine these points before going any further into the history of the Arabs of those times.

FROM: MOHEMED: THE PROPHET

The Building of The Kaaba

WE HAVE SEEN that three sections of peoples inhabited Arabia, and the Muslims claim that The Prophet Mohamed belonged to the Ishmaelites. A little discussion is needed here to show further, that both Abraham and Ishmael having migrated into Arabia, built the shrine of Kaabaat Mecca, and that The Prophet Mohamed is not only descended from them, but also received the ministry of Abraham. Regarding the last statement The Qur'an says in section tenth of Al Haj:

THE FAITH OF YOUR FATHER IBRAHIM,
WHO IT WAS THAT NAMED YOU MUSLIM FIRST
OF ALL

For had Abraham not prayed that his progeny should be of those who had complete submission to the will of Allah – the true spirit of the meaning of the term Muslim –; and according to Sura Baqarah had recited as follows?

Our Lord! and make us both submissive to thee (Muslimeen, is the word used), and raise from our offspring a nation submitting to Thee...

I make those points here especially because non-Muslim writers deny all these statements. Now let us, first of all, endeavour to determine whether Hagar and Ishmael came to live in Arabia or not, and secondly who was it that Abraham wished to offer in sacrifice to his God, whether it was Isaac or Ishmael?

According to the Hebrew traditions, we are told that it was Isaac who was sacrificed, and on that contention the sacrificial spot is pointed out in Syria. But if it could be proved that it was Ishmael and not Isaac who was to be sacrificed, then not only the entire chain of evidence can be linked; but also, regarding the scene of sacrifice we will have to own the authenticity of the Arab writers.

In the Sacred Book of the Jews, we read that the first child of Abraham was the son of Hagar, and the boy was named Ishmael. Isaac was the second son of Abraham from his other wife Sarah. When the two boys grew up, Sarah persuaded her husband to have Hagar and Ishmael banished. After that, in the twenty-first chapter of Pentateuch where it speaks of the Journey Of Birth, we are told the following in the Old Testament:

And Abraham rose up early in the morning, and took bread, and a bottle of water, and gave it unto Hagar, putting it on her shoulder and the Child and sent her away: and she departed, and wandered in the distance.

And the water was spent in the bottle, and she cast the child under one of the shrubs.

And she went and sat her down over against him a good way off, as it were a bowshot: for she said, Let me not see the death of the child, And she sat over against him, and lift up her voice and wept.

THE BUILDING OF THE KAABA

And God heard the voice of the lad; and the angel of God called to Hagar out of heaven, and said unto her, What aileth thee, Hagar? fear not, for God hath heard the voice of the lad where he is.

Arise, lift up the lad, and hold him in thine hand; for I will make him a great nation.

And God opened her eyes, and she saw a well of water; and she went, and filled the bottle of water, and gave the lad drink.

And God was with the lad, and he grew, and dwelt in the wilderness, and became an archer.

And he dwelt in the wilderness of Paran: and his mother took him a wife out of the land of Egypt.

Although the Torah of the Jews insists upon the fact that it was Isaac, and not Ishmael, who was 'offered for Sacrifice' by Abraham, other proof points to the fact that the reverse was the case. It was, for instance, the rule in the earlier ministries that only the first-born was to be thus sacrificed. That command of God Abraham proposed to execute literally and not metaphorically, inasmuch as by the sacrifice, no actual shedding of blood was intended, but of deputing the first-born to serve the shrine and the cause of Allah.

In any case 'when Abraham proceed to slay his son', in the cause of God, so to speak, at His behest; and if that son happened to be Isaac, then it was tantamount to discrediting another command of God in which He had pronounced in the book of Genesis xvii, 19, thus:

And God said, Sarah thy wife shall bear thee a son, indeed; thou shalt call his name Isaac; and I will establish my Covenant with him for an everlasting covenant, and with all his seed after him.

It is obvious from this that God could not issue two orders so diametrically opposed to each other about the one and the same man. The real misunderstanding, of course, is in assuming that Isaac and not Ishmael was the elder brother. Ishmael, indeed, was thirteen years of age when his father attained the age of one hundred, when Abraham is believed to have fallen upon his face and laughed, and said in his heart, shall a child be born unto him that is an hundred years old? and shall Sarah that is ninety years old, bear?

And thus, we found him saying to God 'O that Ishmael might live before thee!' This term really means that Abraham meant to 'sacrifice' and 'offer' his elder son, the first-born, to the service of Allah and not Isaac, to whom he made his heir in worldly affairs. All these facts prove that the 'sacrificed' person was Ishmael and not Isaac.

As regards the place of Sacrifice we must note the Jewish belief which is pointed to be at Marya, situated at Solomon's Temple. A Christian belief has it that the place is no other than where Jesus was crucified. Both of these places are discredited by later researches.

This Marya, or Moarya, or Moreh, is definitely indicated to be within the provinces of Arabia. In the Book of Judges vii. 1 we find '...the host of Midianites were on the north side of them, by the hill of Moreh, in the valley;' and, of course, Midyan is in Arabia. This, then, unquestionably fixes the position of Moreh as being in Arabia; but we might go a step further and quite legitimately assume that the common usage of the word Moreh assumed the form of Marveh, which is no other than the hillock near the Kaaba shrine in Mecca, where Muslim pilgrims perform the rite of Saai during the pilgrimage season.

Imam Malik relates that The Prophet Mohamed, pointing towards Marveh, said: 'All the valleys and hills of Mecca are places of sacrifice.'

Enough had been said to substantiate the belief that it was the eldest son of Abraham – who was Ishmael – that was taken to the land of Moreh or Moriah, to be given as a burnt offering, and that Moriah was in Arabia, and no other spot than the hills of Mecca: indeed so patent is the proof that the entire collection of rites and ceremonies which are enjoined upon the Muslim pilgrims are in strict commemoration of that event of the sacrifice of Ishmael by Abraham.

Let us see how the two approximate. When Abraham had laid the wood near the altar and bound his son, as in Genesis xxii, 10: 'And Abraham stretched forth his hand and took the knife to slay his son. And the angel of the Lord called unto him out of heaven, and said, Abraham, Abraham: and he said here am I.' To this day in the long history of Islam the pilgrims' call is 'Labaik – Labaik – here I am in Thy Presence, here I am in Thy Presence.' In the ministry of Abraham, it was enjoined that during the sacrifice several times circumvolution had to be performed. During the ceremonies of Muslim pilgrimage, the seven rounds of the space of Marvah is the prototype of the same idea. No hair was cut till the pilgrimage was over, this is still the fact in

Islamic pilgrimage practices; also, of course, the cardinal injunction of actual sacrifice is carried out annually during the Haj at Mecca. Do they all not point to the similarity of the two conceptions?

It is sometimes assumed that the city of Mecca and the birth of its ancient history is really imaginary, thrust upon it by the Muslims. The facts, however, are different. The true name of Mecca was Bakka, and it is styled so in The Qur'an in A1 Imran section 4: 'Most surely the first house appointed for men is the one at Bakka, blessed and a guidance for the nations.' In Tafsir-i-Kahir it is spoken of as Tebak, meaning the 'crowding together of men', obviously merchants and pilgrims or a meeting place. Also, a further reference in The Qur'an when Abraham and Ishmael were enjoined to clean up and purify 'My House', must necessarily mean that the House – the Shrine of worship – did not exist before Abraham. These two, the father and the son, according to The Qur'an, 'raised the foundation of the House.'

Even such a great sceptic of all matters Islamic, as Sir William Muir, testifies to the hoary age of Mecca. 'A very high antiquity', he says, must be assigned to the main features of the religion of Mecca... Diodorus Siculus, writing about half a century before our era, says of Arabia washed by the Red Sea, 'There is in this country, a temple greatly revered by the Arabs. These words must refer to the Holy House of Mecca, for we know of no other which ever commanded such universal homage... Tradition represents the Kaaba as from time immemorial the scene of pilgrimage from all quarters of Arabia: from Yemen and Hadhramut, from the shores of the Persian Gulf, and the deserts of Syria, and the distant environs of Hira and Mesopotamia, men yearly flocked to Mecca. So extensive a homage must have had its beginning in an extremely remote age.'

The celebrated Greek astronomer and geographer, Ptolemy, who lived in A.D. 139, according to Musoodi, Ibn Nadim and Yaqut Humwi, gives the dimensions of Mecca as seventy-eight degrees in length and breadth as point three degrees. We must, however, turn to the Oriental sources to find the exact dimensions of the shrine of the Kaaba which Arzaqi provides us. Its height is given as nine yards, in length it was thirty-two yards and in breadth twenty-two yards. This structure of stone erected or repaired was so rough and ready that it boasted neither roof nor doors; and it is not without significance to remember that not till Qossay Bin Kullab – about whom we will have much to say later – of the Quraish tribe received the guardianship of the holy precincts that the building was re-erected, and date palms were laid on it to provide a roof.

Mecca, at this time, lay on the great trade routes over which the merchandise of fertile Yemen passed to the rich lands of Syria. But the doctrines of pure faith were forgotten in the rush of events, in which the wild traits of the Arab race superseded whatever little of religion they had learned. The whole country was in the grips of grossest conceptions of idolatry, over and above the three hundred and sixty idols, one for each day of the year, in the holy shrine of the Kaaba.

The great Hobal, the god of war, carved in red agate, however, retained the principal position in the temple. Around this stood the images of gazelles in silver and gold, also the representations of Abraham and his son. Annually pilgrims thronged the city to kiss the Black Stone built in the shrine of the Kaaba and made seven circuits around the temple.

FROM: MOHEMED: THE PROPHET

Mecca & Beyond

AVOIDING ANY FURTHER contact with the political atmosphere around the Great Mosque, I prepared for the World Muslim Conference, which I had been instructed to attend, should I succeed in reaching Mecca in time for it.

The date of the inauguration was altered no fewer than three times, and it was a great relief when at last we were informed that the Islamic Conference would begin on Sunday, June 6th, at two o'clock. It was to be held in the old Turkish artillery fortification, on the top of a rocky eminence outside the western gate of the city.

As we approached it, I noticed the green Wahabi flag flying from the tower, with the inscription in Arabic in white: 'There is no god but God, and Mohamed is his Prophet'.

Standing alone on grey rocks, the white fort presented a beguiling picture, reminding one of an Arabian knight's castle from the Middle Ages. All around the building, on the rocky ground, earth had been spread and sown with barley and other cereals to produce a green effect like a lawn, and a dozen or so men were spraying water on the young shoots.

At the entrance, white-robed officials wearing white turbans received us and examined our credentials. Then we passed up the wide staircase to the hall upstairs where the

Congress was to deliberate – a spacious oblong apartment some ninety feet in length. There were latticed wooden shutters to the window openings painted green, this also being the colour of the curtains and the covers on the tables. The latter were arranged in the form of two giant horseshoes with a fair space between them.

Most of the leading Muslim countries were represented, though the Turkish delegates failed to make an appearance until later: for Turkey had only recently become a secular State. The USSR had seven delegates; the Hejaz twelve; Java five; India twelve; Nejd five; Asir three; Palestine three, and Syria three. In addition to these, the Wahabi King had arranged for two doctors of theology to appear for the Sudan and three to represent Egypt. In addition to Turkey, neither Iraq nor the Yemen was represented at the Conference until later. The Persians, whose country was one of the very few Islamic ones which was fully independent, never came at all.

Precisely at two o'clock, when all had taken their seats, a muffled explosion shook the building. It was the firing of the salute from the fort announcing that the King was on his way to open the Congress.

'The Sultan! The Sultan!' shouted the usher.

We rose to our feet and saw about a dozen black guards wearing red tunics, white breeches and black knee boots, with the customary drawn swords, ascend the steps, followed by King Abdul-Aziz Ibn Al Saud himself, accompanied by his son the Emir Faisal. Behind them were his ministers, military officials and another bodyguard.

The King went first to the antechamber just behind the President's chair and then took his seat in the middle of the hall at the President's desk. His Chief Secretary, Sheikh Hafiz Wahaba, later Saudi Ambassador in London, stood on his right and read the King's Speech:

'I welcome you, my fellow-brothers of Islam, and I am thankful that you have accepted my invitation to join this Congress, the first of its kind in Islamic history. I hope and pray to Almighty God that year by year we shall assemble to discuss our various problems. In the past, there has been no such thing as Islamic public opinion. Islam has lacked the spirit of reformation and uplift. The government of the Hejaz has been administered by Caliphs or Sultans, who paid little attention to the question of the betterment of this country. There were other Islamic rulers with good intentions who, on account of their illiteracy and lack of knowledge, showed their incapacity to do good to Arabia. Wealthy men, who cared nothing for the future of this country, gave licence and liberty to the people here to such an extent that in this holy and sacred city un-Islamic practices became rife and disturbances began all over the country. Some of the governors of this country have been severe both to the pilgrims and to the inhabitants of this city.

'After the decline of Turkish rule in Arabia, when the government fell into the hands of Sharif Husein and his son Ali, the whole Islamic world became uneasy on account of their inability to govern this sacred land, and every Muslim became anxious concerning the future peace and prosperity of the country. Official papers which have fallen into our hands justify our statement that its late rulers had handed over the independence of the country to foreigners and that they were in their pay. We, the people of Nejd, being the neighbours of the Hejaz, were particularly affected by the cruelties of Husein. He regarded us as infidels and prohibited us from performing our religious pilgrimage to Mecca. Not only did he do this, but he was instrumental in fanning discontent among my subjects of Nejd. When the limit to these cruelties and depredations had been reached and my Ministers and compatriots satisfied me that it was my religious duty to protect Islam from such evils, then, relying upon God and God's support alone, I did not spare my life and property and money to achieve that end. God gave us victory and helped us to purge the sacred land of its oppressors and enabled us, the people of Nejd, to fulfil our promise towards the people of Islam.

'I further fulfilled that promise by inaugurating this International Muslim Congress, and in my invitation to you I spoke of my personal views regarding the future government of the Hejaz. My first invitation received no response, except from our brothers in India. Though disappointed, I issued a second which I am glad to see has borne fruit. You can see with your own eyes that not only are the various sacred places and shrines in the Hejaz safe, but their sanctity is being preserved, and these dearly beloved places are being duly protected. For the first time for many generations, there is peace in the land and perfect security to the pilgrim. This state of peace and tranquillity I mean to maintain according to the strict injunctions of Islam. I invited you to this assembly to discuss and explore avenues for the moral and religious betterment of the Hejaz which may be satisfactory to God and man alike. This Government is being run on the lines of The Qur'an and is free from the vices which had crept into the general practices of the people. I request you to discuss these points. I desire you to make up the deficiency in the morals of the people and to make this sacred land the real fount and cradle of goodness and civilisation, of health and goodwill. Almost everything in this country requires some betterment, and in the betterment of the people of the Hejaz every Muslim must help. My brothers, you are a free people gathered together in this assembly to give free expressions of your views. Islam's weakness today is the wrangling between various sects, which is contrary to the dictates of the Holy Book. And I beg of you to discover means of obtaining a cohesion of ideas and the lowering of those barriers that keep heart from heart. I pray God that He may guide you and me to a serious solution of these difficult problems. May peace be with you.'

The speech was heard in silence. The King rose, bowed to right and left, gave his greetings, went to his antechamber, and returned to his palace, with his guards following him, while all stood.

We were left in a dilemma as to the mode of procedure. As the King had said, we had never had an international Islamic conference before.

Hafiz Wahaba proposed that, for the time being, the oldest delegate should occupy the presidential chair and conduct the business till a permanent president should be elected, and this honour fell to Maulvi Abdul Wahid.

He read a long passage from The Qur'an, after which Mohamed Ali, the delegate of the Caliphate Committee from India, (the man who had shortly before attacked me for such crimes as my marriage and being a British spy and stooge) rose and said it was very regrettable that brothers in Islam – namely the Turks and the Arabs – had been set against one another in that holy city as a result of the revolt of the Arabs against the Turks during the War, largely engineered by the mischievous activities of Husein and his followers.

Now that the reconstruction of Islamic interests was being effected through the agency of that assembly, he thought it only right and fitting that the head of the Turkish delegation should be made president, in order to cement the rapprochement between the peoples of the Islamic world.

Evidently our temporary president, Maulvi Abdul Wahid, could not tolerate this, the more so as no Turkish delegate was present. Jumping to his feet and shaking with old age and emotion, he declared that the suggestion of Mohamed Ali was calculated to widen the fissure and break up the friendly attitude of Muslim peoples. And when he went on to hint that Mohamed Ali was actuated by personal desires, Ali's elder brother as well as other Indian delegates, jumped up and protested vehemently against the charge. There was general consternation and an interchange of uncomplimentary remarks.

Had not someone judiciously hinted that this was a serious gathering of responsible men assembled to solve certain vexed problems and not a vegetable market, matters might have descended to abuse and blows.

The election of President resulted in the victory of Sharif Adnana, who secured forty-four votes. Hafiz got one vote, and the head of the non-existent Turkish delegation nine. There were some blanks.

Generally speaking, many people were glad to welcome Sharif Adnana because he was a man of sober ideas. He had been an exile for some years and had only recently returned to his home, and he was liked by everybody.

Then came the election of two vice-presidents, wherein the Seyyid Suleiman Nadvi secured thirty-two votes and Raz-ed-Din thirty. The former was the chairman of the Caliphate Committee in India and the latter, leader of the delegates from the USSR.

When it was announced that the election of a secretary-general would take place, Mohamed Ali rose on a point of order. Hitherto the Congress had been conducted in Arabic, and to the surprise of everyone Mohamed Ali spoke in English.

This was strange, for the Ah brothers had declared time and again in India that, as well as the British Government, the English language was to be boycotted.

Amid some confusion, it was discovered that the great leader of the tens of millions of Indian Muslims could not express himself in the Holy Tongue of Arabic: and there was some curiosity as to exactly what a 'point of order' was. And whether such a point was an Islamic, or a British, invention.

The sudden introduction, at such a gathering and in such a place, of the tongue of what the Indians were continuously telling the Arabs was an 'infidel' race –in the mouth of a devout and prayerful Muslim divine, one who was an avowed enemy of the British: it was, to say the least, extraordinary in the eyes of those present.

One of the Arab delegates quickly interrupted the rather excited Maulvi, declaring that if he could not speak in

Arabic, the real language of Islam, he had better express himself in Hindustani or whatever language he knew which was not that of his enemies, and an interpreter would be found.

But Mohamed Ali continued in English, after claiming that he spoke English because it was the language of a 'People of the Book', the English Christians, even though they were his enemies. He refused to speak Urdu, his native tongue, because, he said, it was known by millions of 'unclean Hindus, idol-worshippers...'

Having been given permission to continue in the Book People's language, the Maulvi wanted to know on what basis the delegates had been elected. Indian representatives, he declared, should be entitled to more votes than those of Nejd or Asir, because they represented an infinitely larger body of Muslims. When his remarks were translated, there was much talk and whispering among those on the President's right where sat the representatives of Nejd, Asir, the Hejaz and Syria. They did not wish to accept that there was anything in Mohamed Ali's contention. They failed to understand how he dared to make such a proposal, breaching etiquette to such a disastrous degree, in such an assembly.

He wanted, they said, to differentiate between Muslim and Muslim. He was seeking self-advertisement and self-aggrandisement, which the restive independence and individualism of the Arab cannot brook.

Voting papers were then handed round, but once more Mohamed Ali rose and inquired of the President what had become of his proposal. There was no reply, and when he realised he was being ignored he made another suggestion, turning the tables completely.

'We in India', he said, 'are slaves; we are not independent, our necks are bleeding under the hobnails of the English. We cannot justifiably claim to have equal status with the free people of Nejd or the Hejaz. I propose, therefore, that if we Muslims in India have one vote, then the people of independent countries should have four.'

Perhaps he thought this would please the Arabs. But, like the preceding proposal, nobody made any comment. Taufiq Sharif was elected secretary-general by an overwhelming majority.

Next day, the real work began. The first item was that the assembly be called the 'All-World Muslim Congress'; that it be held yearly in Mecca during the time of the pilgrimage. Here, Mohamed Ali rose to propose an amendment.

'Supposing there is war in Arabia', he said, 'and the delegates could not get to Mecca; where is the assembly to sit?'

After some discussion, it was decided that if there were war or disturbances in Mecca then the Congress would meet in some independent Islamic country where Islamic law was practised; failing such a country, then in the best possible Islamic province.

Another proposal was to purchase the buildings surrounding the Great Mosque, knock them down, and make a wide avenue right around the Holy Place. This led to very heated discussion. The majority of the delegates favoured it; but apparently not a few had vested interests in the properties concerned.

However, it was referred to a committee with instructions that it should go thoroughly into the question, draw up plans, and advise the Government of the Hejaz on the subject.

One of the most far-reaching schemes, which was duly carried after three days' discussion, was the proposal to build a railway line between Jeddah and Mecca and link it with the Hejaz Railway at Medina, and also to construct a branch line to Yanbu, the port of Medina. It was also agreed to carry out certain essential improvements at the port of Rabegh, on the Red Sea, south of Yanbu. A harbour was to be built and docking accommodation provided.

An interesting feature of the railway proposal was that the money for the construction of the line was to be provided by general subscription throughout the various Islamic countries, and when the undertaking was completed and running, half of the revenue was to go to the Hejaz Government and the other half to the upkeep of the line.

'Why half the proceeds should go to the Government, when the Arabs were not prepared to spend a penny on it, can best be answered by the Wahabi King himself', added Mohamed Ali.

There was an outcry at this further infraction of good behaviour; but the Arabs have a great sense of humour. A sheikh from Medina restored everyone's good temper, in a doubtless unconscious imitation of the true parliamentary manner, by suggesting that the Indian be forgiven, 'since he was clearly suffering from the unfortunate effects of what he had earlier described as the condition in his country: British hobnails on his neck!'

Other resolutions passed included the decision to establish hospitals and base camps where pilgrims making the Haj could obtain medical attention and comforts; and finally, it was agreed that from next year, every delegate must contribute towards the running expenses of the Congress.

The spirit of good fellowship which existed at the Conference was, however, marred in its later phase when the Ah brothers sharply questioned Wahabi practices.

Many of the customs which were resorted to by the ignorant pilgrims, especially Indians, run contrary to the true spirit of Islam; and these the Wahabis rightly prohibited, thus giving an opportunity to the Ah brothers to raise a storm on that score. Not only did they want to have the repair and guardianship of the shrines in the hands of a body of which they would be a part: they also urged that ah fees collected from the pilgrims should be disbursed by the nominees of the Conference; which was clearly transgressing the laws of hospitality and an interference in the sovereignty of the Wahabi Kingdom – which even a far lesser man than the redoubtable Abdul-Aziz Ibn Saud would never have tolerated.

Throughout, there was an extraordinary demonstration of cultural differences, when the continuous interruptions and adversarial habits of the people of the Indian subcontinent –which they found perfectly normal at home –were met with a wall of silent disapproval from grave-faced Arabs, who had seldom experienced anything like it. It was indeed a striking lesson in culture-clash.

The Conference broke up after a stormy session for the performance of the actual pilgrimage. The full pilgrimage does not consist only of visiting Mecca; close to the Holy City at Arafat many religious ceremonies have to be performed.

On the 8th of Zilhij the pilgrims, wearing only the usual regulation costume of one white sheet, leave Mecca. Taking the Taif road, everyone journeys to the plains of Arafat; and usually a halt is called at the village of Mina after about three hours' journey from Mecca; but many continue straight on to Arafat. Crossing the landmark of Muzdalifa and the narrow rocky defiles, one comes to the Hill of Mercy, at which sacrifices are offered to complete the Haj ceremony.

Smitten with the heat and in the grip of a high fever, I left the Cradle of Islam, after completing my various duties.

Dawn was breaking; its grandeur grew lovelier and more definite as one streak of light blended with another on the ridges far away; and the two-seater car kindly supplied by the King sped on to the shores of the Red Sea.

The moving sand was like the marching of men; and, though ill in body – for I had contracted enteric fever – I had an inner feeling of exhilaration at having performed a visit to a place the like of which exists nowhere else in the world – the cynosure of Islam, the grail of every Muslim's heart.

I was advised to get out of the heat as quickly as I could; and at Jeddah, fortunately, a small craft was setting her sails. With little difficulty, I got standing room on it. The captain of the boat, though not knowing me, was willing to take a chance with a passenger in his lugger-boat as far as Port Sudan, just across the Red Sea.

The Sudanese crew looked at me almost with reverence as I stood bargaining to be taken across to their country. Though they visited Jeddah regularly, they were not able to afford the journey to Holy Mecca themselves.

Every pilgrim back from the land of the Hejaz is an object of respect and envy to these simple and lovable people of the Sudan. But I was too dazed with fever to take any notice of their congratulations on having been to the Cradle of Islam. Jumping into their somewhat unsteady rowing-boat, I bade them hasten. As to what coin I gave them for hire I do not remember; for me it was enough that I was getting to some place where I could find a bed to rest on.

There was only one hotel in Port Sudan, just facing the quay, and it was modern. They wanted to charge me a gold pound a day, and wanted it in advance. I told them I had three sovereigns in my possession. I had little hope of reaching Jerusalem, my ultimate destination, with only three coins and the enteric fever still in the marrow of my bones, the management thought. But I felt rich enough: and I was in a daze. I reeled to a room and, switching on the electric fan, I flung myself on to the bed. I knew no more till fully twenty-four hours later, and whether it was sleep or if I was comatose, I never cared to ascertain.

It was on the third day, when the management found that I could not pay in advance because I wished to retain that last coin, that I had to leave the hotel. There was not much to pack – only a prayer mat and a copy of The Qur'an. I possessed nothing more.

I had a belt with a large brass buckle on it, given to me by my Sufi teacher, who had drawn my attention to the symbol inscribed on it. I had half understood that this device might be recognised by others on the same spiritual path: who might help, but only when one was at the end of one's tether.

Thus, it was that, overcome by heat and dehydration, I sat down in the impoverished souk of Port Sudan like any other of the many exhausted wayfarers who dotted its streets. I found under my hand a small piece of charcoal. Behind me was a whitewashed wall. On the wall I carefully drew the symbol; a sort of double-square. Then I fell asleep, or unconscious…

I woke with a start, to find water being splashed on my face, and a man speaking to me in Hindustani.

In conversation, I discovered that my young friend was a Borah, originally from Bombay, who traded in betel-nuts, wrist watches, cloth – in fact, anything and everything which he could import from India in a small way. He thought I looked forlorn, he said, and guessed that I must be needing help. He carefully wiped the symbol of the Sufis from the wall with a clean towel, and took me to his home, where I was given food and rest for some days.

Then he took me to his warehouse. It was a barn of a place divided into two sections, an office and a store. The building was open at the back like a caravanserai. The office had no files, no pen or ink, no ledgers. All business was done by word of mouth. He did not believe in wasting his time dusting the office, because 'as soon as you dust, another sandstorm would soon make it dusty again'.

For day after day, I sat under the thatched roof in his warehouse, drinking soda-water which was quickly made by throwing handfuls of something into an earthen pot of water beside me.

Our dinner consisted of dried dates, rice and smoked and dried meat soaked in camel's fat. I helped myself liberally and liked it, chiefly because I had been living on rather short, if not non-existent, rations. The pound-a-day at the hotel did not include any food.

A few days later, a score or more Indians and others of the non-Arab population, who were either employed or were trading at Port Sudan, were invited to meet me. Dried dates and curd were served, and even the notionally vegetarian Hindu merchants were eating camel with the rest.

It was astonishing to me to hear how well these crowds of Indian Hindu shopkeepers spoke Arabic. Of course, they pronounced the words with their own Hindustani accent. They were not going to give up all their national characteristics, they said, when I enquired about intonation. Far into the night we sat, talking and gossiping about many lands and many trades. Occasionally, our host had to chase a jackal away from under the floor of the huts, which were built on raised and propped-up wooden platforms.

Perhaps it was that the period of my fever was over; or it was the change in the air from Arabia to Africa; or only that Fate had ordained that I should continue to live. Anyway, I was soon better –so much better indeed, that I actually walked to the quay to see whether there was any prospect of sailing to the Near East. And there was one ship there. They were loading peanuts onto it.

For a consideration, I proposed to the man on watch that his captain might take me to a European port. I was taken before the captain.

'What do you want?' he growled at me. I explained.

'I can't', he said, 'and I would not! Quite a lot of scoundrels want to escape. I am not of those who will give them a lift and get into trouble for it.'

He blew hard his strawberry nose and gulped another dose of a beverage denied to me as a Muslim. I descended the gangway, very much down from my pedestal.

'Besides', he yelled after me, 'you can speak English. Why do you not buy and sell like those blighters who are fore and aft of you?'

Buy and sell! The thought leaped into my mind.

Sheikh Umru, the local bead-and-curio-merchant, had many men working for him. Why should I not sell his wares at the dockside? The Sheikh agreed, and soon provided me with beads and amulets of glass, trinkets of sorts reputedly hand-cut by the best Sudanese workmen; but in fact, imported from Birmingham. Lion claws, hair from the mane of the king of the animals, made into brooches and so on in the workshop of the Sheikh, were sold to the European curio-hunters who frequently passed on British ships through Port Sudan.

When the next steamer arrived, I was ready with dangling strings of beads, rosaries of the Holy Witch, and the claw that warded off evil.

Old and young, mostly women, crowded the rails and yelled at me to come up. My rival tradesmen were more fleet footed than I; they had experience dating back to when they had been urchins. But the British soon found that I could make myself better understood. They clamoured to examine the wares of the native who spoke English so well.

Thus, I made a good harvest. I was bringing psychology into trade. I saw a young courting couple mooning like two half-wits as they bent over the ship's railing, giggling over nothing. Approaching them, I proffered the young lady a ring of elephant hair and dilated upon its wonder-working qualities bringing good luck to the newly wed. Only a few of that kind of ring were made by a Sudanese witch every year. That was the local belief, anyway. Its price was more than one of equal weight in gold. In fact, I could have said more in its praises, according to the Sheikh's advice, but a little was sufficient and the magic ring was promptly bought.

The next customer was a missionary lady from South India. She knew the price of the junk which I carried, for it was her thirty-first voyage back to the East. But one thing she did not know: psychology. The beads she did not want; for the other bric-a-brac also she had no use; but had I a cure for baldness? I did; and the solution was none other than common salt and ammonia, slightly coloured with madder. The people of the-Red Sea coast swore by it...

A sergeant's wife, with what seemed like about nine infants hanging round her, hailed me next, but seeing her encumbrances I did not break my neck to serve her; instead, I edged round to a prosperous-looking middle-aged man.

He was too wise to patronise me, and remarked to his fellow in the next deckchair that in Dundee they could buy my entire assortment for ninepence. 'So you can! But have you seen this stamp which I have? A real Arab stamp, amazingly old?' He had not, and he bought it at a good price for his album, which had incidentally fallen from his lap as I approached him, a fact of which I had made a mental note. By the time I had finished, I counted fully nine gold pounds profit on my sales –not bad for an afternoon's business. For the first time, I realised the meaning of studying one's market.

It was a great evening in the annals of the Sheikh's trading days when he counted the proceeds of my afternoon's sales. We went fifty-fifty. A month of such brisk trading, and I should have enough to pay for my fare to Europe on a cargo ship; so I tarried at Port Sudan, making ready for the arrival of the next steamer.

After a week's weary waiting, the next boat did arrive, but there was a yellow flag floating from its masthead. They had smallpox on board. For the next three weeks, no further ship came into Port Sudan, and my employer found my keep rather expensive.

Then there was another intervention in my life. One dark night, as I was sitting somewhat morosely in the dimly lit shop, an employee of a shipping agency where I had enquired for a passage came to see me. He gave me enough in Egyptian money to buy a ticket to Port Said and a little over; but on one condition did he offer it.

'I am a follower of the Sufi path, a dervish', he said, 'and not a rich man. I want to see that no deserving person is stranded and will help everyone I can: provided you will not mention my name to anybody, and do not return the sum to me, but rather make a chain of this good action. Help someone else in the manner that I have helped you.'

I was so moved with this true spirit of charity that I very nearly wept. Slipping the money into my hand, he was gone, perhaps never to meet me again.

The very next day, I took passage on a freighter. The sum at my disposal could not buy me anything better than deck accommodation. When I had paid even for that cheapest of all rates, I had just two gold pieces left. These I tied in the corner of my handkerchief and wore it under my shirt, next to my skin.

The ship had hardly left the shore, when the thought of food on the voyage distressed me. The purser could not allow any rations to be given to me for less than eight pounds; so, being at my wit's end, I had either to cook my own food with the Lascars and buy flour and butter and other items, which would cost at least three pounds up to Port Said; or fall upon the mercy of the unhelpful-looking Goanese head-waiter on the boat. I chose the latter course. He agreed to give me the leftovers from the table for a pound. The other pound I tied even more securely around my neck, for I wanted to travel beyond the Egyptian coast. Three meals I was given by the waiter.

True to the bargain, they were scraps from the table, half-pats of butter, a nibbled piece of toast, a discoloured, over-sugared and discarded cold cup of tea. These delicacies were placed before me in the scullery of the dining-saloon, and then I ate voraciously, thanking God fervently for His small mercies.

In between the meals, I used to mix with my fellow-passengers on the deck.

There were eight Hindus, all bound for South America to ply some small pedlar's trade.

There was a young Indian Muslim from Kenya with his tiny son, whom he was taking to school in England. Once a rising light at Cambridge University, this young man had incurred the wrath of his conservative Indian father by marrying an English woman.

When the old gentleman cut him off with a shilling, he gallantly went as a trader to Kenya and was doing fairly well.

Then there was another rather sober-looking young Punjabi. A former Sikh, he was now an enthusiastic convert to the Christian Scientists, and was on his way to its centre in Boston.

A long and narrow passage ran along the hold in the ship, and it was there that we 'lived' during the night. All along the length of the space, iron bunks were fixed to the side of the ship. There were no portholes, no means of breathing fresh air. You could hardly breathe at all, unless you opened the iron doors and flooded the interior with foetid air. Everybody did his cooking there, the Hindus took their baths in the place, they spread their washing there to dry, and then we all slept there.

If the Black Hole of Calcutta or a prison cell is worse than the accommodation which I am describing, then all I can say is that you should thank your stars that you have not the experience of that place which I had.

And then the greatest of all tragedies occurred.

One bright morning, while I was admiring the scenery of the coastline, the ship lurched a little; a spray of water rose high and, dashing itself against our lower deck, completely soaked us. It was easy to dry myself merely by donning the pilgrim sheet. During this operation of changing however, I must somehow have loosened the knot in the handkerchief.

As I stooped, the precious coin fell with a tinkle and rolled smoothly, quickly as a ray of light on its yellow glistening body; down it leaped into the bowels of the sea. With it went my sole hope of travelling beyond the Egyptian coast.

FROM: ALONE IN ARABIAN NIGHTS

Government of Pre-Islamic Mecca

THE GUARDIANSHIP OF the Kaaba – the shrine of the Black Stone, records Amir Ali, was originally an appanage of the children of Ishmael, had in consequence of the Babylonian attack, passed into the hands of the Jurhumites. But another clan was gaining strength, that of the Bani-Khuzaa, who issuing from their southern strongholds in the mountains of Yemen overthrew the Jurhumites and made themselves the masters of Mecca.

Gradually the people of Ishmae,l who had suffered almost total annihilation at the hands of the Babylonians, showed some signs of regeneration. It was during the first century before Christ that one Adnan, one of the important scions of the Ishmaelites, had married a daughter of a Jurhumite prince. The issue of this marriage, One Maad, finally re-established his power over Nejd and the whole of the Hijaz.

But whereas the adjoining provinces were thus reduced, the sole guardianship of the holy shrine still remained in the hands of the Kuzaites. Then Fihr, an able descendent of Maad, fell heir to the Ishmaelite clans with a rulership over slightly larger tracts of lands than his progenitor, but yet the control over the shrine of Mecca was not his up to the third century of the Christian era.

The power of the Khuzaites, however, gave way before Qossay, a descendent of Fihr, upon the death of the last Khuzaiter King. Qossay was the fifth in descent from Fihr and was born about A.D. 398. The title of Quraish was given by this chieftain to his people, for henceforth the Ishmaelite sway was absolutely complete over the Hijaz, for the shrine of Mecca had now come within his pale of governance. Qossay, however, accomplished this about the middle of the fifth century of the Christian era. The Quraish had, therefore, come to stay in the land, for it was that section of the Ishmaelite which gave to Arabia The Prophet of Islam. These researches incidently place it indisputably out of consideration that The Prophet Mohamed was humbly born.

Qossay, as an organiser and legislator, had no compeer in his predecessors. Until his rule, the Quraishite families were widely separated, even those who lived in Mecca lived very far apart from each other, and there were hardly any within a close proximity of the coveted shrine of the Kaaba, the protection of which he considered his one aim in life. Perceiving the dangers to which the national pantheon was exposed from its unprotected condition, remarks Amir Ah, he induced the Quraish to settle down in its vicinity, leaving a sufficient space free on the four sides of the temple for circumambulation.

His capacity as a ruler soon brought forth those fruits of peace which come with good government, the wealth of the realm increased, and from his method of managing a state we can gather some interesting facts regarding the government of early Arabia. He was perhaps the first chieftain who has had a house of representatives erected, but only the men of his own clan could be admitted to it. In this Dar un Nadwa or the Council Hall, not only civil functions were held but disputed cases were heard, and judgment was given under the presidency of the head chief, who had a council of elders; none of the members was to be under the age of forty years.

It was, too, at this hall, according to the foregoing authority, that the Quraishites, when about to engage in a war, received from the hands of Qossay, the standard, Liwa. He used to attach the white piece of cloth to a lance which one of his sons bore to the chiefs of the Quraishites. It was during his time, too, that an annual poor-tax was levied, called the Rifada, out of which poor pilgrims were fed. He was then the first man of his race to install the three historical institutions those of the council hall, giving of the standard and charity for the poor pilgrims, respectively known as Nadwa, Liwa and Rifada; and from the upkeep of these institutions the ruling house of the Quraishites was ever distinguishable from all other tribes and clans. These were regarded as the princely emblems: and no one other than the Quraishites was permitted to observe them. This priest, king and judge centralised the functions of the church and the state in himself till he died in A.D. 480, leaving his section of the Ishmaelites, the Quraishites or the Quraish as undisputed guardians and protectors of the shrine of the Kaaba.

After Qossay's death his son, Abdud-Dar assumed the title of the chief of Quraish and the pontiff. But as soon as the uneventful reign of Abdud-Dar closed, then the descendants of his brother Abdu Manaf began to contest the prerogatives of the great chief with the direct descendants of Qossay, namely the children of Abdud-Dar. This dispute arose, let it be remembered, on account of the maladministration of the realm by Abdud-Dar's progency, and by no means due to the jealousy on the part of the other sections of the clan.

A division of duties, however, was soon effected. To Abdus Shams, the sons of Abdu Manaf, the right of controlling and distribution of the sacred well of Zam Zam was given, as well as the collection and distribution of the poor-tax. Whilst the retention of the Kaaba shrine keys, the distribution and presentation of Liwa, the standard, to the army and the presidency of the Council of state was entrusted to the house of Abdud-Dar; that is to say, a sort of dual monarchy was satisfactorily established. This control of the state, however, soon passed into the hands of Hashim, brother of Abdus Shams. Hashim died in Syria in A.D. 510, where he had taken his merchandise, leaving a son named Shayba with his Yathribite wife Salma. It was then Muttalib, who journeyed to Syria to bring home his sister-in-law and young nephew Shayba – later named as Abdul Muttalib – and assume the duties of the state which passed to him on the death of his brother Hasham.

From this period onwards the part of Arabian history goes apace, which has direct bearing upon the story of early Islam in general, and on the life of The Prophet Mohamed in particular. This is a juncture, too, where mistakes are easily made to appreciate the events which continue to play upon the doings of the Quraish, and if essentials of the historical data of this period are not firmly grasped the comprehension of The Prophets' work is rendered almost impossible. By knowing these details fully, one will be enabled to realise the extent of transformation which Mohamed's ministry brought about in the government of Arabia; as indeed, by the study of an earlier chapter regarding the social depravity of the people at that time, the student will be able to judge the influence which The Prophet's labours exercised upon the social side.

We had then, only two men of consequence in the then Arab polity: Muttalib, and his nephew Abdul Muttalib as the leaders of the house of Quraish. The former died in Yemen about the end of the year of A.D. 520 leaving Abdul Muttalib, his 'white-haired' nephew, in virtual command of all that the chiefdom of the Quraish stood for at the time; that is to say, presidency over both the state and the church. It was a presidency inasmuch as the different offices of the government were divided between ten senators, every one of these holding the office as an hereditary favour. Amir Ali explains that facet of it most admirably; and I could very usefully reproduce his analysis here. The dignatories, according to his researches, were as follows:

I.   The Hijaba, or the guardianship of the keys of the Kaaba, a sacerdotal office of considerable importance and rank. It was allotted to the house of Abdud Dar, and at the time when Mecca was converted to Islam, it was held by Osman, the son of Talha.

II. The Sikaya, or the intendance of the sacred wells of Zam Zam, and of all the water destined for the use of the pilgrims. This dignity belonged to the house of Hashim, and was held at the time of the conquest of Mecca, by Abbas, the uncle of The Prophet.

III. The Diyat, or the civil and criminal magistracy, which had for a long time, belonged to the house of Taym-ibn-Murra, and, at the time of The Prophet's advent, was held by Abdullah-ibn-Kuhnafa, surnamed Abu Bakr.

IV. The Sifarath, or legation. The person to whom this office belonged was the plenipotentiary to the state, authorised to discuss and settle the difference which arose between the Quraish and the other Arab tribes, as also with strangers. This office was held by Omar.

V. The Liwa or the custody of the standard, under which the nation marched against the enemies. The guardian of this standard was the Commander-in-Chief of the State troops. This military charge appertained to the house of Ommeyya, and was held by Abu Sufyan, the son of Harb, the most implacable enemy of Mohamed.

VI. The Rifada, or the administration of the poor tax. Formed with the alms of the nation, it was employed to provide food for the poor pilgrims, whether travellers or residents, when the state regarded as the guest of the shrine. This duty, after the death of Abu Talib, upon whom it had devolved after Abul Muttalib was transferred to the house of Naufal, son of Abdu Manaf, and was held at the time of The Prophet by Harith, son of Amr.

VII. The Nadwa, the presidency of the national assembly. The holder of this office was the first councillor of the State, and under his advice all public acts were transacted. Aswad, of the house of Abdul Uzza, son of Qossay, held this dignity at the time of The Prophet.
VIII. The Khaimmeh, the guardianship of the council chamber. This function, which conferred upon the incumbent the right of convoking the assembly and even of calling to arms the troops, was held by Khalid, son of Walid, of the house of Yakhzam, son of Marra.
IX. Khazina, or the administration of public finances, belonged to the house of Hassan, son of Kaab, and was held by Harith, son of Qais.
X. The Azlam, the guardianship of diving arrows, by which the judgment of the gods and goddesses was obtained. Safawan, brother of Abu Sufyan, held this dignity. At the same time, it was an established custom that the oldest member exercised the greatest influence, and bore the title of Rais or Syed, chief or lord par excellence. Abbas, at the time of The Prophet, was the first of these senators.

Abdul Muttalib, the son of Hashim, was the most influential member of the Quraish family: and as is the custom with warrior clans, he was eager to have a large progeny to protect his house and continue his influence as the leader of the tribe. And on account of the fact five of the sons of this patriarch have received fame or notoriety with or in connection with Islam a detailed mention of Abdul Muttalib's family is not without significance here.

His twelve sons were: Harith, Abdul Uzza alias Abu Lahab, Abdu Manaf, known as Abu Talib, Zubair, Abdullah, Dhirar, Abbas, Mukawwim, Jahl, and Hamza, the names of the other two sons are not known; and had six daughters. It should, therefore, be borne in mind that the government of the Quraish, with Mecca as the fountain head, was officered almost entirely by the sons, nephews, sons-in-law or first cousins of this venerable patriarch, Abul Muttalib: he was thus the Father of the Quraish Government at the time.

Beyond the fact that in consequence of what is said above, Abul Muttalib had an undoubted pre-eminence both in the administration of the law and whatever of religion there was at the time, two incidents in his life single him out from the rest of his people. The one is that he wanted to sacrifice his son Abdullah to the shrine, and Abdullah was the father of The Prophet Mohamed; the second is that during his time, the Abyssinian viceroy of Yemen brought his legions on elephants in order to destroy the Mecca shrine.

As a by-product of the former incident, however, we could not lose sight of the point that in the upbringing of Mohamed, this old Chieftain's association is perhaps the most pertinent issue bearing upon the subject of this book: the life-story of the Islamic Prophet. The events of Abdul Mattalib's day will, therefore, more than repay study.

It cannot be said that Abdul Muttalib was unduly priest-ridden or that he wished to emphasise his adhesion to the laws of his idolatrous ancestors in order to gain more influence in the eyes of his people, when towards the latter part of his life as the father of eighteen children he felt progressively drawn to the idea that time had arrived when one of his sons must be sacrificed to the holy shrines of Mecca. That one or other of the members of his household were always falling ill, may be no more and no less than a mere incident in the work-a-day life of a large family, nevertheless Abdul Muttalib could not forget that when young he had taken a vow that he would bestow one of his sons if he were blessed with a large progeny, and that he might live to see them grow into hardy men and women. The gods had fulfilled his wishes, and it was incumbent upon him now to make good his part of the bargain. The insistent illness in his house, which I have likened to mere incident and liable to occur in any large household, however presumed itself ever more rigorously upon his mind as a persistent reminder of the gods to fulfil his vow.

It was in this frame of mind that Abdul Mattalib rose that special day of which I speak, he sent word to Abdullah, his dearest son, to come to him beyond that rock-strewn valley which skirts Mecca on the way to the fruit-laden glens of the Taif highlands. There he confided his purpose to Abdullah, and the latter, true to the Ishmaelite traditions, submitted as readily as did Abraham's son to his father. As the two walked back home, resignation sat upon their brows, and the ladies of the house, being acute observers of human impulses, were not slow to guess the reason for the preparation of a feast which was ordered by their father to be ready at sundown.

Presently, cousins, sons and relatives of Abdul Muttalib gathered in the courtyard of Abdullah's sister. Wearing their proud robes, they were still crowding, for they knew that Abdul Muttalib had not required their presence without a good purpose. The high priest had now entered, and hardly had he taken the salutations of the faithful to the shrine that all eyes were turned towards the stony stairs, cut as they were on the side of the rock that formed the eastern flank of the courtyard. Abdul Muttalib stood there holding the hand of his favourite son Abdullah. Then the tribesmen knew the mind of their chief.

In the name of the three hundred and sixty gods of the Kaaba, in the name of the hoary traditions of the Quraish, he recalled the vow that he had taken. Now as he was growing old and had lived to see his children at the heights of power and glory, he wished them to continue to flourish thuswise. Could he hope to perpetuate the happy condition of life without giving to the gods their due, to those that have blessed him with so much? He then spoke of bestowing Abdullah to the shrine of the pagan gods of Kaaba. Abdullah he chose because Abdullah was his dearest son, for Abdul Muttalib's gods will not be propitiated with the less precious offering than what was the most cherished life in the eyes of the old chief.

There was a tense silence as Abdul Muttalib sat down, whilst the elders touched their beards, and eyed each other not knowing what to say, then one bolder than the rest raised his arm: 'Nay, nay, O! Abdul Muttalib', he protested; 'worthy as thy intention is, Abdullah is just as dear to us as in thine old eyes.' He proposed that camels may be given in exchange to the shrine. It was now the turn of the high priest to speak, who drew their attention to the fact that in the past all questions were to be decided by divining at the shrine; and men's voices were as worthless as salt on sandy hills when compared to the decision of the oracle. The men had not done talking when a batch of women demanded the right to be heard. Near the gate, hefty men were barring the way to the rush of a dozen women who wanted to force their way to the centre of the gathering. They were the sisters of Abdullah and his women relations. Whatever the truth of the story, they were led by a woman who is said to have seen a radiance dart out from the forehead of Abdullah, and the wise women of the desert alleged that that young man was a forebearer of someone extraordinary in the annals of mankind.

In such conservative gatherings, as can well be imagined, when the affairs of one man really interested the whole clan, matters like the dedication of a son to a shrine always tended to become a controversial subject; so that passions were getting enflamed, the gathering soon divided into rival parties, one insisting that the lad should be given to the shrine, the other that he could be rescued in exchanging camels. But Abdul Muttalib was adamant in fulfilling his vow: and, therefore, to decide the issue it was agreed to have the oracle speak about the affair.

A great concourse of humanity filled the holy precincts of the Kaaba. The elders of the tribes filed in one by one and stood around the shrine; the high priest, taking the old chieftain by the right hand and Abdullah by the left, solemnly advanced to face Hobal, the Stone War-God, then he touched the statues of silver and gold gazales, and went round the three hundred and sixty idols. This done, he ascended the steps at the foot of the shrine. The divining spears were drawn with the name of Abdullah in exchange for ten camels.

The oracle spoke about accepting Abdullah in preference to ten camels. A second time the reading was taken, and the number of camels was doubled. The result was the same as the first. A third time the lot was cast, but the gods still retained their partiality for Abdullah and refused an offering of thirty camels. This ought to have decided the question, had the general company agreed not to press the point further, but to a man the tribesmen were determined to persuade the gods.

Even Abdul Muttalib was stirred to the depths of his soul over this inveteracy of the idols; he bowed low to Hobal. 'I shall stake mine last camel, aye the whole flock', he yelled, 'before thee, to see what it is to be to thy ultimate decision. And he read and reread the minds of his clansmen: for a dozen more voices rose after him offering their all to see whether Abdullah could be spared: for the Arabs, idolatrous though they were, nevertheless were simple children of nature with children's single-heartedness towards love and hate with emotions that knew no bonds.

So, the high priest was asked to cast again and again and increase the number of camels each time that he drew the negative spear. What joy, indeed there was, when at last, the gods were pleased to accept a hundred camels in exchange. There are, however, two statements about this offering of Abdullah. Waqidi believes the report of divining to be more authentic, and Ibn Ishaq contends that the elders of the clan were chiefly responsible for arranging their exchange. But judging from the state of mind of old and young of Arabia of that period it is more approximate to truth that oracles were made to speak on the subject.

From where, according to the Muslim Belief, The Prophet made his 'Nightly Journey to the Throne of Allah'.

Abdullah now was again free to act as a sort of secretary to his old father, and was soon married to Amna, daughter of Wahb bin Abdul Munaf, in the tribe of Zuhra. She was considered one of the most celebrated of the women of her time, regarding whose accomplishments such authorities as Ibn Hasham speak at considerable length. The age of Abdullah at the time of his marriage according to Razaqi was seventeen years.

No sooner had Abdul Muttalib settled the question of Abdullah and had married him, when another event threatened the integrity of Arabia and its shrine. This was the march upon Mecca of the Abyssinian viceroy of Yanian, named Abra al Arsham. It has been noticed by the Yemenites that Mecca continued to prosper and grow in strength on account of the trade that passed through it, but more in respect of the shrine to which thousands of pilgrims flocked, and thus diverted all their wealth and interests to the city of the desert in preference to the Church at the Yemenite capital of Sana. The only remedy was to destroy the shrine of the Kaaba.

With this object in view, the Viceroy rode ahead of his troops on a highly caparisoned elephant. The desecrating army had reached almost within the sight of the temple when Abra called a halt, not only to discover about the fortification of the city, but also regarding the resistance which his troops were likely to meet. The Quraish with all their martial traditions were no match to the well-drilled and organised army of the Yemenites; and, therefore, consternation prevailed in Mecca. The appearance of the elephants, animals quite unknown to the people of the desert, where the largest creatures known were camels – added to the havoc amongst the Meccans. The reports of the defeat of a Himyarite chieftain, Dhu Nafar, by the Abyssinian general had already reached the Quraish: and under the stress of the cumulative effect of these matters, the Mecca war-council decided to leave the shrine to look after itself, and the people to abandon the city immediately. In the meantime, Abra's men had captured Abdul Muttalib's camels.

The southern troops remained encamped near Mecca. Knowing the weak position of the Quraish, the Abyssinians were in no haste to attack; till one day an ebony black rider, holding Abra's standard, rode up to the brow of the hill that looked directly on to the shrine of Mecca. He bore a message from his general to the chief of the Quraish, in which Abra indicated no desire to bloodshed, his only wish being to dismantle the Kaaba. But he made it abundantly clear to Abdul Muttalib that should his people show the slightest sign of defending the temple, then the Abyssinians would spare neither the lives nor wealth of the Arabs. The Quraish had already made their decision, they would neither defend the shrine nor would they remain in the city whilst the acts of profanity were being enacted. A reply to that effect was sent to Abra.

The events that followed can be well narrated by what Tabri – one of the foremost historians – records. This appears very fully in The Literary History of The Arabs, thus: 'Then Abdul Muttalib was conducted by the envoy to the Abyssinian camp, as Abraha had ordered. There he enquired after Dhu Nafar, (the captive chieftain of the Himyarites) who was his friend, and found him a prisoner. 'O Dhu Nafar', said he, 'can you do aught in that which has befallen us?' Dhu Nafar answered, 'What can a man do who is a captive in the hands of a king, expecting day and night to be put to death? I can do nothing at all in the matter, but Unays, the elephant driver, is my friend; I will send to him and press your claims on his consideration and ask him to procure you an audience with the king. Tell Unays what you wish: he will plead with the king in your favour if he can.

'So Dhu Nafar sent for Unays and said to him, 'O Unays, Abdul Muttalib is the lord of Quraish and master of the caravans of Mecca. He feeds the people in the plains and the wild creatures on the mountain tops. The king has seized two hundred of his camels. Now get him admitted to the King's presence and help him to the best of your power.' Unays consented, and soon Abdul Muttalib stood before the Viceroy.

'When Abraha saw him, he held him in too high respect to let him sit in an inferior place, but was unwilling that the Abyssinians should see the Arab Chief, who was a large man and comely, seated on a level with himself; he therefore descended from his throne and sat on his carpet and bade Abdul Muttalib sit beside him. Then he said to his dragoman, 'Ask him what he wants of me.' Abdul Muttalib replied, 'I want the king to restore to me two hundred camels of mine which he has taken away.'

'Abraha said to the dragoman, 'Tell him: you pleased me when I first saw you, but now that you have spoken to me, I hold you cheap. What! Do you speak to me of two hundred camels which I have taken, and omit to speak of a temple venerated by you and your fathers which I have come to destroy?' Then said Abdul Muttalib: 'The camels are mine, but the Temple belongs to another, who will defend it', and on the King exclaiming, 'He cannot defend it from me' he said, 'That is your affair; only give me back my camels'.'

As it is related in a more credible version, the tribes settled round Mecca sent ambassadors, of whom Abdul Muttalib was one, offering to surrender a third part of their possessions to Abraha on condition that he should spare the Temple, but he refused. Having recovered his camels, Abdul Muttalib returned to the Quraish, told them what had happened, and bade them leave the city and take shelter in the mountains. Then he went to the Kaaba, accompanied by several of the Quraish, to pray help against Abraha and his army. Grasping the ring of the door, he said:

> O God, defend Thy neighbouring folk even as a man his
>   gear defendeth!
> Let not their Cross and guileful plans defeat the plans
>   Thyself intendeth!
> But if Thou make it so, 'tis well: according to
> Thy will it endeth.

Next morning, when Abraha prepared to enter Mecca, his elephant knelt down and would not budge, though they beat his head with an axe, and thrust sharp stakes into his flanks; but when they turned it in the direction of Yemen, it rose up and trotted with alacrity. Then God sent from the sea a flock of birds like swallows, every one of which carried three stones as large as a pea or lentil, one in each bill and one in each claw, and all who were struck by those stones perished. The rest fled in disorder, dropping down as they ran, or wherever they halted to quench their thirst.

I hesitate to credit the whole of this prodigy of Tabri both on account of the fact that he gives also another reason of the destruction of the invading army, the cause being the outbreak of smallpox in Abra's camp: which, being a new disease in Arabia, frightened the Abyssinians quite as much as the appearance of giant animals like the elephants did the Quraish of Mecca. The outbreak of that pestilence is quite definitely founded on historical grounds. The Qur'an throws more light on the subject: In the Chapter of The Elephants (one of the earliest revelations), it says:

> Have you not considered how your Lord dealt with the possessors of the Elephant;
> Did He not cause their war to end in confusion,
> And send down (to prey) upon them birds in flocks,
> Casting against them hard stones,
> So He rendered them like straw eaten up?

In all likelihood, the version of the outbreak of smallpox is correct, the dispersing of an army in such circumstances cannot be thought to be beyond the range of possibility;

for a similar example we might recollect the manifestation of disease that annihilated Sennacherib's men. The appearance of birds, as spoken of in The Qur'an, is quite comprehensible because after the soldiers died, the birds feasted on their corpses, tearing off flesh from the dead bodies and casting it on the stones. Hence, as Mohamed Ali agrees, it is that in the concluding words their torn flesh was compared to shred, (strawlike) and eaten up. Nor is this use of 'birds descending' to eat up the dead bodies uncommon in Arab literature. We might even go to the ordinary Arab poem for a parallelism of the idea.

Both the Arab proverb and prosody bear witness, says Mohamed Ali, to birds having been spoken of as attending a victorious army to feed upon the corpses of the enemy left on the battlefield. Thus, we have the well-known Arab proverb – May the birds disperse thy flesh – which is a kind of imprecation, meaning 'may the man die, and his flesh be dispersed and eaten up by birds.' The famous Nabighah says: 'When he goes out with the army, flocks of birds, being guided by the companies of the army, hover over his head.' Here the birds are made the attendants of a victorious army, as if they knew that the army which they followed would slay the enemy, and that they would thus feed on dead bodies.

Out of this incident of the Yemenite invasion of the Hijaz arises another important point of Islamic religious law. The story is centred round three ideas, Idolatry, Trinity and Unity (yet to be pronounced), that is to say the matter revolved around the idolatrous people of Mecca, the Christian invaders and the birth of Mohamed during the same period – a Mohamed who was to proclaim the Oneness of God. When the Christian Viceroy believing in Trinity attacked a shrine of idolaters, the God of a people (Unitarians to be) sent a scourge and destroyed the hordes of Trinity; which seems to indicate to a superficial student that God in some way preferred the cult of the idols.

The Muslim Canonists, however, argue that this destruction of the invaders was in the first instance a sign of Mohamed's advent – since he was born in the same year – that such a man will oppose the conception of Trinity and emphasise the One God amongst the peoples of the world. Beyond this portent they aver that it was in fulfilment of the prayers of Abraham to bless the Ishmaelite with The Prophet, a prophet who will 'clean-up' the sacred house, which was built by Abraham. One finds a testimony of it even amongst that pagan society of Arabia that the idol-worship, though it was the only form of religion which they knew, nevertheless the conception that the Kaaba was built and sanctified by Abraham, always lingered in their minds: for it may be recollected that according to Tabri when the Abyssinian Viceroy sent his messenger to the Quraish, Abdul Muttalib replied: 'By God, we seek not war, for which we are unable. This is God's holy House, and the House of Abraham, His Friend; it is for Him to protect His House and Sanctuary; if He abandons it, we cannot defend it.'

Furthermore, it is contended, that as the incident was to pave the way for Mohamed's endeavours – to purify the House of God that Abraham built – a deeper meaning lay in the matter. To the Quraish it was to act as a warning, that when God could destroy such a powerful enemy of theirs as the invading army of the Yemenites, it was well within His power to annihilate the Quraish if they disobeyed the man who professed to be The Prophet calling humanity towards the one and only One God.

FROM: MOHAMED: THE PROPHET

Perils of Man-Smuggling

As I BENT down to unstrap my camel load, someone tugged at the hem of my long, flowing robe. Then the wet nose of the camel touched my bared arm, and I thought that the tail of my loose shirt must have been caught under the bag which I had unloaded. Once again, I felt –yes, this time it was certain: a pull at my clothes.

'In the Name of Allah! In the Name of Almighty God!' and the voice of a prostrate form, gurgling from a hoarse throat, was drowned by the sound of the bubbling camels in the quadrangle of our desert rest-house.

With more than ordinary curiosity, I bent down towards the one who had pulled at my garments, and whose words of supplication had been almost swallowed up in the general din of shouting drivers as they unloaded their beasts of burden.

I flashed my torch at the man. He lay, face downwards now: holding his side, apparently in great pain. His eyes – Oh those eyes! I can't forget them – they had a haunted look. And his face – well, you have heard of the fantastic hawklike features of the desert Sheikh? He could have beaten most, if not all, of his film counterparts, for the aristocracy of the desert was writ large on his visage.

Now a change seemed to come over him, as if he was summoning his last reserves of strength for some action...

Suddenly, he leaped up like a wounded panther and snatched the flashlight from my hand.

'Thinkest thou that in the heart of the desert, people will spare thy life if they see thee making light without a fire?'

A long memory came back to me, for had I not been shot at, once, in a Bedouin encampment as a magician for 'making light out of nothing, like the one cast down from Allah's Palace'.

The man now squatted down beside me. Our backs rested against my sitting camel. From his cummerbund he produced a paper, shading the light of the torch with the skirt of his long robe whilst I read the epistle.

It was a letter from one of my oldest friends in these parts, begging help for this hunted man!

'Peace be to thee, my brother!' I shook him by the hand, 'What a great honour has fallen upon me. It shall, indeed, be my pride to escort thee, the friend of Murad; for Murad once saved mine life's blood.' 'Sh-hhh' – he placed his hand on my lips.

I took the tip, for the camel may not understand a conversation, but Allah only can tell who hides behind the camel: and although my new friend knew that I, as Murad's seasoned commercial agent, could smuggle him even to heaven; yet even here and now, he said there were eighteen men in the rest-house who would almost literally drink his blood.

With what care I could bestow, the Sheikh's wounds were attended to by me. His enemies had only half-buried the point of their blades in his thigh, and he had slain three before he got to where I was unloading my mount.

It is true that as trading goes in Arabia, I was not an ordinary merchant, but the roving commission given me by Murad, the merchant prince of Damascus, had made it possible for me to travel safely for many months into the most covetously guarded parts of inner Arabia where inter-clan fighting is so dangerous that they shoot first and ask later. But indebted though I was to Murad, I would have hesitated a little before agreeing to smuggle his friend to safety had I known then what I was to learn of the facts of the case.

That night, I had intended to rest before taking the long sandy stretch that lay before me from the banks of the River Jordan eastwards. But Murad's letter and the plight of the young Sheikh compelled my departure.

A haze floated over the distant sand dunes, as the silvery moon, like a blazing scimitar, rose higher and higher above the horizon. The sleepy gatekeeper rubbed his eyes as my camel lumbered out.

Thou goest at an evil hour!' he shouted, 'for, beyond the ridge, thy life will be in the palm of thy hand!'

It was fortunate, however, that he did not plunge his spear into the sack that hung by the side of my camel. For a good reason I had accommodated the wounded Sheikh in it; and stuffing hay in another sack, I had placed it at my back to look like someone sitting behind me.

For three hours my speedy camel did gallop. She was the best trotter in Murad's stables, and the Sheikh felt fairly safe, because not until dawn could any man fire on us during those days of the month of fasting, when all the faithful must remain peaceful to one another during the hours of night.

Then the face of the moon began to tarnish, and the sand now showed curious strands of colour in that half-light which betokens the approaching dawn. Then a streak shot up, all along the rim of the desert: the Sheikh wriggled in his suspended cradle but lay still again when I announced the approaching light of day.

With a sense which comes to desert travellers, the Sheikh and I had a presentiment that we were being followed at a discreet distance. Only of the aircraft or armoured cars searching for the fugitive Sheikh did we have fear.

These were the times of the French Mandate over Syria, and the Sheikh was what today would be called a freedom-fighter.

But maybe the French will spare him, I thought; and have just placed a price on his head only to set the Bedouins of the desert on his trail.

If that were the case, I thought, then we were more than a match for the Bedouins. A smuggled machine-gun provided by Murad, and which equalled the balance of my camel's load, would see to that.

Just as I was rounding the bend of Bin Khiza, I could have yelled with delight at the sight of the tent-dwellers not too far below where French territory ceased. But it was still a good three miles. Hard hoofs hit on rock; presently an Arab climbed up the ridge on our right and then ducked down. We were spotted.

Almost immediately, a bullet sang past me. There was no time to lose. The Sheikh crouched behind a boulder, and in a trice, I saw the sack which rode behind me rent to bits by bullets. I was now manning my machine-gun. Knowing that they would not shoot down the camel, I let her run towards the friendly encampments.

Our attackers were spread out fanwise, skirmishing fashion. But our superior arms were playing havoc with their ranks. Muffled faces jumped up and fell before the flailing of the machine-gun fire. Presently their leader steeled himself and stood up with a long-barrelled musket and took aim in the most heroic but foolhardy manner imaginable. A shot from the Sheikh's rifle made him whirl in a frenzied circle, and he dropped on his face.

Now they were closing upon us, now retreating. The automatic weapon barked unceasingly. Then it jammed, as these devil's contraptions seem to love to do.

I appealed to even my game leg to do its best, as I scrambled down, yard by yard, towards the land of friendly Bin Khiza. It was, after all, the nephew of the Sheikh of that tribe who was with me, blazing away for his life. As such he had been introduced in the letter which he had taken from his girdle.

Another attack was launched against us; amazingly, the machine-gun unjammed itself and this attack, too, was repelled. We were crawling to safety as we turned and fired, again and again. Forms of our enemies rose only to be mown down by the devil's own weapon.

Then the burring and whirring sound of aeroengines struck upon our ears. 'What in the Name of Allah...!' I shouted.

They swept down; one could see clearly from their wing insignia that they were the French desert patrol. Within a few moments they had landed a small, armed group. But by then we were already arriving at the outpost of Bin Khiza's tents. Free men, in the territory of the free, in Independent Arabia.

A dozen horsemen, led by the Sheikh of the tribe himself, rode towards us, firing a welcoming salute into the air. The leader embraced me with a mighty bear-hug.

News had reached him, by relay courier, mounted on the country's fastest mares, that Murad was having the Sheikh's nephew escorted to him, it was hoped, by me. He anticipated trouble, but not a pitched battle like the one that we had just been through.

'And let mine eyes that have dimmed with waiting alight upon my dearest nephew's lustrous features!' He pulled the cloak from my ward's face.

A murderous gleam stole into the old man's eyes, as he started back from the sight. The one whom I had smuggled made a wry face.

'Aman –Aman – in the Name of Allah I seek peace, and sanctuary!' he said.

'In His Name I give it' stammered the Sheikh.

Then the stranger spoke, in perfect Arabic: 'Aye, it is true that thy nephew wanted to escape, and he confided in me. Him I had drugged and dressed him with mine own uniform, stole his papers and in his guise, I have reached safely here out of the hands of my regiment. As to me, my name is Krutz', and the German renegade hung his head in shame.

I saw the Arab chieftain's thumb curl over the hammer of the carbine. Then he tarried.

'In the Name of Allah, thou hast asked peace and sanctuary', he said, red mounting to his cheeks: 'In His Name I have given it; but go thee back to thy regiment before sundown, for let infidel kill infidel; I shall not pollute my blade by slaying dogs.'

The deserter's eyes shot with blood.

'I shall not go back to the hell from which I have escaped', he shouted; and as the old Sheikh turned, there was a sharp report. Smoke floated from the mouth of the deserter. In his teeth was the end of the barrel of his rifle. So that, if your way should he one day to the Wadi of Bin Khiza, see a rudely erected tombstone with 'Al Almani' on it.

One lesson which the incident has left with me is that of one thing you can be absolutely sure in desert travel: it is that you can be sure of nothing, least of all your fellow travellers.

I lost my way more than once over the devious tracks of the desert when I trekked back to the south, and I discovered to my amazement that the Arabs of Jordan have hardly any sense of direction outside the area over which they graze their animals.

Fortunately for me, twenty miles to the east of Deraa is Bosrah, a great conical peak which projects prominently from the hills in the background. This landmark proved essential in my final journeyings in Jordan, and it allowed me more than once to correct the failings of so-called Arab guides whom I sometimes recruited from encampments.

If weak in geography, they were always strong in encouragement. Whenever asked where anywhere was, they invariably answered, 'Qarib –it is near!'

Beyond Deraa, one moves into the country of the Druses –a race about whom not a great deal is known and who had a bad reputation with the French for their warlike proclivities, as well as for insisting also that they are originally French and good Catholics. The French constantly complained that the Turks said that, during the days of the Ottoman Empire, the Druses had always sworn they were Turks by origin and good Sunni Muslims.

Personally, however, I found the Druses to be quite pleasant people and not sparing in their hospitality.

The men, especially, are of magnificent physique, and they are great horsemen. They have, however, one curious practice: they blacken all around their eyes. I discovered that this was not out of any desire to adorn the manly face. The substance which is used for this treatment is held to keep away the flies – of which there are positive clouds in some areas – and to safeguard the eyes from the glare of the blazing sun.

The men certainly have magnificent eyesight, rivalling in this respect the tribesmen of the Pashtun lands in Central Asia. They can observe even the slightest movement over incredible distances and they are natural and splendid shots.

Life in the Druse mountains can be exciting for the unaccompanied wayfarer, for the tracks over the mountains are littered with boulders which have been precipitated down from above.

Journeying along these paths, every now and again one hears an ominous rumble and looks up at the hillside with no little apprehension. Quite often, miniature landslides obliterate the tracks and bring down with them rocks and boulders, which fly at unexpected angles. Many of these boulders would be sufficient to crush a man or a mule.

I had several narrow escapes from this kind of unpleasant death, but these were the only occasions when I suffered perturbation. The Druses, as far as I was concerned, belied their generally fierce reputation and I found them almost shy, rather than an aggressive people.

All the time, however, one could sense a certain atmosphere. Here were a people who would remain quiet and law-abiding if they were left to their own devices. Quite obviously, they were resentful of intrusion and suspicious of any interference from an outside power.

The Turks, during their regime, evidently realised this. In any case, their suzerainty was quite nominal.

One thing that makes the Druses a rather difficult people to make conform to modem ideas of administration is the nature of their religion. Its secrets are zealously guarded, and no man is initiated into the mystic rites until he has more than reached the age of discretion. And when he is admitted into his church, he has to make the most terrible and binding vows never to disclose to any who is not a full initiate, any of the secrets of his faith.

Consequently, the Druses never speak of their religion, and little is known about it beyond the fact that it resembles a somewhat curious mixture of Christianity and Islam, and uses secret signs and passwords.

They have one outstanding belief, and that is in regard to transmigration. They believe that, at the time of death, the soul passes into whatever is born on their land at that moment – no matter whether the newborn one is human or an animal. Should death take place at a moment when no living thing is born, then they believe that the soul passes away to China; and the people of the Jebel Druse believe that there are many of their race in China.

These people do not worship in churches, mosques or temples, as do those who have other faiths. They are careful to perform their religious ceremonies in some chamber carefully hidden away from the eyes of the curious.

Most carefully guarded also is their sacred book upon which, they say, nobody who has not been initiated with the full rites of the faith has ever been allowed to gaze.

This secrecy which attends the religious observances of the Druses also extends, in some measure, to their relations with people of other races. Many of the troubles of the past have undoubtedly been due to a disregard of this trait.

Farther on northward, when working toward the Iraqian frontier with the Jebel (mountain) Druses left behind, I had the misfortune one night to stay in a small house where a man became sick. Apparently, he was taken seriously ill in the middle of the night, for my sleep was disturbed by the shuffling of many feet.

Those who have been taught to respect the sickroom and to enter it only when bidden or by permission of the doctor, would view with amazement that which transpires in this part of the Near East when a man is unfortunate enough to be ill.

The noise in this house was such that sleep was impossible. When I rose to investigate the cause of the confusion, I found the place filled with friends and curious neighbours who had been hastily summoned to render aid. This motley crowd was busily engaged in prescribing all manner of incredible remedies and charms, mostly at the tops of their voices.

The man's bed, a hard pallet on the floor, was literally surrounded by those anxious to try their medical skill. It was quite obvious that the patient was seriously ill, for already two freshly killed chickens had been applied warm to his feet.

Every few minutes, the unfortunate was dosed with an evil-smelling concoction declared, by the old lady who had apparently dispensed it, to be capable of restoring any but one who was actually dead.

It was in my heart to believe her, too. I should have had to have been on the verge of coma not to have arisen and hurriedly fled from that noxious smell.

Others who assisted plied the patient with charms made of earth, and yet others were deliberating whether or not one should be despatched for a lamb which could be sacrificed for the good of the patient.

The wife of the man demurred and suggested that the company should at least await the mom before embarking on such desperate measures.

It was easy to understand her concern. Chickens, charms and potions cost money or its equivalent and already she had mortgaged a goodly part of her household goods in acquiring remedies for her man.

Whether or not it became necessary to slaughter a lamb I shall never know, because I thought it expedient to change my quarters. I could do little more. I could not possibly have intruded into the circle around the sick man, even though I was aware that the treatment he was receiving was probably hastening him to his death.

Indeed, his friends and neighbours evidently worked with thoroughness, for I was told, early the next morning, that the man was dead.

Going to collect the belongings which I had left in the house the previous night, I found that this was indeed so. The poor widow was bewailing her lot. I could only attempt to console her by contributing to the burial fund.

A long strip of muslin had been resurrected from somewhere; and from the smell of camphor which it gave off it was reasonable to assume that it had been used at more than one burial already. The body of the man was wrapped in this shroud, and it would be little more than this which he would require.

Later that day, I saw the remains being carried away in a rough wooden box – for the dead have to be interred quickly in the East.

The box was carried from the house by the friends who had done so much to expedite the man's end; they performed this service not from any sense of remorse, but because those who act as pallbearers acquire great merit.

As the cortege proceeds, the first person of the same religion who is met is expected to relieve one of the mourners and thus the burden is shifted from shoulder to shoulder until the burial place is reached.

The coffin or box, with the shawl which is placed over it, are not interred. These are hired for the occasion by the poorer people and returned to the hirer after the body has been placed in a deep grave with only the muslin shroud as a cover. A priest was hurriedly summoned to recite from the New Testament in Arabic.

At yet another village, I came across an occurrence which was more pleasing – nothing less than a wedding. The ceremonies attaching to marriages differ from country to country, sometimes in vital respects; sometimes in lesser. Invariably, however, they are of interest to onlookers, if not always for the principal participants.

Here the wedding is divided into two distinct ceremonies –the actual betrothal and the wedding ceremony proper. In Muslim law, both ceremonies are legal and binding. Consequently, there is more involved in the initial function than the light-hearted bestowal of a ring which may, or may not, already have adorned the finger of some earlier fiancée.

The ceremony of betrothal is a very serious one, into the preliminaries of which the families of both contracting parties have entered with zest, for it is one requiring the exercise of much business acumen.

Quite often betrothals are arranged by marriage brokers, many of whom are old women. They receive a commission from the two parties for their services. Much the same practice is observed by many of the Jewish fraternity, even in London, and it has not been unknown, I was told there on good authority, for Mayfair hostesses to receive a valuable 'present' for arranging a match between some wealthy social aspirant and a member of the peerage. The arrangement in every instance is mainly commercial.

The peoples of this part of the East, however, have one practice which may or may not commend itself to brides of other nations.

In the betrothal ceremony which I witnessed, the bridegroom-to-be was the Sheikh of the village and the girl the daughter of a neighbouring chief. They were not wanting in worldly goods, especially as the bridegroom's father was also a merchant who had journeyed to England and had taken to himself a Feranghi, a Frankish wife. But of that more presently.

The bride, her mother and other feminine friends were accommodated in one room while the bridegroom and his friends occupied one adjoining.

The presiding elder (he is not a priest: marriages are civil contracts) took up a position in the doorway between the two rooms and read from a list detailing the property of the bride.

It had not been prepared merely to impress the neighbours and the friends of the family, or from any sense of false pride. There was a real purpose to this part of the proceedings.

All the articles named by the elder were to give her a sense of security. In later years, should the man desire to divorce the bride, he would be unable to send her away penniless. He would have to provide her with all the goods and chattels mentioned in the list.

This practice may seem curious to some Western minds; nevertheless, it has its counterpart in Western marriage settlements. In Germany especially, it is frequently the practice for the groom to cite in his marriage settlement the cars, the houses and other items which one day *might* come into his possession. There is a close association between the two forms of contract.

I remained in this village long enough to witness the second part of the ceremony, since this took place only a few days after the first.

The bride lived in a flat-roofed single storey house and, in common with half-a-dozen other such structures, it looked out upon a courtyard. In Europe you would say that it was but one of a collection of cottages which shared a common backyard.

All the neighbours came to the assistance of the bride and freely loaned carpets which were laid over the stone slabs of the court. These loans were augmented with gifts of flowers, with which the court was further decorated.

A huge tea-urn had been obtained and this was kept bubbling the whole day. It was greatly in demand; its only rivals being long pipes of sweet sherbet which were passed from hand to hand. The court, by the way, was given over entirely to the women.

The bride was attired in a new silk robe and her neck was adorned with a string of glass beads amongst which were interspersed a few gold and silver coins.

This trousseau was the gift of the groom – another pleasing practice, some fathers-in-law will say.

The bride had not disdained cosmetics. Her cheeks were rouged, her eyes had been blacked with kohl and her garments had been plentifully besprinkled with scent.

The hostess of the occasion –quite an old woman – seemed to be serving in a professional capacity. Obviously, she augmented her income by providing her services in this way. No mere amateur could have carried off the role as did she.

As the guests entered the courtyard they peered around for this woman and then advanced upon her, enunciating the words: 'May this wedding be blessed.'

And the hostess, with supreme gravity, would respond: 'In the Name of God enter; your kindness in coming to assist us is indeed great.'

In the adjoining house, where the guests of the Sheikh were assembled, a somewhat similar scene was being enacted. Here, however, the masculine temperament made for a little more verve and vigour.

A wandering minstrel had been imported to amuse the guests, and he sang songs in a shrill, minor key, the words of which were improvised to meet the needs of the occasion.

Masculine humour, at such events as weddings, is cruder and much more direct than the feminine, and judging from the roars of laughter which the minstrel produced from the guests and the obvious discomfiture of the groom on sundry occasions, the man was well worth his fee.

The entertainer's voice was shrill and piercing, and I could not but notice with amusement that, when he introduced some sally at the expense of the bridegroom, the feminine chatter from the nearby courtyard suddenly ceased, and the hidden audience there was patently listening to the words with appreciation.

Once even, the fair ones so far forgot themselves as to echo the boisterous laughter of the men when the minstrel had been particularly audacious.

The formal part of the ceremony –a brief affair –had taken place earlier in the day and the singing and the laughter and the drinking of tea, coffee and sherbet proceeded until a late hour. At dusk, candles and lamps were produced and the whole assembly was served with a repast consisting of coloured rice, mutton, pomegranates and sweets.

Later, as the party showed signs of breaking up, a medley of particularly efficient bandsmen appeared as if by magic, and the surrounding roofs of the nearby houses became crowded with those anxious to witness the final phase of the ceremony.

The male guests assembled around the groom as an escort and a procession was formed which made its way slowly to the home of the bride.

As the groom reached the threshhold of his bride's abode, a lamb was sacrificed, and then the bride was led to the doorway and given over to the bridegroom amidst the plaudits of the spectators and the raucous blowing of trumpets.

In all these proceedings, Sheikh Abdullah, the bridegroom's father, was, I felt, taking but a half-hearted interest. His mind, it would seem, was flying back to some distant scenes, some former experiences. At first, I thought that a man past middle age could hardly be expected to raise enough enthusiasm about an affair which warms young hearts; but the reason was different. He was recollecting his own former, Feranghi, wife: the mother of the boy whose wedding he was celebrating.

FROM: ALONE IN ARABIAN NIGHTS

The Birth of The Prophet

THE STORM CLOUDS of Yemenite invasion were hardly lifted from the Quraish when the world was called upon to witness a notable occurrence, commonplace in itself, the incident of childbirth – but this birth has a meaning to the story of nations.

When The Prophet of Allah was born, extraordinary portents are reported to have been seen in Mecca and beyond. Traditionists have it that fourteen minarets of the mighty palace of Cyrus fell from their proud places; the flame that burned in the holy Persian temple was extinguished; the river Sadah was dried up.

Even now some accept without questioning the sighting of the star which the Wise Men of the East followed in search of Jesus, even now some believe the inexplicable manifestations heralding the coming of Buddha; and more pertinent still, we hold by common consent that the hand of God shows itself in the course of things, the reason of which leaves the wisest of us dumbfounded and guessing.

Even The Qur'an, when we claim to discover the causation of most doings, very frequently certain occurrences are still labelled by us as the 'Act of God', because they surpass human comprehension. Is it then justifiable not to accord a sympathetic consideration of such happenings, which are reported at the birth of The Prophet Mohamed; for it can be indisputably admitted that that man was clearly an exceptional personality; one whose life and work was to act as the guiding star for nearly half of the world, so that an especial stage must have been set upon which this Master actor was to perform. In the light of these circumstances, no astonishment is to be expressed that nearly fourteen centuries ago, men beheld phenomena that may be likened to the finger of God pointing to the clearly marked destiny of Islam.

On the most authentic calculation of Mahmud Pasha Falki, it is now proved that the birth of The Prophet took place on Monday, the 20th of April, A.D. 571. The infant was named Mohamed by his grandfather Abdul Muttalib. His widowed mother Amina fed the child from her breast for two or three days. Then Toyaba acted as his wet nurse. Here we might usefully recount the genealogy of The Prophet.

It was customary in Arabia then, that the names of only those ancestors were remembered who had distinguished themselves in some way in their national lore. As a general rule, they began counting the names from one Adnan downwards, for the fact that Adnan was directly descended from Ishmael was recognised on all hands. The historian Tabri is said to have stated that Adnan was the fortieth descendent from Ishmael, thus connecting The Prophet Mohamed with Abraham.

Here we may mention those from Adnan upwards, they are:

Mohamed.
Abdullah.
Abdul Muttalib.
Hashim.
Monaf.
Qusay.
Kallab.
Morrah.
Kaab.
Lowaey.
Ghalib.
Fahar.
Malik.
Nadar.
Kinana.
Khazema.
Mudrika.
Ilyas.
Modarr.
Nazar.
Mad.
Adnan.

Further in reference to what I have said regarding the curtailment in the number of names above Adnan, and the reason thereof, in Bokhari the following names are also given to join the genealogical table of The Prophet with Ishmael as follows. It should, of course, be remembered that not all the forty names according to Tabri appear here:

Adnan.
Oad.
Almaqoom.
Tarah.
Yashjib.
Yarab.
Tabit.
Ismail.
Ibrahim.

When Toyaba was feeding the infant Mohamed, The Prophet's mother Amina heard of the exodus of Bedouin women, who had been paying their biannual visit to Mecca, as was the wont of the desert folk. On such visits, according to the custom, many women offered their services as wet-nurses to the mothers of such children as belonged to the highest social strata of the town.

This custom had a mutual advantage to both parties. The Bedouins nursed the children of the aristocracy not entirely on account of the good remuneration which they were to receive, rather they hoped that when a boy of the ruling house was reared amongst them, preferential treatment would be given to their tribe above all other people of the desert.

The parents availed themselves of it because they wished their sons to learn the purest Arabic language – which is only spoken by the tent-dwellers in the heart of the desert – also, the children, whilst with the Bedouins, would get used to hard living, imbibe that spirit and appreciate that fire which should characterise a desert-born from a soft-living town Arab. Not the least interesting point regarding it, is that such children were taken away by the Bedouins to their encampments, where they were kept for some years to live and breathe the free air of that vastness which is called the Arabia of the real Arabs.

This practice of sending the children for a hard training was so universal amongst the Arab aristocracy, that even during the glorious days of Banu Omayah, when their power and grandeur rivalled the might and splendour of Persia and Rome, Arab princes were brought up in the homes of the tent-dwellers. We have a notable exception in this regard in Walid Bin Abdul Malik, who for certain reasons never saw the Bedouin upbringing, with the result that he did not speak Arabic with fluency and use apt phraseology. Iman Sahayli dilates on this subject at considerable length, and even quotes the words of The Prophet in which he is said to have attributed his skill in the use of ready expression to his stay with the Bedouin tribes of Bani Sad.

The Bedouin lady named Halima Saida, who belonged to the tribe of Howazan, was at first not particularly eager to take Mohamed – a fatherless boy – but as tradition did not permit going back without a charge whilst one awaited her, she at last was persuaded to nurse a child who was to become a Prophet, and took him with her to the encampments of the tribe. When Halima had other work to do, her daughter Shima, a comely and gentle girl, looked after the boy, little knowing what a remarkable personality those tiny feet that pattered on the hard sand around the tent in the desert were supporting.

For two years, Mohamed lived with the Bedouin nurse in the desert. He would have been kept there a little longer, but even during those short months, curious happenings began to unnerve the tent-dwellers. Such manifestations their eyes had never seen, such light playing about the boy, such straying of the infant Mohamed who always found his way back to the tent, such whisperings in the air as were passed beyond what has ever been experienced by man. What could be the reason of it all if not the presence of the wondrous son of Amina, they thought? So, they decided to hasten his departure to his mother in Mecca, lest more doings of such an unaccountable nature baffled them.

As Halima sought the door of Mohamed's mother, she saw many corpses borne away, men were crowding before the idols in the Shrine beseeching Hobal to ward off the plague that had visited them. A word from Amina was enough to emphasise upon Halima the necessity of taking the boy Mohamed back to her encampment, for Mecca was no safe place for whosoever had to stay in it at that time when the pestilence raged in the city. Thus, Mohamed found himself back in his temporary home amongst the Bedouins. Ibn Ishaq gives the duration of The Prophet's stay with Halima as six years.

Mohamed had attained the age of six years when ultimately Halima brought the boy to his mother. Soon, a journey to Medina was arranged, so that the boy and his mother could see the tomb of Abdullah, the father of the man who was to thrill the world with a Message. No more than a month did they stay at Medina, when with Om Aman, the maid servant, The Prophet and his mother, their caravan started Mecca-ward. But Amina fell ill upon reaching a wayside village known as Abwa, and died there, where she lies buried. It was thus the duty of Om Aman to escort the orphaned Mohamed home to Mecca to his grandfather Abdul Muttalib.

This old chieftain of the Quraish received Mohamed with love and affection of which the people considered him quite incapable, but Abdul Muttalib had ever nursed the memory of the day when he had bartered his son Abdullah for a hundred camels; and being a merchant whose carriers were no other than these ships of the desert, loved camels dearly: it was then the sign, the reminder of his lovable son Abdullah that he saw residing in the shining eyes of young Mohamed. He, therefore, bestowed particular and unrelaxing care upon this orphan boy; which is important in the light of the fact that Abdul Muttalib was already the sire of eighteen children; and others in the ordinary way of thinking must have claimed a considerable amount of the old gentleman's attention and regard: nevertheless, Mohamed remained always his best beloved.

Although the official primacy of Abdul Muttalib was still supreme during his waning years, when his years were passing beyond eighty, yet it was growing increasingly patent to him that the other branch of his tribe was gaining strength, and the lot of those upon whom his mantle was to fall may not be so free of cares as his; so far, at any rate as the leadership of the clan was concerned. He wished to solidate the position of the house of Hashim. This desire obsessed him greatly with the advancement of his age; yes, indeed, as

Young says: 'Like our shadows, our wishes lengthen as our sun declines.'

And it was as the old chieftain feared, for at his death in A.D. 579, shortly after his return from a journey to Sana where he went to represent the Quraish at the court of Saif, the house of Hashim was definitely under a cloud. Not that Abu Talib, the old gentleman's son, an uncle of The Prophet, was an incapable man, but the rival factions were far too strong.

The Prophet was eight years old when he passed into the guardianship of his uncle, Abu Talib. The two offices which Abdul Muttalib exercised directly in the Government of Mecca were divided between his sons. The administration of the water of holy Zam Zam was given to Abbas, whilst the collection of the poor-tax remained in the hands of Abu Talib; the latter retained the leadership of the house of Hashim in his hands, being the elder son of the old chief, Abdul Muttalib. The presidency of the whole clan, however, fell to the share of the rival tribe of Omoya because Harab, the son of Omoya, was elected in place of Abdul Muttalib.

The orphan son of Amina and Abdullah assisted his uncle Abu Talib in his mercantile interests. When Mohamed had attained the age of twelve, Abu Talib proposed to take his merchandise to the markets of Syria. When this biennial caravan was ready to start, Abu Talib was distinctly distressed as to who would look after the orphan during his absence: for the intense affection which the uncle Abu Talib bore for this nephew Mohamed has passed into legend. He would not touch his food without Mohamed sitting beside him, he would even start up at night in his sleep and call to

Mohamed to ask whether he was safe. This being the degree of attachment between the two, Abu Talib could not dream of leaving the boy behind him in Mecca till his return from Syria. So, Mohamed accompanied his uncle to the fertile regions of Lebanon.

By easy stages the Meccan caravan journeyed northwards. The desert tracts of hard sand were now behind them, wending in and out of the many passes of the Syrian uplands the caravan of Abu Talib was nearing its destination. Perched on one of the spurs of Jabul Haroon was a monastery, stark and naked it rose above every peak beside it, and this is where the celebrated Christian monk Bahira worshipped.

Twisting and bending, the long line of Arabian camels zig-zagged its way below in the pass where Bahira looked out. He strained his eyes to see whether they were deceiving him: for lo! according to some reports, the trees and stones beside which a particular camel rider of that caravan passed inclined as in salutation and greeting; according to what others say, in that hot noon day sun, a fleecy cloud hovered over a rider to protect him against the sun's scorching rays.

Inch by inch the cloud moved over this especial rider, so add the traditionalists; yes, shifted its position as an umbrella high above the hills and cast a shadow upon one of the camel riders. The rest covered their heads with their head-sheets, knowing nothing of the protection accorded to that especial fellow-traveller of theirs.

'Is that the man, about whom I have read the prophecy?' asked Bahira, but he continued to stay unbelieving by. The caravan was now resting in a pocket of the hill. He could see them pitching their camp for a night's rest. They were unloading the packs from their camels. It thrilled Bahira. An opportunity had at last arrived to test his knowledge about the advent of The Prophet.

Bahira had made up his mind. A messenger was hurrying to invite the wayfarers to a hearty dinner at his monastery. Bin Ibrahim relates that the messenger returned in company with the men of Mecca, whom the monk greeted at the gate of the monastery: 'By Lat and Uzza, our stone-built Gods of Mecca Shrine!' said the leader of the caravan, 'thy conduct doth puzzle me, O Bahira! many a time and oft have we passed by the convent; yet until now thou hast never heeded us; never didst thou dream of showing us the least sign of hospitality.' Bahira, however, replied briefly by some non-committal words, and invited them to be seated at the table. While the men feasted, Bahira walked about the room seeking one in whom he was interested. But none seem to give the description given in his Book: for according to the Muslim historians, he must have been looking for one regarding whom Jesus spoke in John xvi. 12-13.

'I have yet many things to say unto you, but ye cannot hear them now. Howbeit when he, the Spirit of truth, is come, he will guide you into all truth.

'Nevertheless, I tell you the truth; it is expedient for you that I go away; for if I go not away, the Comforter will not come unto you, but if I depart, I will send him unto you.'

The Muslim theologians do not refer to these statements as meaning the Holy Ghost, for they contend that John was filled with the Holy Ghost even before he was born; and then it speaks of Jesus receiving the Holy Ghost in the form of a pigeon: so that the above Bible references are, to the

Muslims, clear enough Christian allusions indicating the appearance of The Prophet Mohamed. It was, therefore, the fulfilment of these and similar prophecies which Bahira was searching: indeed, upon witnessing those abnormal phenomena of nature's protection, the monk considered himself justified in instituting a search amongst the Meccan merchants.

To the narrative of the feast then, when Bahira could not find any of them to answer to the description that was in his mind, 'O men of the Qutaish tribe!' he said, 'is not one of you remaining in your tents?' – 'Aye, one only;' was the reply; 'we left him alone at rest on account of his extreme youth.' The monk insisted upon having the lad brought to share the feast.

As Mohamed strode through the hall, the monk could not but be impressed by his free and easy gait; and when he had finished his dinner, Bahira approached him, and taking him on one side 'O young man!' said the monk, 'I have a question to ask. By Lat and Uzza – thy great Gods of stone – wilt thou consent to answer?'

Bahira desired to put him to test at the outset by invoking the idols of the Mecca shrine; but Mohamed was of a different persuasion. 'Address me not in the name of Lat and Uzza, for I owe no allegiance to them. Question me in the name of Allah – God that is one – and by Allah I shall answer thee.'

Bahira asked him many things about his family, about his experiences in the desert, about those extraordinary manifestations that good men can only understand: and finally when the youth rose and gathered up his cloak, the collar slipped down his shoulder, and lo, there was a patch – a dark patch – the seal of Prophecy – at the exact spot where Bahira's sacred manuscripts had indicated as the sure sign of the coming Prophet. The monk had at last seen the mark, as foretold.

Sooner than it takes to relate, the learned Christian monk was before Abu Talib. 'What relation is this lad to thee, Abu Talib?' he asked, and he replied, 'that he was as a son to him'.

'Yes, as dear as a son the lad may be to Abu Talib, but he is not thy real son.'

'Mark then my words', thus spoke the venerable monk solemnly, 'and mark them well, for this is no ordinary man, this Mohamed thy brother's son, but a Prophet he shall be; so heed my words and watch over him with constant care, thy charge is precious to humanity.'

Day followed day more or less uneventfully in the life of young Mohamed upon his return from Syria, but he now could appreciate the panorama of Arab vice as complexioned in the licentious mode of living of his people. In a Mecca where tribal jealousy clouded and blackened men's hearts, where people reeled in the dust beside the wine-bibber's tavern, where gambling tables gathered the young and old; Mohamed's finer faculties revolted, but here he lived and did some hard thinking.

Now and then he would betake himself into the wilderness to brood over the misery that sat upon the Quraish, and in deep contemplation something seemed to say that the dawn of righteousness would break soon. It gave him hope, but no sooner did he return to the city and found his kinsmen in the entanglement of the vilest of sins, than those hopes woven by the reflective moonbeams were shadowed by what he saw in the wine-seller's booth, in the shameful scenes of the wayside dances; whilst men so earnestly rose and fell before the stone gods of the Kaaba, praying for victory in battle, or women supplicating for the blessing of a male child, so that he could sing the poems of Arabian lore laden with that pleasure which bestows the highest praise to satanic majesty. And in the midst of this wretched environment, the sensitive mind of Mohamed would fall into a bewildering sleep, till at dawn he saw one line of light as sharp as the glistening edge of a sabre, for Mohamed always had a hope, a horizon of boundless good which must one day banish the wicked practices that even now before his Call made his heart loathe so utterly.

To the arts of reading and writing Mohamed was a total stranger, but his capacity for trade soon won him fame. His truthfulness, correct attitude to all men, his steadfastness were acknowledged to the extent that he was styled as the 'Most Trustworthy'. He was considered to be the best man amongst them on points of honour and virtue. Everyone looked upon him as a worthy scion of the proud and distinguished clan of the Quraish.

An incident which throws light upon his character and resourcefulness may be cited. It was about this time that his fame as a righteous person was in the mouths of all men, when he had acquired a considerable influence in business. The necessity for repairs of the Shrine of the Kaaba arose.

The sacred Black Stone proved the bone of contention, for it was considered to be an especial honour to a clan to be able to build it at its former place.

Every section contrived to have that honour, till the peace of the tribes was threatened, all seemingly having an equal claim to that honour. It was, therefore, resolved that on the morning of the next day, whosoever entered the holy precincts first should have the honour of replacing the Black Stone. By an odd, and a very lucky coincidence it happened to be no other than that Prince of Peace-Makers – Mohamed. He was asked to perform the ceremony as agreed.

Another man would have applauded his good fortune, and, considering it a personal triumph, might have precipitated a tribal war by taunting his rivals; but not so Mohamed. He spread a sheet on the ground, placed the Black Stone upon it, and asked the elders to take corners of the sheet, thus lifting the stone to its place; all thereby shared in the honour, and no one man could say that he alone did it. Even the cleverest brains cannot think out compromising schemes like this on the spur of the moment; it must have been a gift – and such gifts have deeper meanings than superficial observers are inclined to credit.

To those who consider the narration of such incidents trifling and slight, I should ask them to picture the gathering of tribesmen before the shrine, a shrine for which they were willing to shed the last drop of their blood, a gathering of desert warriors who would slay a man and not regret it. Such men crowded into the precincts, with determined faces they raised their eyes to the residence of their idols: the Bani Abed-Dar had joined the powerful tribe Bani Adiyy-bin

Kab, they had filled bowls with their own blood, dipped their fingers in it swearing that they would sooner die than relinquish the privilege of resetting the Black Stone, and for four nights and days the contest lasted.

At any moment an intertribal war might have broken out, it would have blazed to the other end of Arabia and might have lasted for generations as a blood feud. Different people look upon the items of their religion in different lights from the Arabs of that time, much indeed as the Muslims of The Qur'an hold to these matters with a passion unrivalled by any craving of the materialist world. This early behaviour of Mohamed is possibly the first milestone of his ministry towards an endeavour at peace making: and possessing a totally Oriental mentality – for whatever it is worth – I feel that that device of The Prophet saved his nation from a ruinous war.

FROM: MOHAMED: THE PROPHET

Merchant & Citizen

AS TRADE AND commerce had become a family avocation of life of the Quraish, and The Prophet's Sire, Hashim, the merchant prince of Mecca, had established business connections with countries as far distant as Iraq and Syria; these connections were very greatly enlarged by Abu Talib, in which Mohamed acted as his chief helper.

The many qualities of personal character, which distinguished Mohamed from the rest of his countrymen, were responsible for making him not only a general favourite amongst the people of Mecca, but in the business community his solidarity of contract and fair-dealing became a byword, so much so that men would come and trust their all to him, repose their secrets in him, and seek his advice, knowing that his judgment was so excellently executed that it must have welled up from some divine hidden source.

Abdullah Bin Abialhumsa, a merchant of Mecca at that period, relates that once he was transacting some business with Mohamed, when leaving the business half-finished, the former had to go suddenly to attend something else, promising, however, to return presently to complete the work. For three days, Abdullah did not come: other matters absorbed his attention to such an extent that he forgot all about the affair in hand with Mohamed. Recollecting his promise after three days, Abdullah sought the other party with whom he was negotiating, and to his astonishment found Mohamed still waiting for him. To us who have lost the real glow of virtue and are unmindful of the high traditions of our engagements, such a long wait may appear a sheer waste of time.

But it is the dross amongst us that speaks thuswise; for there are men even The Qur'an who value their words more than the discomfort of a long wait; they are not the clod and stones of the earth; they have not divorced things of the Spirit and merely cultivated the flesh – flesh born of dust. Think what an impression that waiting for three days left in the mind of Abdullah, an impression so deep that such an incident has passed into history, recorded in every worthwhile book for the last fourteen hundred years, a classic example of what man is and should be capable of doing. Yet The Qur'an if a man waited for such a long time, he would be called mad: but it shows how much nearer madness we ourselves are as compared to the real issue of man's destiny.

Mohamed had now attained to the age of twenty-five years. A fine manly figure he had, of medium height, sallow of complexion, with colour showing in his cheeks, a wide forehead, with eyebrows meeting above his rather prominent nose, set proportionately over a large mouth in a rather thin face, he was considered to possess the best type of Arab physiognomy. He had a fairly long neck, crowned by a large head with rather curly hair, eyes of dark grey, he wore a thick beard. Much more minute details are given in Tirmizi, Muslim and in Bokhari; but for our purpose the above may suffice; although it may be added here that between his shoulders there was a reddish growth, which has given rise to many legends that it was the place where Allah's Seal could be read; though there is no authority for this statement.

A rich widow lady Khadija was informed in Mecca of the increasing popularity of Mohamed in the town, and particularly regarding his business capacity. Distantly related to Mohamed – (a cousin by a relation in their fifth line of ancestry) – Khadija was more or less of a merchant princess and carried on a large export trade on her own. As a capable and virtuous woman, she was styled Tahira, or the Chaste, as Mohamed was known as Amin, or the Righteous. She engaged him to superintend her caravan and take the merchandise to the far-off markets of Syria. Mohamed was to receive a higher commission, due to his better qualifications.

Abu Talib, the uncle of The Prophet, was not quite at ease regarding this journey of his nephew, for although Mohamed had arrived at man's estate, nevertheless there was a strong attachment between the two, and the uncle feared for the safety of his nephew during long and arduous travel, for had the Christian monk Bahira not warned Abu Talib to protect his nephew against the Jews, according to Suliman Bin Ibrahim? He confided his fears to Maisarah, the servant who was to accompany Mohamed on his journey to Damascus, and bid him watch the safety of Mohamed, and record every incident that occurred by the way: and so, Khadija's caravan laden with the merchandise of Yemen and the Hijaz started northward in charge of Al Amin, the Righteous Mohamed.

A long line of lumbering camels wended their way in and out of those dry and parched sand dunes, which seemed to stretch to the other end of the earth. In that interminable waste of soft sands, the inexorable heat of the desert sun dried up the water-skins before the travellers reached their next water holes or resting-places. Flames of Jahanam itself danced and floated over the rocky defiles under the fierce noonday heat, but the caravan moved on. Mohamed now riding, now walking, led this train, the price of which surpassed even the amalgamated wealth of the whole of Mecca merchants.

And Maisarah, like a faithful servant, watched over his master. During the time when the sun's rays were hottest, and their weary way lay between boulder-strewn passes, where no shade was possible, and rocks lay throbbing with heat, beside which a tuft of grass sheltered, even the beast of burden had a taste of hell-fire itself: 'but' so says Bin Ibrahim, 'the servant of Mohamed was startled to see that his master did not even throw the end of his black turban to shade his eyes. He was quite comfortable.'

Maisarah would look up and see a light cloud, like the giant feathers of a bird float in the blazing sky. These clouds, he avers, increased and met, then they were stretched out in long strands resembling the beam-feathers of enormous wings. They cast a shadow over the leader of the caravan. And thus they remained over him throughout their long marches; but when the sun's rays began to lose their intensity, the mass disintegrated into feathery shapes once again and disappeared in thin air; giving place to the azure and saffron sky till stars began to peep through the blue black vault of the heavens, and calmness settled on the vastness, such as it can nowhere, save in the desert; giving rest to a weary caravan of men and beasts of burden.

Then soon night enveloped them, men lay in between their loads, the camels munched their fodder in deliberate fashion, the campfire was now glowing embers; yes, indeed night had descended upon them, a night of enormous silence, of mystic quiet, with a sky bejewelled with steady bunches of stars, the soothing gold-dusted desert air breathing on them like a soft caress.

But Mohamed was awake, wondering. His thoughts a hundred marches away, dwelling upon the work of man, trying to discover the purpose of creation, the whys and wherefores of life's bitter drama: while palm trees in yonder oasis beside the pool swayed back and forth as the gentle breeze wafted through them, making their lofty heads now meet, now part, like men in consultation; and thus gathering up velocity, lifting moving sands to a distant dune; but all remained silent, like the calm of heaven, whilst Mohamed brooded in the stillness of those desert nights as his fellow-travellers slept, the sleep of the weary.

From his journey to Syria, Mohamed returned successfully, for he had disposed of Khadija's goods at greater profit than his predecessors had done. The father of the merchant princess had died by then, and although Khadija was senior in age to Mohamed, she sent a message of proposal of marriage to him. In this regard, the women of Arabia had complete control. Three months after his Syrian journey, amongst great rejoicing in which all the elders of the clan participated, Khadija was duly married to The Prophet. His uncle Abu Talib read the marriage service and a dowry of five hundred gold pieces was fixed for the bride.

Although after the marriage Mohamed had to shoulder a greater responsibility of the Mecca trade, and business circles saw more of him, the reflective aspect of his mind began to show itself the more clearly. His desire to peer into the hidden mysteries of life and death became more intense, he pondered more seriously about the chaotic condition of his kinsmen. In the seclusion of Mount Hira – now called the Mount of Light – near Mecca, he began to pay visits the more frequently for meditation. Gradually, contemplation hardened into a passion, till by and by it became his practice to betake himself for days together to the cave of Hira, and plunge into solitude to think out the riddle of this panorama of existence.

Deep contemplation began to bear fruit, for it was during those lonely nights that sensations which beggar description sprang up in his mind. Voices now rose from even the inanimate objects around him, and died away in distant whisperings. His mind blended in tune with the infinite. Something was taking shape; an epoch was dawning. As Ibn Hisham so aptly puts it, 'in the oft benighted worldly pathways of material existence, the inner self of every lofty person has been awakened to influences unseen, but felt.' Such were the moments that came to Samuel of yore, to Jesus in the vastness of Palestine, when they poured out their very souls to comprehend a way to save their people from the darkness; and in this pondering these uplifters of humanity found a way. The process was the same with The Prophet of Mecca; the habit of the Great Influence is ever unchanging.

In the stillness of the cave of Hira, sat Mohamed contemplating; it was day, the sun dipped behind the crags without interrupting the thoughts of the thinker. Then came the darkness, swallowing everything, wrapping even the naked spurs of the Mecca hills with a suddenness which is the magic of the desert, till stars were hung down from the velvety blackness like radiant bunches of grapes; but Mohamed's contemplations were deeper than to be affected by the change of light and darkness. This night, as a hundred or more before it, he was alone in the rock-hewn cave of Hira, alone with his thoughts, his ear attuned to a far-off symphony.

It was the faint ray of light that now shot up, pale yet a while, then adding another strand to it, like a pointing finger of light it grew; gradually the crest of the rocky mountains lit up. The dawn, breaking in its majesty, spreading like a river of liquid pearl growing lovelier and more gorgeous like a golden torrent; but yet the sun was hidden when a Voice spoke to Mohamed; yes, a voice like a whispering in the hush of some great Cathedral. 'Thou art The man', it said, 'Thou art The Prophet of Allah.' To 'explain such matters human argument and causation strikes its limitations, explain how a man gathering up rose petals cannot affix the flower to its original stem and make it blossom, explain what is it that whispers into our hearts, aye, into the hearts of the most wicked of us – that we have done wrong when we have erred.' Such manifestations are not the things for the discernment of the eye, the nose, the brain, the Voice is of the House whence came the command, saying: 'The voice said, "Cry." And he said, "What shall I cry?"' as in the Book of Isaiah.

FROM: MOHAMED: THE PROPHET

The Golden Caravan

THE LITTLE WIND which heralds the sun's rising stirred among the sands. A loud call resounded through the caravanserai, the cry of the muezzin calling to men to awake so that they might engage in morning prayer.

'La Illaha Mallah (There is no God but God)', he repeated. 'Worship is better than sleep!' he continued in his holy chant.

In the red rays of the first hour of day, our devotions were hastily offered, for we had far to go before the Imam gave the signal for journey's end that day.

As a perhaps over-devout fellow pilgrim of mine from Konia said, the uproar of the caravan getting under way is like that of Eblis, the Devil, flapping his wings. The peculiar ululation of the camels, the incessant yelping of dogs, the cries of the camel-drivers and water-sellers urging travellers to see that they are well supplied with liquid refreshment, and the noisy farewells of friends combine to make a volume of sound such as few who are not used to travelling in odd corners of Asia can imagine. Mounting my camel, I ride some hundred yards or so out of the crowd so that I may see the picture in its entirety.

THE GOLDEN CARAVAN

From this distance, I receive a much better impression of the caravan as a whole than when in its midst. At first, it gives the impression of a dull-bright mass of colour in which the primary hues – reds, blues, greens – predominate, with here and there a splash of gamboge or snowy white. The several races which make up the people of the pilgrimage are easily discovered. There are the dreamy-eyed, visionary men of Turkestan, the stalwart, soldierly Afghans, the placid Turks, the more volatile Egyptians, each in the garb of his community.

The caravan forms up into a long line of colour. The time has not yet come to cast off bright garments for the white and grey of the pilgrimage. As the sun climbs slowly upward, it strikes on the garish pageant of our pious column, turning it into a flower garden. The guards, mounted on horseback, and with rifle on knee, take their places at the head of the procession. The caravan is ready to start: only the smouldering fires are left in the caravanserai.

But then, there occurred the usual delay.

The caravan master must be interviewed by a hundred anxious folk as he rides from end to end of the column. Many of these people come from districts the most unfrequented, and are quite unused to travel. They are out of their environment and cannot understand conditions. Their questions are not put very clearly, or are, perhaps, couched in a language unknown to the leader.

Others pray incessantly, hoping that this will add merit to their pilgrimage. Again and again, they repeat their prayers or verses from holy literature. The clamour of their vociferation fills the ears like the drone of a myriad of bees; occasionally a voice, louder than the rest, rises above the hum.

Suddenly, there is a roar from the front of the train. A pack-camel has run amok, has bitten the animal in front of it and kicked it in its rear. Uproar ensues. The owner of the beast is deluged with pious curses, and with much ado drags it by the halter out of the column.

A rifle-shot rolls over the plain in a series of reverberating echoes. It is the signal for departure. We are off. But it is slow progress at first. The camel is a beast which takes a long time to get under way. The digestion of his morning meal and the absorption of the large quantities of water he drinks before starting on a journey occupy an unconscionable time, and until then he is likely to be surly and even wicked in temper. Those who know him best do not seek to chastise him, but to humour him, if possible – a difficult task. The rocking of the camel from side to side is like that of a boat on the sea, and occasionally has the same results.

The caravan, as seen by an outrider like myself, keeping clear of its flanks for some miles of its progress, has the appearance of a great coloured serpent as it winds over the desert sands. It seems a rainbow fallen flat to earth and moving slowly across the plain, and which, having no wings to bear it back to heaven, must crawl these sands until their golden dust heap over it and bury it deeply – until some poet finds it and by his magic restores it to the skies. On, on it drags, under the now merciless sun, constant prayers arising from its straggling ranks.

In this brilliant column is packed all the romance and wonder of the East; it is the Arabian Nights in motion, an epitome of the marvels of the Orient. At night such tales are told around its campfires as a novelist would give years of life to hear, tales told by artists who are yet amateurs, life-histories of adventure in every land of Asia, adventure often so seemingly incredible that one not belonging to this wandering brotherhood would laugh aloud, could he follow its recital. But there is no laughter here. These bronze-faced listeners comprehend the nature of the artist's task and know full well that few stories are worth the telling unless gilded by gorgeous words, and that, as like as not, they have an inner meaning. And again, the incredible does happen in the East, is happening there every day.

All day, the caravan trails its length along the golden plain, slowly, but with all the certainty of fate. At the hour of sunset it halts, the azan is called, and devotions are engaged in. Then the evening meal is prepared according to the strict regulations of pilgrimage and the several national customs of the pilgrims. The most extraordinary concoctions are made, the most extraordinary quantity of water is consumed.

There is very little sleep. All night long, pious and perfervid men repeat their prayers or texts incessantly. The staying power of some of the aged patriarchs is enormous. They appear to be made of hammered steel. Neither the fierce solar rays, the lack of good water, hunger, nor the want of sleep affects them in the slightest degree. They rise in the morning, straight as poplars, fresh as palms in an oasis, with supplications on their bearded lips.

The caravan is the symbol of religious sacrifice. What inclusion in its ranks means to the devout cannot be said in mere words. In many cases, it implies a lifetime's hoarding and strenuous toil, so that a man may behold the city of his desire. And for a season, he becomes again the nomadic patriarch who lies behind the history of his faith and fervour – the man who walks in Allah's way.

Thuswise we had started on our long, long trail on the pilgrims' way: and, at the end of the day's journey, rested at another caravanserai.

Although none formed permanent groups or separate parties within the caravan as such – as all men are one in the eyes of Allah – nevertheless some of us threw our worldly goods together as we rested at night: I was with a professor and a wandering merchant.

'He is sleeping, if ever a man slept', said the copper merchant to me, nodding towards a placid-faced man in the shade of the balcony of the caravanserai.

'No, my brother-in-faith', said I to the corpulent merchant, 'the professor is like that always. I have often thought that he indulged in deep daydreams: but he merely meditates!'

'Leave alone, leave alone, sheik of sheiks!' whispered our camel-driver; 'such men are better asleep, for they talk like books.'

The three of us sat in a cell of that caravanserai in Old Istanbul, where, in days gone by, much merchandise passed to the lands of the West. Carpets from Bukhara, spice from Ind, salt and vinegar from Trabzon and goodly loads of dried fruit from Izmir were brought thither by a million lumbering camels.

But now, its glory had faded. New routes, newer methods of carrying goods were in vogue, and we pilgrims were among the five guests in the old caravanserai that night.

The man whose trance was the subject of our remarks was no other than Sheik Ahmed Bey. He had written more books than he had read: and, in the lore of the ancient East, few equalled him.

Like me, a globe-trotter pilgrim, who sought nothing better from life but to bend his steps from shrine to shrine of Old Asia, from Holy Mecca, to Meshed Sharif, to Kerbala Moala, Bukhara Sharif and much further, the Professor of Philosophy was a pilgrim – a pilgrim not only in the sense of performing the sacred rites at Mecca, but a seeker who sought more than the outwardness of a green turban as the reward for his Haj to the sacred shrines.

FROM: THE GOLDEN CARAVAN

In the Veiled Mecca

A HUNDRED THOUSAND or more Muslim pilgrims crowd in the desert city of Mecca for their annual pilgrimage. By far the largest number of them dwell under the British flag; yet they come from every part of the globe in quest of that Grail of a Muslim's heart.

They travel singly, or with their families, in motor cars, on camels or merely trudge the sun-baked regions of Arabia. The city is open only to Muslims, and my recent visit to the mystic shrines of that veiled town of the desert has left very vivid impressions upon my mind as I took to the Pilgrim's Way to Mecca, which lies some fifty miles east of the Red Sea port of Jeddah, where the pilgrims leave their boats to journey on camels or how they will to the City of Prayer in the heart of the desert.

From Jeddah, our long caravan journeyed Mecca-ward. With my head shaven and wearing only one white sheet, the pilgrim's costume, I nestled down in my mat-covered litter which was tied on the back of my camel. The rocking movement to and fro of my litter kept time with the recitation of ninety-nine names of Allah. 'I am in Thy Presence, O, the Mighty', I prayed, and my tongue seemed to cling to the roof of my mouth with thirst, but imbued with an intense feeling of religious fervour, I continued, 'Lead me in Thine own way, O Allah, as I approach Thy Throne.' And the ship of the desert moved on with his fellows, munching all the time, quite oblivious of the scorching heat that beat upon the brown rocks, painting everything now violet, now red, now grey.

An indescribable feeling came upon me on seeing the two whitewashed pillars which stand some three miles outside the city of Mecca, to mark the inviolable sanctuary of Islam, within which no blood may be shed; and all of a sudden, in the lap of encircling brown-grey hills, appeared Mecca.

Its buildings stand in the midst of a distant violet haze, and a huge cry of prayer from the thousands of the faithful rose to the skies. Then we plunged into silence, a silence of reverence; some prostrating, others kneeling and lifting our tear-dimmed eyes to the city towards which we had prayed five times a day all our lives, as our ancestors had done for over a thousand years of Islamic history.

Wearing the regulation costume, I waited in the sullen heat while the sun beat down on my shaven head, till I found room to approach the holy precincts. Thousands of pilgrims packed the Harem Sharief, or the Great Mosque, waiting to kiss the mystic Black Stone which, set in silver, is built in a wall of a small room covered by the Carpet. Around this structure, wide marble floor is laid, on which the faithful walk as they encircle the Kaaba seven times on entering the Mosque.

In the midst of this vast quadrangle of some two hundred and eighty paces long and eighty paces broad, surrounded as it is by the double arches of the colonnades, stood Kaaba, where the bending and swaying of the worshippers, the loud recitations of the Egyptians as they faced the heart of the Mosque, or clung to the curtains of the mystic Kaaba, appeared to me a world of its own.

For ten days or so, our world-congregation was engaged in prayer in Mecca. From early morning till late at night there was nothing but one round of prayer and meditation. There is no lighter side to life in Mecca. From the point of view of strict Islamic injunction there should be nothing but that spirit in the city, because this exclusiveness of the atmosphere is considered to bring out the real essence of the faith, the more so to its followers in contrast to their life prior to taking the pilgrimage.

We stayed in pilgrim rest-houses which, towering to six or seven storeys, are built on the slopes of the hills. They are let by the Meccans in apartments during the season of the pilgrimage. Their rents vary from three pounds to ten times as much, according to the nearness to the Shrines. All food is imported from the Red Sea ports to Mecca, as none can be grown in that part of the desert. Everyone cooks his own food and buys his own rations of water. This latter item is of great importance, because there is only one sweet water well in the whole city, and when the difficulty of satisfying the need of over fifty thousand pilgrims is taken into account, it is not surprising that sometimes one pays as much as a shilling for a small bucketful of water.

Its price might even increase with fresh arrivals of pilgrims, for Mecca is known to have housed as many as a hundred thousand pilgrims at one time. It is, even, not uncommon to import water from Jeddah, especially when the day temperature in the shade rises to 133 degrees and more. Generally speaking, there are no arrangements for cooling the houses either by electric fans or other methods used in the tropics. Ice is sold out before the sacking is removed from it, so to speak, for probably it is the rarest commodity.

Only in the evenings, when the heat of the sun abates a little, yet leaving the rocks still warm with the day's heat, could we walk in the many covered bazaars and examine those wonderful silks and beads that are made in and around Mecca; or climb up the adjoining hills, particularly when the moon rises, to see Mecca lying in the hollow as a fairyland of silver, solemn, still, mysterious; glowing with no electric lights, but tallow candles paling away in the distance. The scene robs one of the fatigue of the stiff climb. Later we ride, not in motorcars, for none is allowed in the Holy City, but on gaily painted donkeys, their tiny bells suspended on their hairy necks and jingling all the way to our respective rest-houses.

The most remarkable spectacle which met my eyes there was, when thirty thousand Wahabis of the desert, mounted on their camels, in the full blaze of the heat, were at prayer with us near Mecca. Their warrior king, Sultan Ibn Saud, dressed in the humblest garb of the pilgrims, stood in front, leading the prayer. It was three in the afternoon, according to the Western method of time calculation, when the intensity of the rays of the sun was at its greatest. The heat waves passed in and out of the ranks of the Wahabi soldiers, their faces stern and immovable, as if steel-graven, lifted to the wall of the mighty rocks enshrining the memories of early Islam, as they heard the deep intonations of their leader's prayer. He was reading aloud:

'Meekly do we approach Thee, O The Mightiest of the mighty. Lead us to the path trodden by the faithful and the accepted ones.' He prayed loud and long, and then stopped, as if choked and overcome with religious emotion. The terrific rays of the naked desert sun poured down upon him, and over it all sat a great silence. But he was reading again, 'Give us strength, O Allah', he began, 'to march in Thy way so that we might be of some service to Islam.' Thirty thousand voices of the Wahabis mingled in one mighty 'Amen', and rumbled and echoed through the hills beyond into the parched sands of the desert. Then they sank into mute prayer again for three hours at a stretch, till the Call of the evening prayer dispersed them, and Ibn Saud, that warrior ruler of Arabia, that enigma of the desert, took his place in the humblest ranks of the faithful.

Then in the gloaming, which quickly was swallowed up by the darkness of the desert, our caravan moved to the shore. Men and women, all we pilgrims appeared to be dazed; we seemed to drop suddenly into a vacuum completely cut off from all life of moving humanity. A joy filled our hearts for having performed the holiest action of Islamic religion. New feelings thrilled our minds, and as the moon rose and hung like a scimitar over the crest of the rocky defiles, a thin streak on the pale face of the limitless sands was our pilgrim caravan, as that moving thread of life trekked in and out of the desert hills to the shores of the Red Sea at the close of our pilgrimage.

FROM: THE GOLDEN EAST

The First Voice of Truth

WITH MUCH CONTEMPLATION, the reflective mind gets supersensitive to impulses, which a barren mind cannot respond to: and thus, great souls overcharged with this refulgence see visions to which the uncultivated eyes are blind. Messengers of God are of such make and build.

A Western scholar, who contributed to Oriental Religions, I should like to quote, for he is free from that blight of bigotry which has settled down upon most of them, even of great names in their countries. That fair-minded scholar is Johnson. 'The natural relations of Mohamed's vast conception of the personality of God', he says, 'is the only explanation of that amazing soberness and self-command with which he entertained his all-absorbing visions'; and then he continues, 'it could not have been accidental that the one supreme force of the epoch issued from the solitude of that vast peninsula round which the tides of empires rose and fell.

'Every exclusive prophetic claim in the name of a sovereign will has been a cry from the illimitable vastness of desert. The symbolic meaning given to Arabia by the withdrawal of the Christian apostle to commune with a power above flesh and blood became more than a symbol in Mohamed. Arabia was itself the man of the hour, The Prophet of Islam its concentrated world. To the child of her exalted traditions, driven by secret compulsion out into the lonely places of the starry night, his mouth in the dust, the desert spoke without reserve.'

A few days later, however, in the placidity of the desert night in the Cave of Hira, the Voice whispered again. It was a night in the month of Ramadan or fasting (609th year of the Christian era) when the vision spoke, once, twice and yet a third time the angel Gabriel insisted. But overwhelmed with divine magnificence as Mohamed was: 'How can I read? I do not know how to read!' he replied.

And here the first revelation occurred to Mohamed:

Read in the name of thy Lord...
spoke the angel, and The Qur'an has it:

Read in the name of thy Lord who created,
He created man from a clod.
Read, and thy Lord is most honourable,
Who taught (to write) with pen,
Taught man when he knew not...

This over, Mohamed woke from his trance. A great trembling had seized him; for God's Messenger had had speech with a mere man: and fear stole into his heart. Presently he was walking back home, in a paroxysm he lay on his bed all a-quiver, for he knew not what he had seen, or what its significance was. Like a comforting wife, Khadija was at his bedside, and listening to her husband's experiences. 'From thy lips never have I heard a lie', she said, 'nor have I doubted thy virtue', and she added, 'what thine eyes have seen, and ears heard, of a truth, is odd. But it is as thou sayst that a Mission is placed in thy hands, thou art heralded as The Prophet of Allah.'

And as Bin Ibrahim says, no man in Mecca was more conversant with the Holy Writ than Waraqah Ben Noful, an Arab convert to Christianity. Mohamed's wife took her husband immediately to the scholar's home. No sooner had he heard his cousin Khadija's story about her Prophet-husband than he cried: 'By the most Holy God! If what thou sayest is correct, He who manifested His Voice to thy husband is the very same great Namus, that is Allah's confidant, the Angel who appeared to Our Lord Moses. Doubt me not, O, Khadija', he added, 'but thy husband is The Prophet risen out of the clan of Quraish. Go, and be of good cheer!'

Bent by age, and blinded by long years of study, the Christian sage Waraqah henceforth could go to the shrine of Mecca to see The Prophet regarding whom he had read and for whom, like the Syrian monk, he waited. Again, he asked Mohamed of his experience at the cave of Hira, and again he tested it with his knowledge of the ancient lore and found it true. 'Ah! I should like to be still in the land of the living', he would address The Prophet, 'when your kinsmen will send thee to exile.' Mohamed would feel surprised by what Waraqa said, to exile, outside Mecca was quite the most remote possibility for a respected citizen of the Holy City, and he a merchant-prince to boot. 'Of a surety, they will drive thee to exile', insisted Waraqa, 'for never hath mortal man brought what thou bringest without falling a victim to the most dastardly persecution. Ah!' he sighed, 'if God deigned to lengthen my days until then', relates Ibn Hishem of Waraqa, 'I would devote all my energies to helping thee to triumph over thy enemies!' But Waraqa died soon after.

In the beginning, The Prophet had to tally his activity with the personal safety of his adherents. The plant was delicate, it required deliberate and slow growth, for the Quraish idolators would not tolerate any other form of worship, and the Quraish were a powerful, and bloodthirsty people. The earliest conversation to Islam was, therefore, limited to the immediate group of The Prophet's friends and relatives. His wife, Khadija, was the first person to embrace Islam; then Abdullah, surnamed Abu Bakr, an important merchant of Mecca, and Ali; other notables followed them, the chief amongst them being Osman, son of Affan of the Ommeyya family; Abdur Rahman, son of Auf; Saad, son of Abi Wakkas, afterward the conqueror of Persia, Zaid, and Zubair came within the fold at an early stage. Many people of humbler station in life also became his first disciples.

But although The Prophet's preaching had gripped the minds of many, and the circle of his adherents was growing, nevertheless all ostensible steps to popularise it were kept strictly within narrow bounds. The faithful met and prayed in a house belonging to Arqum, some distance removed from the hub and bustle of the city of Mecca. In the valley of that sun-smitten hill of Safa, the followers of Allah held their secret prayer-meetings. A while too, they will go to the far-off folds of the Mecca hills and engage in their devotions hidden from the eyes of their idol-worshipping kinsmen. It was during one of these Islamic retreats that Abu Talib, The Prophet's uncle, saw his nephew praying with his son Ali.

He watched the two standing with folded hands, facing towards Jerusalem, standing mute for a brief period of time, then reciting, and then bending and finally prostrating on the bare rocks: and Abu Talib looked on with amazement at this form of worship. When they had finished praying: 'What form of devotion is this, the son of my brother?' he asked The Prophet. It was time for keeping no secrets, and Mohamed's duty was now clear. 'The prayer is of the religion of Ibrahim, Ibrahim our grand sire!' he replied. 'The single-heartedness with which his nephew and son had prayed, and the confident tone of Mohamed's speech so forcibly effected the old chief of the Hashim Clan, that he permitted them to continue their worship; 'for none shall harm you, I aver', he asserted, though he would not himself embrace Islam. That was the way of Abu Talib.

For three years, this preaching was carried on with utmost care and secrecy, till the duty of The Prophet was emphasised by the Command: 'Make known the Command which has been given to you.' In another Revelation, he was ordered to warn his kinsmen. He called the men of Quraish from the heights of Safa. 'O, men of my clan!' he raised his voice, 'if I tell you that an army is advancing towards us from behind the hill, would you believe me?' Men eyed each other, not knowing what Mohamed's real meaning was, but they had already great faith in all matters on which Mohamed made himself heard, for he was known to all as the righteous, Al Amin, one who spoke nothing but the truth. To the simple question put to them from Safa, however, they were now willing to reply unreservedly: 'Aye, Aye. Of a truth, if you said that an army advanced towards us from the folds of Safa, we shall all believe you; for thy word has never been found to be wanting!'

In this atmosphere, when his people had testified to his veracity, Mohamed declared that if they did not believe in One God, and in him as the Messenger, then Allah's wrath will descend upon them. But the minds of the men of Quraish were rusted through generations of idolatry, the tarnished disc never reflects back the glorious radiance of a mirror aglow with the light of spirituality. The Prophet's hearers, who a short time previously had set seal on his merit as a truth-teller, were not inclined to listen to a matter which cut deep down into their hoary traditions. They got wroth, says Bokhari, shaking their heads in disapproval and disgust, they dispersed. Mohamed's uncle was also amongst them.

A few days after this, a huge feast was prepared to which the young and old of the Quraish were invited. At the conclusion, The Prophet rose to speak. 'I have brought to you, all men of Quraish, indeed to the whole world', he said, 'that which is a standby both in this world and the next. In carrying on this onerous task who will assist me?' Men's tongues were tied with amazement to see how a mere man, a man whom they had seen grow amongst them, a man feeble and humble like all men, should dare stand before them; yes, before them, who would slay a man at sight if they found him speak ought against their idols, yet here was he standing before them preaching rank sacrilege about their stone gods, gods who had given them victory in battle, had blessed them with rain when drought came, and whose house they had defended for centuries together. And here a man of their own flesh and blood was defying what a great empire could not do with impunity. 'Who will be with me', asked Mohamed, 'in carrying on this great task?' Who would you think now stood up? No other than the son of Abu Talib. 'Mine eyes are sore, my legs may not be strong, and tender in age though I be', said Ali Bin Abu Talib, 'I shall abide with thy mission, O! Mohamed, the Messenger of God – that God Which is One.' There was a roar of laughter amongst the guests. Stalwart men who had wielded the battle axe and the spear all their lives nursed their swords, these warriors of Quraish rocked with laughter. Forsooth, a weakling like Ali, and only Mohamed to carry out defiance against the might of their ancestral religion! It was ludicrous, a joke.

Gradually, the number of Mohamed's followers increased to forty. There was nothing to be done by stealth now, for injunctions to The Prophet were unequivocal: henceforth he was to go forward fearlessly preaching the truth. Presently he was addressing the worshippers in the shrine of the Kaaba itself. No greater offence against the Established Church could be committed. There were tumultuous scenes in the sacred precincts, angry voices were rising, jeering vituperations were hurled on the preacher; skirts were being torn off their long trailing abaya, the preacher was forgotten, the cause was forgotten, only pandemonium remained, arms were rising and falling on their tilted turbans. Haaris Bin Abayhala ran to the sacred precincts, thinking The Prophet in danger of his life. He was tearing through the tumultuous crowd of angered men, calling 'Ya! Mohamed! where art thou'; hardly had he gone ten paces through shouting, yelling men when leaping swords descended upon the rescuer of Mohamed. Haaris was the first martyr of Islam.

FROM: MOHAMED: THE PROPHET

The Quraish

It is pertinent here to examine the reasons which prompted the Quraish to an inexorable hostility against Mohamed's message.

First of all, we should know what conditions obtained in Mecca regarding the prestige of the Quraish, and other important clans at the advent of The Prophet. The city of Mecca was revered throughout Arabia primarily on account of its shrine of Kaaba where dwelt three hundred and sixty idols. The ministrants of the precincts were the Quraish, and thus they were called the Celestial Family. Incidentally, it helped them in trade, and in the government of the realm, too, theirs was the whole say.

Let us note who were the officials whom the voice of The Prophet sought to dethrone. There was first, Osman Bin Talha, the custodian of the Keys of the Kaaba; from the family of Nofal, Hurs Bin Amir looked after the disbursement of the funds for the poor; from the house of Hashim, Abbas had the right to distribute water to the pilgrims; Yazid Bin Rabiatul Aswad was the Councillor; from Tameen was Abu Bakr who arranged the reparation; the standard-bearer was Abu Sufyan from the rival clan of Omayah; Walid Bin Mogheera from the Makhzoom family was in charge of the transport; Omar Bin Khattab, the scion of Aday, acted as the plenipotentiary; the diviner and soothsayer was Sufyan Bin Omyah, and the treasury was in charge of Haars Bin Qays. I have given these names with their family connection because some of these dignitaries embraced Islam and became staunch supporters of The Prophet, whilst others took very conspicuous part in opposing the ministry of Mohamed both in peace and war. The names of most of them, as we shall see later, will occur frequently as the drama develops; and therefore, the above details will be very useful as a reference.

There are, however, half a dozen other names as well which ought to be mentioned in this regard, for although these men were not actively engaged in the discharge of any ministerial duties, nevertheless, they exercised enormous control over the people. Like the others, their names will also start up in the doings of early Islam, and therefore a familiarity with them is necessary; they are: Abu Sufyan Bin Hurb, whose father had led the Quraish army in the battle of Fijar; the next name is that of Abu Lahab, The Prophet's uncle, junior to Abu Talib, under whose protection Mohamed had enjoyed security; the third man was Abu Jahl, a nephew of Walid Bin Mogheera, and a leader of his clan; next in order was Walid Bin Mogheera, now the undisputed head of the Quraish, then Aas Bin Waal Sahmi, a rich merchant, with a large following and many sons, and lastly Otla Bin Rabiyah, another merchant of considerable fortune. Around these personalities centred the influence and prestige of the Quraish, which held the whole of Arabia within its grasp. This dual monarchy of State and Church was all-powerful.

Having regard to what is explained above, the first reason which can be ascribed to the hostile attitude of the Quraish against Mohamed's doctrine is that it sought to dismantle the belief which had been handed down to them for long centuries, a belief, indeed, which had given them, like their forefathers, the excuse to rule over the bodies and souls of their countrymen from the north to south of the Arabian Peninsula. If that belief was endangered, even in the slightest degree, their rulership would be seriously damaged, the very existence of the Quraish as an entity in Arabia would be destroyed.

Side by side with this common menace, there was the question of acute rivalry which existed amongst the two clans of the Quraish, the House of Hashim and that of Beni Omayah. So far, the latter section held the most important posts in the government. Delicate matters of statecraft could not envisage the appearance of a man from the rival section of Hashim, and by gathering a large following make the scale weigh heavily on the side of those whose competition was resented by Beni Omayah.

They argued that even supposing the conception of One God, as preached by Mohamed, was tantamount to sacrilege in the eyes of everyone, yet if Beni Hashim saw that Mohamed had gathered so much strength as to help them to overpower Beni Omayah, then Beni Hashim would not have any scruples in aiding Mohamed, the man of their own clan, his 'excesses' towards the idols notwithstanding.

It is, therefore, hard to discredit the opinion of many writers that the thought of their being pulled down from the pedestals of the state and trade always lingered in the minds of the Omayah's sons who so vehemently opposed Mohamed's mission. The contention, however, in no way throws in the shadow another cause of animosity, that of the dismantling of stone idols from the Kaaba.

The next cause appertains to the uneasiness felt by the Quraish about having restrictions placed upon their moral turpitude. In addition to the base and despicable licentiousness of the general public of Mecca at that time, we have evidence to show that even amongst the keepers of the shrine, depravity and vice were common. Who but Abu Lahab himself stole and sold the golden idol of the gazelle, which was kept in the temple of the Kaaba. Other instances of the degeneracy of the moral conduct would not bear mention.

Incidentally, also the other reason of the opposition was that the Muslims then prayed, directing their faces not towards idol-infested Mecca, but towards Jerusalem, a city revered by the Christians. The devotee of the Kaaba thought that what Mohamed sought was to accomplish by preaching what Ibraha, the Christian general of Yemen, had failed to do by force of arms, that is to say, implant Christianity. And through Ibraha's invasion of Mecca territory, to the Quraish had been bequeathed the greatest hatred for Christians and Christianity. The Meccan had on that score been 'bestowing their sweetness' upon the sun-worshipping Persians, and shunning the Christian Romans of Syria: so much so that when the Persians proved victorious against the latter, the Quraish rejoiced.

The struggle between Persia and the Roman Empire, says Mohamed Ali, had existed for a long time. The great struggle, in which Persia was victorious, began in A.D. 602 when Chosroes II of Persia battled with the Romans. The Persians overran Syria, Asia Minor and had reached Chalcedon in 608. In 613 and 614, both Damascus and Jerusalem were taken by Shahabraz, and the Holy Cross was carried away in great triumph. Soon after, even Egypt was conquered.

When the news of this conquest reached Mecca, adds this Muslim scholar, the Quraish were jubilant, as in sympathies they showed undoubted preference towards the fire-worshippers in opposition to the Christians, who in common with the Muslims were the 'people of the Book, and thus enemies of pagan Arabia.

In the year A.D. 615-616, The Qur'an announced, 'that whereas the Romans were defeated they will again rise and be triumphant': 'The Romans are vanquished', says The Qur'an in Surah Ar Rum, 'in a near land, and they after being vanquished shall be overcome within a few years. Allah's is the command before and after; and on that day the believers shall rejoice...' We have the testimony of known history that it was exactly as told in The Qur'an; the Persian Empire sank to earth within a very few years.

The causes and their effect enumerated above, one will presume had enough in themselves to produce more militant opposition to The Prophet and his fellows. In a country where life was cheap, and dark crimes were not considered crimes at all, it would have been quite an easy matter to slay Mohamed and thus stifle his movement; especially in the beginning the smothering of Islam's messenger could not be fraught with any particular dangers. Any ruffian might very easily have put Mohamed away. It is so in ordinary matters of the world. Different laws govern the universe in regards to personalities who bare a torch in their hand, a torch before whose radiance the gloom of vice is to disappear. These, however, may be my own feelings; but viewing the question from the angle of vision of the Quraish, superficially looking we could not escape the conclusion that they made some tactical mistake in not taking drastic steps right in the very first break of the Islamic dawn.

A more serious study of the conditions then prevailing shows us that the Quraish had made no mistake. They knew their business. To kill a man was an easy enough matter; but its consequences were far-reaching. It precipitated a clan war, a blood feud that would have raged for generations, for Mohamed belonged to the tribe of Hashim, and his kinsmen could never have left the matter alone till the blood was wiped out with the sword. Furthermore, men of other clans had also embraced Islam by now. These followers of Mohamed would have shed their blood in the way of their master, thus practically the entire Arabian Peninsula would have been embroiled in one great national upheaval of internal wars. Besides the wicked state of the Mecca society notwithstanding, there were still some men left who desired to have the differences arranged amicably.

THE QURAISH

A delegation of the important men of Quraish waited upon Mohamed's uncle: 'O! Abu Talib', they said, 'thy influence is appreciated throughout Mecca, thy respect we cherish in our eyes and hearts; but this nephew of thine is incorrigible. He mocks at our idols and flaunts the traditional worship of our grandsires. Wilt thou rid us of him, or shall we take the law into our hands, deal with him in our own way?' Abu Talib dismissed them with a conciliatory reply: but Mohamed could not be muzzled, his orders were not orders of a human being; he obeyed no laws of the vice-ridden people of Mecca, and he continued to warn the idol worshippers, and invited them ever more zealously to tread the path of Allah.

A second time, the delegates of Mecca came to Abu Talib to give him the final warning: 'Range thyself along thy nephew O! Abu Talib', they shouted, 'so that we may deal with thee as well, for Mohamed's ways are beyond toleration.' The old chief promised to speak to his nephew, and sending for Mohamed, he said, 'my beloved nephew, place not so much burden upon mine old back which I may not be able to bear.' Abu Talib's appeal moved The Prophet deeply.

On one side, you have the filial regard for a venerable uncle who has watched over Mohamed when he was a helpless orphan, on the other the mighty call of God's message. On one side, the entire weight of the powerful Quraish, men with glistening swords and proud lances, who rule the heart of Arabia and beyond, who could exterminate a hundred times more the followers of Mohamed before the day dipped in the golden west, and on the other the promise of Allah's words; yes, Allah whose power was impersonal, hidden, mysterious, known and appreciated only by those who were fit enough to behold it.

But feelings did not battle long in the mind of Mohamed, with his characteristic boldness in such matters, 'In the name of God – who is One – I swear', replied The Prophet to his uncle, 'if they will place the moon on my right hand and the sun on my left, even then I cannot, will not, turn from my Mission.' The pronouncement had something of that directness and intensity which truth can only impart; and Abu Talib was palpably impressed. 'Go thy way, the son of mine brother', he said, as reported in Bokhari, 'none dare touch thee!'

The Quraish thought of another stratagem. Is this son of Abdullah really so dear to Abu Talib that he could not be persuaded to part with him? Could monetary considerations not affect the decision of Abu Talib? A third time, a few leaders came to the uncle of Mohamed. 'O! Abu Talib', they said, 'here is Ammarah Bin Walid, son of the most accomplished and handsomest man of Mecca. We bring him to thee. Adopt him for thy son, and let us take away Mohamed, for our souls hunger for his blood.' Abu Talib refused the offer. He did not want another man's son – even with financial backing – to clothe and feed, whilst giving up the one who shared the flesh and blood of his own kinsmen. The bargain was all one-sided.

Next, they went to Mohamed. They offered him one of the offices in the Mecca state, 'a rich wife thou mayst have, a share in the business of the merchant-princes, indeed anything that thy mind craveth for. But leave alone your ways of preaching. O! Mohamed, for the pleasure of thy clan thou shalt win thus wise: or prepare for the wrath of Quraish!' Mohamed, in place of accepting their terms, reiterated the warning of Allah: 'Take heed O! men of Mecca', he replied, and fear the wrath of God. Banish your idol worshipping, and incline towards right living to which Islam invites you.' And then they let loose their passions, murder was in their eyes, men foamed with rage, tugging at their beards, the youthful amongst them greeted Mohamed's words with derisive laughter, a few swords flashed in the noonday sun, spear heads showed above the turbans of the Elders who could with difficulty quieten down the more fiery elements amongst them.

There were other ways to bring a man round to think as they thought, chuckled the wise acres of Mecca. To thrust a spear in the side of their culprit was not one of them: at least, not quite that till it be in a pitch battle, they reasoned.

FROM: MOHAMED: THE PROPHET

The Persecution & Ascension

THE PERSECUTION OF The Prophet now commenced. His followers fared no better. Many a time when the sand was baking under the intense heat of the Arabian sun, Muslims were taken to those stretches, where they were made to lie, a large boulder having been placed upon their chests.

Others were branded with hot irons; others were immersed in the water till they were just about to be drowned. Ibn Saad gives these and other details about the atrocities inflicted upon the Muslims.

Even women did not escape the wrath of the Quraish. Simeyah was killed by Abu Jahl, Zanerah, another pious woman, was beaten till her persecutor himself collapsed; and after taking a rest, began to beleather her till she became unconscious, and ultimately lost the sight of her eyes. Men, like Abu Fakiyah, were dragged through the streets by their feet, passers-by were asked to spit on them and then they were placed over the burning sands. The treatment meted out to Mohamed was scarcely less severe. One day, while he was praying, a man throwing his sheet round the neck of The Prophet dragged him with such force that Mohamed fell on his knees. On another occasion Abu Jahl caused some camel intestines to be thrown over him at the time of worship. Thorns were strewn in his way, men even cast their slops and rubbish upon him from their windows as he passed by.

The persecution of the Muslim was getting unbearable, when The Prophet advised some of his followers to abandon Mecca and seek refuge in the neighbouring Christian Kingdom of Abyssinia, where justice was done and hospitality was shown to the refugees. In the first Hijrat, or exile, four women and eleven men left their homeland during the fifth year of Mohamed's Ministry in A.D. 615.

Later, others too left Mecca, and Ibn Hisham gives the total number to be eighty-three men and eighteen women. Osman, the fourth Khalifa, was one of the first batch which had left Mecca, but he returned later to rejoin The Prophet.

The Quraish, however, saw a further danger to their position by this voluntary exile of the Muslims. They feared that the followers of The Prophet would acquaint the powerful ruler of Abyssinia with their excesses and weaknesses, and this might prepare the mind of the Negus to repeat the invasion of Mecca. But chiefly did they resent this flight because the mission of Allah, so far circumscribed in Mecca, was now going to be spread beyond the confines of Arabia. They forthwith resolved to send a delegation to await upon the Negus in order to have the Muslims expelled from Abyssinia. The charges which the Meccans brought up against the helpless refugees were that they had abjugated their ancestral religion and had adopted a new faith.

I cannot do better than to quote from the oldest Arabic biography of Ibn Hisham regarding this, a great milestone in Islamic history: 'Then he, the Negus, sent for the followers of The Prophet', says the biographer, 'when they came before the Emperor, he had convened his bishops with their books, and then he inquired, 'what is this religion by reason of which you have separated from your people: a religion which is neither my own, nor like any other?''

Jafar, son of Abu Talib, who was their spokesman, narrated how they were leading a barbarous life, worshipping idols, eating carrion, violating the ties of consanguinity and how the strong man's hand was always lifted against the weak: thus, they continued to live, he asserted, till the Apostle of Allah rose amongst them to summon them to God, declaring his Unity and offering prayers only to Him. The Prophet bade them be truthful, God fearing, performing neighbourly duties towards their neighbours, respect the property of orphans, to give charity and abide by the moral laws; and, above all, associating none with God.

In details did Jafar mention the cruelties inflicted upon them at Mecca, how they were induced to go back to the pagan life of idol-worship. Then the Negus asked the leader of the Muslims to recite some passages of The Qur'an, and he read the Sura of Maryam which, like others, was revealed to The Prophet. The Negus and his bishops were so overcome that they wept bitterly: 'Verily', said the Negus when the recitation was over, 'verily, this, and that which Moses brought emanate from one lamp. Go!' he addressed the Muslims, 'for by God, I will not suffer them to get at you, nor even contemplate this.'

Amru Bin Aas, the head of the Mecca delegation, refused, however, to be defeated in his purpose. During the evening he saw the Church dignitaries and told them that although the followers of Islam did not believe in the form of their ancestral worship, they did not in the like manner owe allegiance to the Christian ethics, more especially the followers of Mohamed had no faith in the Trinity and in the Divinity of Jesus. In their estimation, Bin Aas stated, Christ was no more and no less than a mere man. The Abyssinian bishops were persuaded to use their influence in exhorting upon the Negus the necessity of banishing the people from his realm who entertained such ideas about the Saviour.

The stage was set the next morning, when the Negus assembled his court. The machination of the pagan Arabs had apparently conquered. The bishops sat on the right-hand side of the King's throne, the officers of the state stood on the left, an oppressing feeling was abroad, many heads were bent in whispers as the Muslims were asked to present themselves again before the mighty ruler of the Abyssinian warriors and declare their views about Jesus. Amru was certain that what the Muslims would say could not but favour his cause.

If Jafar gave an evasive reply, then the leader of the Meccans would at once denounce him as a liar, for The Qur'an could be quoted to say that the Divinity of Christ was not to be believed by the faithful; and if the Muslims were truthful then the Emperor, with the connivance of the bishops, would be angered, and command the expulsion of men who in his eyes would be painted as heathens. 'Say what your belief is about Christ', thundered the Negus to Jafar as stated by Shibli, and the leader of the Muslims repeated what was told to them by The Prophet, that Jesus was to them a Voice of God, a slave of Allah and His Prophet.

The pagan Arabs chuckled in their beards, at last their manoeuvring had succeeded, and they watched with assurance the expected command from the Negus. But the Emperor picked up a piece of straw from the ground: 'By God Almighty', he said holding the straw in his fingers, 'Jesus was no more than what you state, you have not exaggerated about Him as much as this thin piece of straw.' The effect of this extraordinary pronouncement struck the bishops mute with wonderment, with difficulty they were able to control their wrath-born amazement. The Arab pagans felt as if the earth was swallowing them, were they hearing and seeing aright? There could be no doubt about what the Emperor of Abyssinia meant: 'Go, to thy dwellings!' the Negus swayed his hand towards Jafar, 'and live and worship in thine own way, none shall interfere with you.'

As a humble tribute to the justice of the king of Abyssinia the Muslim, refugees strove to help the Negus against his enemies. Though small in number, they could withal be of some service to the cause of their benefactor. The Negus had taken the command in person against those who had invaded his territory. Zubair, a young Muslim was deputed to go to the battlefield, and inform the refugees if help was wanted, for they were ready to show their gratitude. Ibn Hisham gives an account of how the young lad swam the Nile by means of inflated goatskins, journeyed to the scene of war; and returned to inform his co-religionist of the victory of Negus over which the Muslims greatly rejoiced.

Upon the return of the Quraish delegation to Mecca without the Muslim refugees from Abyssinia, the flames of revenge burnt the fiercer in the heart of the Meccans against the followers of The Prophet. An organised system of persecution was now set on foot; and even the more important men of that persuasion were maltreated: despite the fact that such strong men as Omar and Hamza had embraced Islam, and there was almost a daily addition in the ranks of Mohamed's followers.

Concurrently with his ever-growing molestation, other steps were taken to boycott not only the Muslims but also the entire House of Hashim which gave birth to the movement of Islam. A large meeting of all the clans was held to devise the means of this ostracism, wherein it was agreed that no one shall give his daughter in marriage to the men of Beni Hashim, and vice versa, no one shall carry on any business transaction with them, none shall provide them with water or any articles of food. This shall remain in operation till the Beni Hashim see their way in giving over Mohamed to them to be slain. Munsoor Bin Akramah having inscribed these resolutions, says Mawahib Ladunyah, suspended them on the Kaaba shrine of three hundred and sixty idols.

And whilst the thraldom of this excommunication sat heavily upon the clan of The Prophet, the ill-treatment was increasing without restraint upon the Muslims. For three years Beni Hashim had to bear the brunt of all the doings of Mohamed, and true to their tradition bore hardships cheerfully. Towards the later part of this social boycott, limits of starvation had reached: people ate leaves, dried up, and cast-off leather was soaked in water and roasted for food. When children wept for food, the persecutors hailed their distress with glee.

During this period of trial, the Ascension of Mohamed to the Celestial Throne of Allah occurred, of which I shall speak presently; and it was at this time, too, that the Muslims were commanded to offer their prayers five times a day. Eventually the pagan Arabs of Mecca, who had many blood ties with Bani Hashim, on their own accord lifted the ban, and The Prophet's clan was again free to occupy its former quarter in the city; but soon after both the beloved wife of The Prophet, Khedija, and his uncle Abu Talib died. There is still a controversy whether Abu Talib embraced Islam on his deathbed; but, of course, we know the spouse of The Prophet was the first Muslim and died as such: and now for the last ten years, Mohamed had been carrying on his mission under turbulent circumstances with such fortitude.

As the storm of opposition raged the fiercer against the Muslims, Mohamed's resolve grew stronger. The Quraish were on the warpath, and they meant to extirpate the cause which had brought disgrace upon their idols. If Mohamed was the Messenger of God, the pagans demanded, then let him bring down the heavens in pieces, shift mountains, erect a palace of gold or ascend to the skies by means of a ladder, and bring down a complete Book of his Laws.

Nothing short of these miracles will satisfy the Quraish. Nor was this demand of asking for miracles a new demand from The Prophet; for the same was asked of Jesus; as in the words of Professor Momerie, 'His immediate disciples were always misunderstanding Him and His work: wanting Him to call down fire from heaven; wanting Him to declare Himself King of the Jews; wanting to sit on His right hand and His left hand in His kingdom; wanting Him to show them the Father, to make God visible to their bodily eyes... This was how they treated Him until the end. When that came, they all forsook Him, and fled.'

Or at Alquds, as the Muslims call the city, which has been rendered holy to them by The Prophet's association with it.

It is impossible to escape the comparison that Mohamed's disciples never asked for miracles, they accepted The Prophet on his own merits as a model man, whose life story was not the life of a god but of a man. In an age says, Amir Ali, when miracles were supposed to be ordinary occurrences at the beck and call of the most ordinary saint, when the whole atmosphere of Arabia and the countries encompassing it, was countenancing supernatural and occult practises, The Prophet of Allah unhesitatingly replied to the miracle – seeking heathens of Mecca: 'God has not sent me to work wonders. He has sent me to preach to you. My Lord be praised! Am I more than a man sent as an apostle? Angels do not commonly walk the earth, or God would have dispatched an angel to preach His truth to you. I who cannot even help or trust myself, unless God pleaseth.'

Here you cannot but observe the clear note of directness, with no embellishment of speech, no effort to shroud himself in mystery regarding his personality or mission: a plain man speaking in plain language the gospel which God put into his mouth: 'I am only a preacher of God's words, the bringer of Allah's message to mankind', and here I may again quote the passage which Professor Momerie attests, that at no time during his life The Prophet made any statement 'which could be construed into a request for human worship.' His miracle was contained in the tenets of his teaching, and his attitude towards mankind.

It was during this time too, as stated above, that the phenomenon of the nocturnal journey to Jerusalem and the

Ascension of The Prophet took place. Before endeavouring to understand the nature of the occurrence, it is necessary to recapitulate what the doctors of Islamic law have reported about the actual happening. Al-Isra, the nocturnal journey and Al-Miraj, The Prophet's Ascension are variously described. Some think that this miraculous journey, says Bin Ibrahim, was physically accomplished, whilst others rely upon the most accredited traditions – among which is that of Ayesha, the wife of Mohamed – that The Prophet's soul alone undertook the journey, and that the phenomenon should only be looked upon as a veracious vision.

There is really no authoritative date of the journey, but according to Bin Ibrahim, who no doubt bases his statements upon the Arab writers, it was the night of the twenty-seventh of the Muslim month of Rabial Awwal that the angel, upon whom devolved the duty of directing the heavenly bodies, was ordered by the Almighty to increase the moon's brilliancy by adding a part of the sun's radiance, and that of the stars by a share of the moon's brightness, so that the firmament that night should be resplendent with light. The Angel was then to descend to where Mohamed was sleeping and carrying him to Allah through the seven zones of Heaven.

Quoth The Prophet, as reported by some biographers: 'I was in a deep sleep when the angel Jibrail (Gabriel) appeared to me.' The angel, taking The Prophet to the Sacred well of Zam Zam, it is related, opened his chest and washed the heart of Mohamed with the holy water of that well. Then the angel brought Al Buraq, an extraordinary bird-like animal, so that The Prophet may ride on it on his celestial journey. The Buraq is described to be a quadruped larger than an ass and smaller than a mule. His coat was whiter than snow, his face was a man's face, but the animal was dumb. He had wings like a giant bird on the mane, and upon his breast precious jewels were sparkling. As soon as The Prophet mounted on it, the creature flapped his great wings, and rose above the clouds careering on and onwards.

From the sacred temple of Mecca, The Prophet's mount took him to the Masjid al Aqsa in Jerusalem with great rapidity. Alighting from the Buraq, Mohamed fastened the bridle to the ring used by The Prophets of yore in Jerusalem, and now one appeared before him holding two cups. One contained milk, and the other had wine. The Prophet took and drank the milk and refused the wine; and the angel, who had accompanied him to Jerusalem and had thus offered him the two cups, spoke approvingly: 'If thou hadst preferred wine to milk', said the Angel, 'thy people would have preferred Error to Truth.'

After visiting the mosque, The Prophet climbed up to where the great rock of Sukhra lies near Al Aqsa, in the sacred Harem of Jerusalem. He remounted the Buraq and, being led by the angel, proceeded towards the skies. During his ascent, he is reported to have met many prophets of old, Adam, Abraham, Jesus, Moses, Idris; there he saw the paradise in which the believers will be lodged, and in it rose an edifice of pearls, the earth of the paradise being of musk and The Prophet's grandsire Abraham was reclining against the wall of the Noble House, in which seventy thousand angels entered every day.

Proceeding further, a 'station' was reached where he could hear the Pen scribbling the account of world's destinies and work of nature; beyond it he spied the Tree of Eternity, and beyond which nothing can penetrate. The refulgence of God's radiance played upon the Tree; and this Light of Heaven enveloped The Prophet as well. The Great Angel here disclosed himself in his true lambent light; for Allah's nearness was now in sight. It was here that the Command to perform fifty prayers every day was conveyed to Mohamed from the Celestial Throne.

On his way back The Prophet was asked by Moses regarding the orders which had been given to Mohamed. 'Thy flock is too weak to bear the burden of fifty prayers', said Moses to Mohamed, 'go back and seek a reduction in their number. To the Throne of Allah did Mohamed return and begged for the reduction in the number of prayers. They were reduced by five; but Moses again reminded The Prophet of the frailty of his people, and again did Mohamed go before the Throne seeking further reduction. The request was granted; and yet a third time Mohamed found himself before Allah's Celestial Light till the number of prayers were reduced from fifty to five; but whereas, it is stated – the number of prayers is thus reduced, the virtue of fifty is vouchsafed into five.

This concluded, Mohamed returned to Jerusalem from the skies and found all the previous prophets awaiting him. Moses and Abraham were already bending low in prayer. He described Jesus as a man of medium height, fair complexioned with long flowing hair. He looked as clean as one that emerges from the bath: the physiognomy of Moses was mentioned as of a tall man, with sallow complexion and curly hair. The Prophet Ibraham resembled Mohamed himself. As the dawn was breaking, all filed up to offer the morning prayer, The Prophet leading the congregation; and ultimately Mohamed found himself in the great Temple of Mecca.

> 'What eyes can pierce the veil of God's decrees?
> Or read the riddle of earth's destinies?
> Pondered have I for years threescore and twelve,
> And can but say these things are mysteries.'

So far, the reports of the many biographers have been set down. Much of it, if taken literally, may sound as a legend; but it can admit of an explanation. In the history of the philosophy of Islam, we have ample evidence to show that this 'transportation' is possible, as this flight has been of the nature of a trance which are not unusual manifestations with men gifted with the powers of the occult. Mohamed, as we know, was an extraordinary man, his message had already singled him out from his fellows; and there can be no shadow of doubt that during a time when hebetation settled on the body, and he was just about to sleep, a feeling of other-worldliness crept upon him, which in essence was of the nature of the Divine.

Whilst Mohamed was in this state of mental and spiritual exaltation, his mind's eye became opened, he had gained possession of knowledge beyond human comprehension, his soul was soaring high above the clouds of sinful humanity as he lay beside the Kaaba in the temple of Mecca. Step by step, he proceeded unveiling mysteries of ages, into the unknown region of thought on and onward towards the grail of true searches, to the Throne of Allah. Meditation, constant prayer to the One God had exalted him in purity and holiness to see and experience things which are inaccessible to men of the common herd. Long flights of spiritual thought transported him to the highest realms which only a mystic can reach, those wings of spiritual ecstasy bore him into that rare atmosphere where he could perceive the Light of the Divine Cause and the Origin of All: and so what is described about his journey with such a glory of colour is nothing but the illusions of a wondrous soul endeavouring to interpret to the profane that impulse which prophets can only comprehend.

Those facets of this stupendous journey where the travel of The Prophet to Jerusalem is spoken of, and the injunction of five prayers during the day was made absolute, are of especial interest to us; because, whereas they lay the cornerstone of the Islamic form of devolution in one case, in the other they explain the reason as to why the Muslims turned their faces towards Jerusalem when in prayer. Finally, they mark the turning point in the career of Islamic preaching, for during this period The Qur'an warned the people of Mecca for the last time before the wrath of Allah might descend upon them: and in it the ground was paved for the Hijrah, or the Flight of the Muslims, from idol-ridden Mecca to Medina.

FROM: MOHAMED: THE PROPHET

The Flight

THE STRUGGLE BETWEEN the Muslims and the Quraish was now open and often violent. Incidents of molestation of The Prophet's followers were growing in number, but the Torch of Truth was fully alight, Mohamed remained steadfast towards his duty.

In spite of the growing strength of the Muslims, they were not allowed to recite The Qur'an aloud nor pray in the Mecca temple freely, till The Prophet went to the uplands of Taif, near Mecca, to preach his gospel of One God. The agents of the Man of Sin had forestalled Mohamed, and his words, therefore, fell upon deaf ears; indeed, it was not without difficulty that The Prophet was able to return from idol infested Taif with a whole skin. He was spat upon, stones were thrown at him, he was jeered at, in short, his peracute reception at Taif was on par with that of the Mecca disorder which took place when The Prophet described his journey to Jerusalem to the pagans.

Nothing daunted, this apostle of Allah returned to his hometown even more resolute in his mind to proceed with the Mission. The pilgrim season was drawing near, and the Quraish feared that at those gatherings Mohamed could not but preach to all and sundry, which would be positively harmful to the cult of the idol-worshippers. At a public meeting of the clans, it was decided to depute men from the Quraish who should warn the pilgrims of the desert regarding the 'sacrilegious' beliefs of one of them – Mohamed – and his followers.

They were to style him as a wizard, his mission as a farce; and if they found him to be capturing the attention of the men of the desert by reciting the passages of The Qur'an, then one of the Quraish should immediately pronounce the Holy Work as a man-made poem with no religious motive, but calculated for the self-aggrandisement of The Prophet.

Mohamed, however, was prepared, for he reposed his trust in the duty before him. Preach, he would, he thought; and let the world judge of his words on their own merits. On the healthy soil, the seeds which he would cost should grow, and thuswise his mind was made up.

The pilgrims came to Mecca from the far-off corners of Arabia. They trekked from the green uplands of Yemen, from the burning sands of the Arabian no-man's-land, from the Red Sea littoral and from the heart of the desert, they came to rejoice and to pray before the three hundred and sixty idols of the Kaaba; and to seek from their stone gods the gift of children, or rain where drought dried up their crops, or victory over their wandering enemies. During the ceremonies, they sold and bought in the marks of Mecca, made merry at the taverns, drank wine till their legs could not support them; and in the midst of it all a call startled them. It was Mohamed who was speaking.

A man was reeling in the dust in an inebriated condition, clinging to the curtain of the shrine of the stone gods, he uttered incoherent prayers that he might win at the gambling table, another kicked him saying how dare he beseech in that manner when the gods had already promised him success, a woman wailed under the swaying curtain supplicating to the god Hobal to give her back her dead child, the haughty Quraish pranced about collecting offerings from the poor pilgrims; and here Mohamed rose to speak in a thronged courtyard of the Temple.

He invited the pagans to come to the way of One God, he warned them of the evil day which they will see if they did not mend their ways, he gave them the glad tidings that the Light of Truth has been ushered in, and that no man had any excuse to grope in the dark any further: 'Come to Allah, the Compassionate, the merciful', he called out again and again.

Men stared at him with eyes of astonishment; what have they heard? What force more potent than their ancestral idols that presided at the shrine had made him so bold as to utter such profanity? The noise subsided as birds quieten down before a thunderstorm: and then the Quraish realised what had happened. Mohamed could have been torn limb from limb, but something stayed their hands, that very thing before which unrighteousness withers and dies. But whereas the time was not yet for these words of Mohamed to sink into the minds of the desert-born; the seed was cast; for shortly afterwards he spoke to some men of Yasrib or Medina about his mission. They were the people of the Khazraj tribe.

These six men of Medina, with whom Mohamed now conversed at the hill of Aqabah, were not entirely ignorant regarding the advent of a Prophet, because a number of Jews living in their town had often related to them the prophesy about the coming of The Prophet. When, however, they heard The Qur'an recited with such glow and warmth which Mohamed only could give, they felt convinced that the verses were no other than those from a Holy Book, and the reciter the man spoken of before. They embraced Islam and undertook to carry the message of peace to their people.

The new converts to Islam, upon reaching Medina, worked for their new faith with such zest that during the next twelve months their original number was doubled. At Aqabah, again they met The Prophet and took an oath of fidelity; but although not wanting in energy themselves, it was felt by these men of Medina that if The Prophet could depute a religious teacher of Islam with them it will undoubtedly provide a greater vigour to the preaching of Allah's religion; consequently, Musab Ibn Umr was sent to Yasrib with them.

In the beautiful city of Medina, the air was free from those sordid influences which hovered over the Quraish at Mecca; the teaching was favourably received, people were more amiable to reason and Islam began to thrive in its new environment with great rapidity; till there was hardly a single family in the town of Medina, where dwelt the two clans of Khazraj and Aus, in which some of the members did not adopt Islam, for now the number of the converts had reached to seventy-five.

In the full blaze of their zeal, the Muslims of Medina trekked to their usual meeting-place of Aqaba to meet The Prophet. Not only had they heard of, but seen the atrocities inflicted upon Mohamed's flock in Mecca, they had witnessed the gleam of truth in the mind of their religious teacher Musab, and Musab was but a particle of the Sun that Reflected the Master Mind, the life of that Fountain Head of Islam was in jeopardy, and it stirred up feelings of racial and religious pride which showed themselves in the desire to have The Prophet amongst them, where in Medina they could guard him and what he stood for with their very life-sap.

This request, of having Mohamed in Medina, was placed before The Prophet during the night preceding the second day of Tashriq. Bin Ibrahim repeats the narrative of one of the Muslim pilgrims. 'We made up our minds', Kab Ibn Malik related, 'to keep our movements secret from our idolatrous fellow-citizens, amongst whom we slept till one-third of the night was passed. We then went out, one after another, stealthily, making our way, slowly and silently, towards a pass on the slopes of the Aqaba, where we all met together to await The Prophet. He soon arrived, accompanied by his uncle Abbas Ibn Abdul Muttalib.

'He had not yet abjured the religion of his ancestors, but he had great affection for his nephew from whom he wished to ward off all misfortune, following the example of his brother Abu Talib. Having been informed of the plans of the people of Yasrib, Abbas wanted to see for himself what amount of confidence Mohamed could have in their proposals. Abbas was the first to address the meeting and spoke as follows: 'O, Assembly of the Khazraj and the Aus! my brother's son, as you know, holds high rank amongst us, and although we do not share his convictions, we have hitherto protected him against his fellow-citizens. In our "qawm" he finds honour and safety. Nevertheless, at the present hour, he turns towards you, and desires to settle in your midst.

'Reflect! if ye decide to remain faithful to your promises and shield him from all dangers whatsoever, it will be well. But should ye fear to be forced one day to throw him over, and give him into the hands of his enemies, it would be better, now at once, to confess that your purpose is not steadfast by withdrawing your proposals and leaving him with his own party.'

'Without the slightest hesitation', says Kab, 'we answered Abbas: "Thou hast heard what we proposed. Thou canst rely on us absolutely!" Then we turned to Mohamed: "Speak, O Prophet! What dost thou want of us, for thy Lord and for thyself?"

'After having recited a few passages from The Qur'an, and recapitulating the fundamental principles of Islam, The Prophet added: "Swear that ye will fight to defend me and my disciples, as ye would fight to defend your wives and children."

'We took the required oath with unanimous enthusiasm: By Allah! we are war children, and our fathers have taught us how to manufacture all weapons – "O Prophet" broke in Abul Hasham, "there exists a compact between the Jews of Yasrib and us, which we shall have to break, perhaps, in order to uphold thy cause. What would be our position, in our land, if, after being victorious thanks to us, thou didst go back to thy 'qawm'?"'

Let the observer pause and think here, whether in this private and secret parley only material gain prompted these simple lovable children of Arabia to speak in the manner in which they were speaking. Was it bargaining? Were the people who were willing to shed their blood to protect The Prophet hungry for the spoils of war? Abul Hasham had made it abundantly clear. They would be slain before any harm could reach The Prophet, and as the reward for their services all they wanted was to retain his presence amongst them; no more and no less. Can human affection attain nobler heights? And let us note as to what The Prophet replies!

'The Prophet smiled', writes Kab, 'and protested: "Rest easy on that score. Your blood hath become my blood, and your honour, my honour. He who wrongeth you, wrongeth me. I will fight the enemies you fight, and support whom ye support. Ye are mine and I am yours! Choose then twelve Najibs amongst you as leaders." Nine Khazraj and three Aus having been selected; 'when we brought the twelve men to him', adds Kab, 'he said, "ye shall be my delegates in your Qawm, as were the apostles of Jesus, son of Mary, among their people."

'The Najibs pledged their words, but just as the solemn oath was about to be sworn, Bin Zarara rose and said, "O, Assembly of the Khazraj and Aus! Have ye reflected seriously about the consequences of the compact ye intend to make with this man? In his sake you swear to go on war with white, brown and black men. But if, in days to come, seeing your property pillaged and your nobles massacred, ye were to forsake him, shame would be brought upon you in this world and the next! We are resigned in anticipation to the loss of our property, and to the death of our best men, if such a sacrifice is useful for the cause of Islam", we replied unhesitatingly, but may we ask The Prophet what shall we receive in exchange?' 'He replied: "Paradise!"'

The oath of fidelity was then taken. First of all, the leader of the Medinites, Abwal Hasheem, placing his hand in The Prophet's hands, swore allegiance. Then followed Al Bara and the others. They promised to protect The Prophet, undertook not to acknowledge any partnership in God's prerogatives, desist forever from theft, adultery, killing of their children and speaking untruths: and henceforth were entitled Insar or the Helpers. The whole pact was so well carried out that the pagan Arabs who travelled with the Muslims from Medina had no knowledge of it; so that when the Quraish complained about the secret negotiations, the non-Muslims refused to believe that such an understanding was sealed whilst they slept in that camp. As to what potent instrument this negotiation at Aqaba was, the succeeding chapters of Islamic history will amply reveal.

The embracing of Islam and the appointment of twelve nobles of Medina as The Prophet's delegate created a situation wholly unthought of by the Quraish of Mecca. Clans after clans in Yasrib flocked to the preachers of Allah; the Ansar, or the converted Medinites, were working with passion, so that The Prophet may find it convenient to be with them and rid himself of the dangers which played on him at Mecca. The enemies of Mohamed were not unaware of the preparation which the people of Medina were making to receive their master; and when the reports of the rapid spread of Islam in Yasrib became frequent in Mecca, a large meeting of the pagans was called to discover ways and means to deal with the new menace which they now felt.

THE FLIGHT

Elder after elder rose to speak in the infuriated gathering beside the yawning mouths of their stone gods in the temple of the Kaaba; each had a new and more gruesome device for destroying the creed of Mohamed. They suggested his being burnt alive, others thought of torture, for anger had seized them as a tempest seizes a slender tree; yet the meeting broke up, having arrived at the only agreement that the people of Medina are to be warned not to assist their archenemy and his faith. The Ansar knew their mind and took no heed of what the Quraish demanded; the Mecca threat dropped at their feet like a spent arrow.

From under the gathering of this storm at Mecca, The Prophet and his followers were watching the clearing sky at Medina. The day, however, came when it was evident upon the Leader of the Faithful to advise his disciples to leave Mecca for Medina: with care and deliberation a slow trek of the Muslims began from the land of the persecuting Quraish to the friendly town of the Ansar; till a very large number of the followers had left Mecca without exciting any undue suspicion of the Quraish. Amongst his immediate friends, however, only Abu Bakr and Ali remained. Repeatedly did his staunch supporter, Abu Bakr, request The Prophet to betake himself also to Medina, but Mohamed waited, waited for the Command. The time passed on, Abu Bakr would remind him how the Ansar awaited him; The Prophet would, however, sit in the temple like a craven figure, lost in silence and meditation, with his face in his hand, and waited and let the time roll on, for his Orders had not yet come: and he could only obey the God of Islam.

Then the Voice came. Abu Bakr was to accompany his master to Yasrib, a joy like the morning sun entered his heart, for were they not going to a city where Islam's standard was fluttering, where the slim and tender creed of Allah was to find a root, from which would arise the tree of One Supreme Being, casting its shade upon the weary and sore-hearted, and from whence the light would dart out to the four corners of the world to let people sift right from wrong? And Mohamed was happy too, for, in Medina, he would enthuse men and women with greater vigour, so that he could share the blessings of The Qur'an with all mankind, because as the sun shines not only for a few trees and flowers but for the wide world's joy, so God sits effulgent in heaven, not for a favoured few, but for the universe of life: so action was forthwith taken, for the future of Islam was contained in that resolve during the thirteenth year of the Ministry of Mohamed.

Call it coincidence or what you will according to worldly imagining, but it just so happened that at the time when The Prophet was preparing to leave Mecca, the Quraish were engaged in a secret conclave to put a stop once and for all to the activities of Mohamed. Once again, they were suggesting, and had ultimately agreed, to kill the father of the Islamic movement, so when someone pointed out the danger of starting a tribal war on account of the assassination of Mohamed, Abu Jahl jumped to his feet with a ready reply. He had been thinking over the matter for a long time, and had now hit upon a plan, whereby the dark deed could be done without implicating any one person. The scheme was that one man from each clan should be selected, and composed of all the tribes, the assassins should waylay The

Prophet, and let all their swords descend upon him at one and the same time. In this manner, the blood of Mohamed could be shared, and no one man could be held responsible.

This decided, they hied forth to Mohamed's house. The night had now gathered and spread itself over the crags of Mecca, plunging the city in the gloom of darkness like a threatening shadow of a storm. Just round the bend of the house of The Prophet, the swordsmen waited, passion burnt in the heart of one bolder than the rest upon seeing the doorway of the man they were seeking. His scimitar leaped out of the folds of his robe as he ran towards Mohamed's door. He would slay the man himself and alone: 'Tarry a moment, you fool!' spoke Abu Jahl, clutching the man by the sleeves, 'tarry a while, he will come out, Mohamed I aver will not see the dawn of another day.' But other plans were made for Mohamed.

And whilst the Quraish waited and foamed like tethered cubs beside the house, Ali had occupied The Prophet's bed and Mohamed, together with his friend and compatriot Abu Bakr, was away out of the town. After winding up The Prophet's affairs Ali was to come to Medina. Beyond the hills of Mecca, the two men of God wended their way through parched valleys of the desert, for their friends in the northern city of Medina were eagerly awaiting them. In the stillness of the night, these two gentle wayfarers trod the earth with lightsome heart, hearts full of hope and joy of what was before them – the growth of Islam – and then the moon rose, touching the distant rocky heads with pale cold silver, and the stars smiled with that languorous smile of aloofness which only the stars possess, and the coolness of the desert increased till it was chilly; and now the night air was distinctly cold as the sun-smitten particles of sand always lose their warmth at night: and the two lone Muslims were wrapped in the magnificence of thought born of solitude; for

> ...All form a scene
> Where musing solitude might love to lift
> Her soul above this sphere of earthliness;
> Where silence undisturbed might watch alone –
> So cold, so bright, so still.

The two distinguished refugees hid themselves in a cave about three miles right of Mecca, in the folds of Jabel Soor. When the morning dawned, and the Quraish found Ali in place of Mohamed in bed, there was general consternation. 'And what are you here for?' thundered the leader of the Quraish to Ali, 'thy master has fled, and thou?' The youthful companion of The Prophet stated that he was there according to his instructions. They dragged Ali before the shrine of the idols. 'Slit his tongue', shouted one, who bound Ali to a log, and, when the Elders had gathered, their wrath knew no bounds. The victim had slipped from their very hands: 'and leaving a weakling like thee, he fled. Bah!' they jeered.

It was then that Ali spoke. He reminded them that although their thirst for Mohamed's blood was unsatiable, every man of Quraish considered The Prophet the most honest man in Mecca, or else why did they deposit everything of value to them with Mohamed? Even at that hour, said Ali, there were such deposits of the Meccans in Mohamed's house, and it

THE FLIGHT

was to return those that Mohamed had instructed him to remain behind, for The Prophet was scrupulous to a fault regarding other's property. With gnashing teeth in evidence, a man ripped his sword from his girdle; the noonday rays making its silver alive, he advanced to slay Ali. But they held him back: for Ali was to return their goods, and, after all, Ali was not the man whom they sought to kill.

At last, he was freed.

Presently, search parties were out in the ravines, over the sun-baked face of the desert, looking for Mohamed. Camel riders dipped and rose amongst the sand dunes to discover the trail of those who had escaped. Savage-looking men of Quraish, maddened by the defeat, sang war songs as they rode up and down the hill where The Prophet hid. Then there was a patter of feet, a camel grunted, its rider was leading his party; in hot chase, the voices of men could be heard, their remarks very audible.

Just round the shoulder of the rock, 'Ahay', shouted a pagan soldier, 'I see some traces of feet', he thrust his face forward, two cruel eyes scanned the pathway, he was now within an ear shot of where the two sat in the cave. A few yards ahead of him lay the cave, a cave where Abu Bakr felt a little anxious for the life of Mohamed: 'Allah is with us!' whispered The Prophet to his companion: and there in a few moments a man with a bared sword in hand was drawing nearer and nearer their hiding place. Had he got the scent? He was sure of it, they are here; but anon! He stopped, rubbed his eyes, was he seeing aright? The trace of human feet on rocks was a phenomenon which he had never seen; and suddenly that trace was gone; the man was frankly puzzled. The ugly marks of his face burnt in the midday sun, in wonderment he looked around; he was following no trail. Again, it baffled him, his features stood out as if they had been chiselled with a very blunt instrument and he retraced his steps: for God's ways are very mysterious.

How men passed to and fro, near and round about that cave, how one almost hit the trail, how an open and unprotected cave, with no trees, shrubs, or stones sheltering it kept its secret hidden from the eyes of even such as had believed to have seen human footprints are matters over which no further emphasis is necessary. Whose hand worked from behind the Veil, who threw a curtain before the eyes of the assassins are points which demand reflection; such occurrences are not normal, the meaning of all these manifestations can be comprehended by the mind's eye rather than described. And so, the futile search ended.

For four days did The Prophet and his companion remain in hiding. Every day, the young son of Abu Bakr went to the city to find out as to what further plans were being made by the Quraish. According to Bokhari, the slave boy of Abu Bakr brought his herd to the cave to provide milk for the refugees, and The Prophet's sister-in-law sent food regularly to the cave. On the fifth day, the two started Medina-ward, knowing that sixteen marches lay between them and their friends, the Ansar. But the Quraish were not yet beaten. Every tribe in the neighbourhood was informed that whosoever could capture Mohamed alive or even bring him dead to Mecca, shall be given the reward of a hundred camels.

Distressed with thirst and munching dried bread and corn, The Prophet and his companion continued their journey. Their trust was in Allah, and indeed how different this journey as compared to his former leadership of the camel train bearing rich merchandise to the fertile regions of Syria! But now both the value and purpose of Mohamed had grown. During his youth he was only an agent, however respected as a mere man engaged in commerce, a man of little better significance than a merchant-prince; but now he held the standard of a movement destined to change the face of the world. His name was now in the mouths of men in the four corners of Arabia.

When swaying in the saddle with the lumbering tread of his camel, Allah's name and prayers on his lips, the blaze of the desert sun was naught to him. On the way he would see signs and portends, his mind in communion with God eternal, hundreds of miles of sand stretched right and left of him, but the wilderness was peopled with that which his prophetic eyes could only discern:

> and thus our lives, exempt from public haunt,
> Find tongues in trees, books in the running brooks,
> Sermons in stones, and good in everything.
> Till all of a sudden, a cloud of dust rose in the far horizon.

It was rolling on towards Mohamed: it became enlarged by the fact that now, towards the evening, a slight haze arose from the surrounding hills, and when within the distance of two or three arrow-shots, the dust was seen to envelop a horse rider, gauntly did he sit in his saddle urging his mount forward. He had no doubt that the men who journeyed towards Medina were no other than The Prophet, his companion and Abdullah the guide, and Siraqa, as was the name of this wild warrior, was bent on possessing the prize of a hundred camels by slaying Mohamed, but just at that instant his horse stumbled and fell.

It was a bad omen for the prize-seeker, and he drew his arrows to divine whether he was to attack the defenceless refugees. The oracle spoke in the negative. But the allurement of a hundred camels was great; leaping into the saddle, he spurred his mount towards The Prophet, this time the horse's legs sunk into the soft sand. Siraqa alighted to divine anew, and again the reply was against attacking the wayfarers. It had a marvellous effect on the man, for humbly he approached Mohamed and begged forgiveness, which was ungrudgingly given.

The people of Medina had already been informed of the coming of The Prophet. Both the Ansar and those Muslims who had arrived from Mecca were anxiously awaiting the arrival. From early dawn till late at night people sat on the parapets of the city walls, staring into the vastness of the desert, their eyes straining to behold the one whom they loved. Day passed day in this anxious uncertainty. Some went further to the plains of Hira on the southwest of Medina, shading their eyes from the glaring sun, hoping to catch a glimpse of the Apostle of Allah, but only the blackish grey boulders deflected the rays, and the bouncing waves of heat rising from them, melting into the shimmering sands beyond with no sign of the approaching Man of Allah. On the other side of the town, they now cast their glances, but here also nothing but vacant and glimmering sand and shale glowed in the distance, without a trace of the noble caravan from Mecca. And thus, will men come and wait and go back home without having welcomed the man of their longing.

It was thus wise when the Muslims had waited one day the whole morning, and at last returned to their homes; that a Jewish scholar looked out of his window into the desert. Two men, clad in white flowing garb, were but a speck in the far distance, their progress was slow, and the Jew watched them awhile: then he cried, 'O ye the Men of Islam', he ran through the town, 'the one that you seek is coming, in yonder direction he and his companion are now approaching the city.' There was a joyous roar of compliments throughout Medina, men buckled up their armour and, putting on their best clothes, were now running in the direction from which Mohamed was approaching. A more sincere welcome is hard to conceive.

About three miles from Medina, that part of the town which lies on a higher plain, is Quba, where many Ansar had their houses. In that quarter of the city The Prophet, according to Bokhari, stayed in the house of Amru Bin Uof. Many other important Muslims, who had arrived in Medina from Mecca, were also staying in the same house. In all, for fourteen days Mohamed is reported to have resided there. The very first thing which engaged The Prophet's attention was the erection of a place of worship.

In an adjoining plot where dates were dried, Mohamed laid the foundation of a mosque with his own hands. Like the ordinary labourer, he worked to have the building erected: he carried stones, mixed the mortar, dug and levelled as one of his flock. This day of The Prophet's entry into the suburbs of Quba is authoritatively indicated to be on the eighth of Rabial Awal in the thirteenth year of his mission, and as the fact of Emigration definitely turned a new leaf in Islamic history, the Muslim Calendar is counted from that date of Hijra, which according to the European method of calculation corresponds to A.D. 622.

Lest the significance of the romance of this first mosque at Quba be lost in the study of that plethora of events which now followed, it should be emphasised that the Leader of the Faithful was not above rolling up his sleeves to work in the building of the first real Temple to Allah's Truth, and in striking at the very root of social or official superiority in the discharge of a common duty. In the eyes of Allah, all Muslims are brothers: the master and the servant, with no distinction of colour or nationality, all standing on one plane, before one Supreme God, and dwarfed by no material status of social rank. For as labourers go, it would have been quite possible to engage local labour if not for all the Muslims, certainly to substitute the Master Teacher of Islam; but it was not resorted to, The Prophet desired to have it deeply stamped in the minds of his followers that Islam has no distinction of that kind. The merit, too, of the prayer and building of this mosque was particularly great, for regarding this 'Mosque of Fear' – Taqwa – as it is called, The Qur'an says:

'... certainly, a mosque founded on piety from the very first day is more deserving that you should stand in it; in it are men who love that they should be purified, and Allah loves those who purify themselves.'

FROM: MOHAMED: THE PROPHET

Entry Into Medina

AFTER TWO WEEKS' stay at the house of Banu Amr, The Prophet was now ready to make his formal entry into the city of his refuge. The streets were lined by men before Mohamed mounted his camel.

The youth of the town, holding banners and slashing the empty air with their glistening blades, pranced about leading the procession; warriors resplendent in their shining armour strode proudly forward, but when the populace saw The Prophet's camel, a roar of 'Allaho-Akbar' ('God is great') rose from the throats of hundreds of men and women. They were holding onto the gear of the camel as a mark of honour to themselves, and women shouted greetings from the tops of the houses, young girls were chanting the praises of the Man of Allah: the Ansar, some time together, sometime singly, welcomed The Prophet, again and again the shouts of 'Allaho-Akbar' rose and fell like notes loosened by the different stops of a giant organ as Mohamed, sitting meekly on his camel, responded to their felicitations as he passed from street to street. But where was he going?

There was not a single man amongst the Ansar who did not wish to have the honour of being a host of The Prophet. To every man who begged to lodge him, he replied: 'Let my camel go where he wishes. I shall stay where the camel may sit'. And the camel, his reins loosened, wended his way through many street twists and turnings before stopping in an open space. There he knelt down, but as The Prophet did not alight, he grunted and rose; but again sat down, where Mohamed decided to stay. It was a barn of one Abu Ayab Ansari: and henceforth he was the proud host of The Prophet.

Abu Ayub's double-storied house was then the residence of the Leader of the Faithful for seven months; and shortly after that period when the Mosque of Nabi was erected, living accommodation was built near it, The Prophet moved to those quarters. During that period too, Zaid was sent to Mecca to bring back with him various female members of the family to Medina. But the very first item which engaged the attention of The Prophet, now as he was in Medina proper, was the building of a mosque. The space in which it was to be built belonged to two orphans, who wished to offer the piece of ground free of charge, but Mohamed had more than ordinary regard for the property of orphans, so the ground was bought from them, even though it was to be used to erect a house of worship. The building itself was unpretentious enough. Its walls were of mud, the pillars of ordinary date palm tree trunks, and for the roof nothing better than mere thatch, and it faced towards Jerusalem. On one side of the quadrangle of the mosque, a room was provided for such Muslims as had no home, and around the mosque existed the living quarters of The Prophet's family. This is really the birthplace of early Islam. Scornful of worldly trappings, an utter disregard, even an abhorrence to the things of luxury, in which the simple and direct mind of Mohamed felt that true and pure living can only be maintained by doing without the tarnished dross of the earth, which wealth has ever proved itself to be since the beginning of time.

When a state of tranquillity was thus secured in Medina, the organised form of worship was ordered. Various devices of sounding the horn or ringing of bells in order to summon the faithful to prayer, which were suggested, did not appeal to The Prophet. The calling of the worshippers to prayers five times a day in a loud voice was the form fixed, also the form of prayer when standing in a row behind a leader, as adhered to up to this day were prescribed. The question of worship having thus been commanded, The Prophet next turned his attention towards the organisation of the Society of the Muslims; that is, the relations that were to exist between the Muslims of Medina and those who having left their all at Mecca had left their native town with, after or before Mohamed.

As the financial capacity of the Meccan Muslims was practically nil, The Prophet gathered together all of them, and asked the Ansar as to what they proposed doing. The people of Medina were willing to give the half share in all their property, land or business to the immigrants from Mecca. Every one of the forty-five immigrants was 'connected into a brotherly accord' with forty-five men of Medina: if an Ausari was a business man, he took an immigrant as equal partner in his trade, in case of his being a farmer, half of the lands he gave to his co-religionist from Mecca, till the system grew so common that when a man from Medina died, his whole property fell in the share of the Meccan immigrant, for the verse in The Qur'an commanded:

'Surely those who believed and fled (their homes) and struggled hard in Allah's way with their property and soul, and those who gave shelter and helped – these are guardians (brothers) of each other.

And thus, the relationship was determined between the men of Medina and those of Mecca. The world's record shows no parallel to this.

But noble-minded as the support of the Ansar was, the Meccans were loath to take undue advantage of their hosts. The example of one Abdur Rahman Bin Auf is a case in point: when offered half of the property of his Brother Ansari or Helper, he declined the offer with thanks, and only asked the way to the marketplace, where he soon opened a small shop, and before his career was over, the refugee had a flourishing business.

No one, of course, wished to burden himself upon the Muslim friends in Medina if he could rationally help it, not even excepting The Prophet, for one day when Mohamed could not find it within his means to entertain a guest, he reluctantly asked Abu Talha to see whether he could do anything. It so happened that Abu Talha had not a greater store of food; so, he put out the light in the house and placed his own and his wife's food before the guest, sitting away in the dark they made gestures, such as in eating, so that the guest should consider that they were also partaking of the food.

This welding of Islamic federation naturally produced significant influence in the civic activities of the people of

ENTRY INTO MEDINA

Medina: so, it was thought important to establish a more thorough working arrangement between the Muslims and the non-Muslims. To this task The Prophet addressed himself next: for what a few months ago was only a scattered and loose batch of poor and helpless refugees had taken a shape of a well-disciplined civic unit of Muslims, showing every sign, both on account of its growing numbers and its efforts in trade and husbandry, of wielding a mighty power. It behoved the leader of this organisation, living and spreading as it now was, to proceed in the direction of forming an alliance with its neighbours.

The Jews of Medina had a decided voice in many matters. They used to enter into alliance with the tribes of Aus and Khazraj, says Mohamed Ali, and to take part in their internecine wars. Though Arab by descent, they formed a distinct unit by reason of their adoption of Judaism and were, therefore, divided into three clans of Banu Qainuqa, Banu Nazir, and Banu Quraiza. Unfortunately, the two Arab clans of Aus and Khazraj – those who were not Muslims – were always at war with each other, and two tribes of the Jews, namely Banu Quraiza and Banu Nazir, sided with the Arab clans of Aus and Khazraj respectively.

A very large number of the above-mentioned Arab clans had now embraced Islam, so that the voice of the Aus and Khazraj became the voice of The Prophet. In the light of new events, since the arrival of Mohamed in Medina, it was necessary to have a treaty with the two Jewish clans: therefore, The Prophet contracted a pact with the men of Banu Nazir and Banu Quraiza. As this was the first political understanding between the Muslims and the non-Muslims, the mention of its terms here is not without interest. The first clause of the Instrument provided that the Muslims and the Jews are to live in peace henceforth.

Secondly, the contracting parties may keep to their own faiths and be unmolested in consequence. The third laid down that in the event of war with a third party, each was to come to the help of the other, provided always that the latter were the aggrieved and not the aggressor; the fourth clause had it that in the event of an attack on Medina, the city was to be defended by both parties; fifthly, that in giving the peace terms to the enemy the other party shall be consulted; sixthly, that Medina was to be considered holy and sacred by both, and all bloodshed within its bounds was strictly prohibited; and finally, that The Prophet was the final court of appeal and arbitrator in all matters in case of a dispute. The Jews set their seals gladly to the document: and the foundation stone of an Islamic State was thus formally laid.

Soon after taking up residence in his new environment, it was now beginning to be borne upon The Prophet that although the Muslim position had apparently assumed a more peaceful and organised form, yet deep currents of intrigue, distrust and possible menace for his followers were to be discerned by the seeing eye: indeed, the situation, if anything, was even worse than at Mecca.

In the city of his birth, a unified system of laws existed amongst the people that lived in and around Mecca. Their traditions were the same, the evolution of their history had marched on parallel lines, in national outlook and aspirations they were not different. In short, a unity of purpose and mind existed amongst the people of Mecca.

ENTRY INTO MEDINA

That that unity was used against The Prophet is beside the point, what is important to note is that Mohamed knew his people well; and, therefore, he could in a measure safeguard their interests by employing means which he, in virtue of his familiar knowledge of his own folk, could devise the more effectively.

But here in Medina, the most generous hospitality of the newly converted Muslims notwithstanding, he and his flock of seventy-five Meccan Muslims were strangers, and may perhaps be sympathetically regarded if they did not find things in Medina exactly in the shape and form to which they were used in their own town. I do not refer to the method of ordinary living, or avocations of life, food or clothing or the like; but to matters of a more profound nature with which the new Muslim community had to reconcile itself at Medina. Amongst others, we must first of all note that in Medina there were several peoples who had a say in the affairs of men's lives.

There were three different clans of the Jews; two Arab tribes. The body of the citizens, therefore, was now composed of six elements, namely, the Jews, the non-Muslim Arabs and the Muslims both of Mecca and Medina. In such a mixed society, presided over though it was by Mohamed, as the Leader of the largest party, working at cross purposes could not be wondered at. But it was more, some men of Medina, mostly Jews, had embraced Islam, not for the sake of the religion, but to act in their own interests, to get whatever they could secure out of it, and perchance to help the enemies of Islam if it suited their purpose. The element within the gates of Medina was a greater danger to the people of the town than an attacking army of the Quraish of Mecca.

The Monafiqeen, as these sections of Medina population were called, were helped in their duplicity by the fact that the Muslims like them turned their faces towards Jerusalem, hence by dissembling thuswise they stood to lose nothing towards their real faith. A rival Arab chief like Abdullah, feeling that his importance in the town was dwarfed by the advent of Islam in Medina, was not slow to grasp the opportunity of inciting his kinsmen, the Jews and others against The Prophet. In the meantime, of course, a tremendous change occurred when a verse of The Qur'an was revealed, in which the faithful were commanded to turn their faces towards Mecca – the Qibla – instead of towards Jerusalem. This, being a Test Case, showed the hypocrites in their true colours, and the Jews and others were now frankly inimical towards the Muslims.

A point of considerable importance springs up in the minds of serious students regarding the appointment of Mecca, towards which the Muslims were to pray. Mecca at the time was pagan, its shrine was idol infested, and Mohamed, who proclaimed the Unity of God, preached the abhorrence of all idols and sought to dismantle the cult of heathenism, was now not only commanded to have his flock pray towards Mecca, but had himself prayed in the quadrangle of the shrine there, even before the above-mentioned verse of The Qur'an. Moreover, many of his followers used to go to perform pilgrimages at Mecca such as Saad Bin Maaz. How can it be consistent with the preaching and tenets of Islam?

Here we must examine what exactly was the object which the Muslims were to worship in Mecca. Was it the courtyard of the Great Temple, its bricks, stones or mortar, the structure called the Kaaba, its idols or walls or the Black Stone, which is built in the wall of the shrine? From all available authority of Muslim writers, it can be deduced that the Muslims prayed to none of the above-mentioned structures of earth, and stone and mortar, least of all to the idols.

The only thing of importance was that House of God which Ibraham and Ishmael had built, as a memory of what sacrifice man is capable of making; that is, the highest sacrifice, the blood of his own son – and rendered the occasion and the House holy by that Association. It is now, as it was then, the sacredness of that offering which invests Mecca's shrine, with the holiness of which the descendants of Ibraham – the Muslims – bow their heads. The fact of all the faithful turning their faces towards that Emblem emphasises the idea of Unity of God and His Purpose. Hence it was so that Mohamed prayed in the courtyard of that shrine. It was, too, on this account that his followers went on a pilgrimage to Mecca; and precisely for that reason the Qibla, or the Temple where a Memory Lingered, was made the place to which all Muslims must turn when in worship.

In addition to the fact that Allah intended to make all Muslims as one people by having them turn their faces to one direction, so as to set one goal before them, and establish a unity of purpose with Mecca as the centre, it is justifiable to deduce other reasons for the Command: '...

then turn your face towards the sacred mosque (Qibla at Mecca).' The reason is that God wanted to fulfil His promise of accepting the prayers of Ibraham when the Father of the Faithful prayed:

'Our Lord! Make us both submissive to Thee, and raise from our offspring a nation submitting to Thee... And raise up in them an Apostle from among them who shall recite to them Thy Communications...'

This prayer was accepted, according to the Muslim belief, an Apostle was sent, he was Mohamed (as argued elsewhere in this book), the Book which he brought was The Qur'an; and the place which Ibraham built as preferred was, therefore, justly accepted as worthy of reposing a memory of Sacrifice and the acceptance of Ibraham's supplications. The House was then the Qibla on that score. If, during the progress of time, that very same association was darkened by the heathenish ways of the myriads of pre-Islamic generations, it should not necessarily disturb the continuity of the Purpose, especially when regarding the advent of The Prophet, it was clearly pointed out that he was to purge the House of God of its loathsome idols and bring the people back to the original Call of Ibraham. Secondly, as pointed out above, this re-establishment of the Qibla distinguished the real Muslims from the Pretenders; who stood out clear before the faithful as people not to be trusted as so remarkably told in The Qur'an: 'And even if you bring to those who have been given the Book (both the Christians and the Jews are called the People of the Book by the Muslims because the original Bible and the Torah are considered as the Holy Work of Allah) every sign they would not follow your Qibla, nor can you be the followers of their Qibla... (their Qibla obviously was Jerusalem): so that after sixteen months of constant facing towards Jerusalem in prayer, the Muslims turned their worship Mecca-ward. The above discussion was necessary to explode the fanatical theory that the Muslim adoration of Mecca was a remnant of Pre-Islamic polytheism, because the idea of Muslim worship avowedly begins from the time of Ibraham: and the Father of the Faithful was anything but idolatrous.

FROM: MOHAMED: THE PROPHET

The Establishment of Other Islamic Injunctions

THE TURNING OF one's face towards Mecca when in prayer having thus been settled, instructions were given as to the actual method of the prayer.

The faithful shall first wash themselves, then he will attend the mosque where the Muezzin or the Caller of the Prayer Call shall be chanting in a loud voice certain formulae. The faithful shall thus range themselves in a row behind an Imam or the leader of prayer; folding their arms over their abdomens, they shall stand, then bend, and finally touch the ground in front of them in unison following their Imam, and then sit, folding their legs under them, to the end of the prayer. The various movements in the prayer, together with what is recited at each move, and their philosophy and meaning will be described in a later section of this book.

The next Command was the observing fast during the month of Ramadan. Prior to this period, says Bin Ibrahim, for three days did The Prophet fast every month: till the verse was revealed: 'As to the month of Ramadan, in which The Qur'an was sent for men's guidance...as soon as any one observeth the moon, let him set about to fast....' Total

THE ESTABLISHMENT OF OTHER ISLAMIC INJUNCTIONS

abstinence from food, drink, smoking, or using anything 'to feed the body' was enjoined upon between sunrise and sunset during the entire month of Ramadan, or the Month of Fasting. As to its reasons and usefulness I shall speak later. Wine was also prohibited in all shapes and form; the Revelation Commanded:

'They will ask thee concerning liquors, say:

In them is great sin.'

The third Commandment lays down the rule of Charity, or Zakat, which was to be given on the assessment of a man's property and earning; it was intended only for the poor. Gambling too was banned: 'O, Believers!' says The Qur'an, 'wine and game of chance, and statues and divining arrows, are only an abomination of Satan's work! Avoid them, that ye may prosper.'

But whilst these orders were being enforced, and men's morals were being brought in line with the way of Islam, storm clouds were gathering fast and furiously in and around Medina against The Prophet and his followers. The local dignitaries, led by Abdullah Bin Ubay and helped by the Jews, were intriguing with the Quraish of Mecca, and the Bedouins of the desert, who lived on the Mecca-Medina route. They were being made to instigate trouble in order to nip in the bud a movement that threatened to dismantle the power of the idol-worshippers of the Kaaba and was incidentally a thorn in the side of those non-Muslim Medinites who had suffered in their overlordship since The Prophet and his men had come to Medina. The trade was passing from the hands of Abdullah, the Arab chief of Medina; the Jews found that they could lend money only on justifiable interest, the magisterial power of the non-Muslim Arabs was not permitted to deal out justice in its own way. And in the midst of it all lived Mohamed, trusting, hoping and confident in his prayer for the cause he had at heart and the men who clung to him. His prayer had a force and life and wisdom, for

> 'More things are wrought by prayer
> Than this world dreams of. Wherefore let thy voice
> Rise like a fountain for me night and day.
> For what are men better than sheep or goats
> That nourish a blind life within the brain,
> If, knowing God, they lift no hands of prayer
> Both for themselves and those who call them friends?'

Presently matters progressed much beyond the limits of endurance; the security of the Muslims was now definitely threatened, wild sons of the desert had already been seen brandishing their swords near the walls of Medina, that they were in league with the non-Muslims in the town was also patent. The Quraish had invited the Bedouins to attack Medina first on the wake of those marauding parties, the Meccans planned their own organised attack; and, of course, concurrently the anti-Muslim population of Medina would fall upon its Muslim townsmen. With utmost secrecy and deliberation, the whole scheme was thought out. Advance parties of the enemy were already sighted in the neighbourhood.

The anxiety of The Prophet could be imagined. With such a small and unequipped following, a handful of refugees to battle against the mighty forces of the Quraish with men and resources ten times as much as those of the Muslims was at first nothing but courting disaster. And then the thought of bringing their peace-loving hosts into a fight – a fight which could not be called, racially and nationally, that of the people of Medina appeared to Mohamed an unnecessary burden to impose upon the Ansar. Finally, what can be said about the Jewish population, who were ready to fall upon the men of Islam as soon as the enemy thundered at the gates of Medina?

Moreover, the very name by which the faith of Allah is known, being Islam, meaning Peace and Resignation, connotes humbleness and not the ferocity of war or clashing of sabres in the heat of battle. Mohamed was clearly puzzled, but not for long as the Revelation, came to him:

'...And fight in the cause of Allah against those who fight against you: but commit not the injustice of attacking them first.' The Command was clear, and war preparations were begun to defend Medina, yes, the Defence of Medina was the point of view but let it be well remembered, so far as the Muslims were concerned, they did not invite battle first.

FROM: MOHAMED: THE PROPHET

The Battle of Badr

RELATIONS BETWEEN THE Muslims and the Quraish were already strained; now actual skirmishes began to take place between the reconnoitring parties of the Medinites and the enemies of Islam.

The Meccans were exerting strong pressure upon the headman of the non-Muslim Arabs of Medina, vowing that unless Mohamed was expelled from the town, the Quraish would attack the city. The most notorious war lord of the Quraish had actually threatened a Muslim pilgrim with death at Mecca if his people did not get rid of The Prophet, and as clear evidence of the state of war, which the non-Muslims precipitated, was the action of one Kurzur Bin Jabar who had raided Medina grazing grounds, and had decamped with The Prophet's camels.

The Muslims, however, still hoped that if the Mecca caravans could be harassed as they passed in the vicinity of their town, a pressure thus exerted might bring about the Meccans to a more amicable frame of mind, and that they might make peace with the Muslims. For The Prophet above all wanted to avert war; but as these excesses had already taken place, his followers were taking all precautions.

THE BATTLE OF BADR

When such tension prevailed, rumours of an oncoming war were in the air. All sorts of reports added to the nervousness of the opposing parties: news, however, reached Mecca that the merchant prince Abu Sufyan, who was bringing his merchandise from Syria, was maltreated near Medina and his caravan looted. The report, of course, was not true, but before it could be counteracted, mischief had been done and incited the Quraish to speed up their war preparations. In the meantime, about the end of the month of Jamadul Tani in the second year of Hijra, The Prophet ordered a party to go into the desert, look round, and report the results of their reconnaissance. Sealed orders of this mission were given to the leader, one Abdullah Bin Jahsh.

When the Muslim party reached Nakhla, and the instructions were read – instruction for only reconnaissance – these were unfortunately not fully acted upon, for the blood of the leader of Medina troopers boiled to see three Mecca merchants on their way back to the city of the idol-worshippers. Hot words were exchanged, then swords leaping into their hands worked their way into the body of one of the Meccans. He was slain, and his two companions brought in chains before The Prophet.

And then did The Prophet get wroth, for the over-zealous officer had exceeded his orders. This incident was very gravely looked upon by the Quraish. In the ordinary way the matter could have been settled quite easily by paying blood-money, but the Quraish were in no mood to make peace. War was declared on Mohamed and his followers, and the Quraish vowed that Medina would be razed to the ground, and its people butchered in cold blood before their swords seek their scabbards, a pretext for revenge had been found and it should be war to the finish, thus resolved the war lord of the Quraish. This is the story of Badr.

A thousand warriors gathered in the shrine of the idols, and a hundred horsemen lined outside, when they placed their arms near the foot of the temple. Lifting their arms in supplication, the Quraish looked at their god of War which resided in the idol of Hobal. To him they sang hymns and sought a sign for victory against The Prophet of Allah, but no sign came.

That the idol did not lift an arm to bless them is readily comprehended; but could that discourage the men of Mecca, and they eleven hundred strong? Holding their spears and swords aloft, they burst into one mighty song of war as the foot soldiers marched out of the town behind the cavalcade of their cavalry. Their shining armours, set and determined faces, and gleaming swords was a pageant of colour, for now the groups of dancing girls with sparkling eyes, radiant faces, and bedecked in their gala dress, thumping on their tambours, came dancing along the line of the soldiers. The poets recited heroic poems of old, the bards were there too, to sing the war tales of long ago, and so the army of Quraish marched on to meet the foe – a foe small in number, weak in defence, ill-fed and ill-equipped and loving no idols. Thus, day by day, they marched in proud array to win victory.

Here in Medina, The Prophet was not unmindful of what was in the air. As a leader of men in peace, so a leader in battle, Mohamed had now the situation well in hand. On the twelfth day of the ninth of Fasting, with his three hundred and thirteen followers, he emerged from Medina. They were journeying towards a village of Badr some eighty miles from Medina, where the Syrian caravan route is sandwiched by high and rocky mountains. On the way, The Prophet held a war council to make sure whether the men of Medina were prepared to fight. Need he have asked them? The Ansar were prepared to shed the last drop of their blood in the cause of Mohamed. By five easy stages, the Muslims were in the neighbourhood of Badr, and the leader of the Faithful was informed that the Quraish had already taken their position on the other side of the ravine; so the Muslim warriors encamped on the near side of it.

With the dawn, the opposing armies faced each other. The Quraish, resplendent in their shining armour, with sparkling battle axes, sabres and scimitars ablaze with the rays of the sun. Pinions flirted from the tall lances of the horsemen, their leader rode in between the lines a hundred strong. On the other side, only three hundred and thirteen men of Islam stood erect, gaunt, their hearts aglow with the warmth of the faith. Mohamed, their general, arranged them in rows.

There was to be no war cry raised by the Muslims, no savage yells of pre-Islamic time were to be employed. War was a serious matter, a life and death struggle at any time, between any two rivals; but this was no ordinary battle: here the question of a mighty faith was involved, glory in being victorious at Badr meant the dispelling of gloom, death meant dying in the cause of Islam, a worthy reminder of the sacrifice which Ibraham made at Mecca, and which gave

Islam its name. That tradition The Prophet was called upon to uphold. A feeling had pervaded the soul of Mohamed on that fateful day. He was praying, earnestly beseeching for the termination of strife, so that as few lives as possible should be destroyed; for bloodshed was the one thing The Prophet abhorred.

Presently, the Quraish were within striking distance; phalanx after phalanx of their men strode forward, confident of victory. The swordsman, Utba the renowned soldier of Mecca, stepped forward into the arena with his son and brother. Three Muslims went to meet them. The proud Quraish inquired the names of his adversaries. 'O! Mohamed', he shouted to The Prophet, 'what three men to battle with us, three soft men of Medina.

'Nay, send those amongst thy ranks that belong to the warrior blood of Mecca, and be worthy adversaries of mine blade.' The three best fighters, namely Hamza, Ali and Obayda, were now facing the pagan Arabs. They whirled round, they jumped about, avoiding each other, blade beat against blade, the women of the Quraish yelled, shouted, singing war songs, urged their warriors till the sword of Hamza made a clean slit in the side of the leader of the Meccans. Ali despatched the other, but the third Muslim was wounded till Ali, turning round, was able to slay the remaining swordsman and bore his wounded compatriot back to the rank of the Muslims: and the two opposing armies watched the duel, with yells on one side and prayers on the other. Another round was now fought, in which the victory of the Muslims was repeated. Then the attack became general.

THE BATTLE OF BADR

Maddened with the adverse results of combat, the Quraish fell pell-mell upon the Muslims, a force of eleven hundred rushed towards a mere handful numbering three hundred and thirteen men, a proportion of less than three to one. Sabres and scimitars rose and fell; lances and spears and arrows were doing their evil work, the shouting and yelling of warriors blending with the thud thudding of women's drums, their cymbals crashed, war chants rent the air, moans and battle cries mingled. Again and again the Quraish charged to dislodge the Muslims; each time they were repulsed, then the din of battle began to grow less, it lessened further for the mighty legions of Quraish were now retreating, fleeing as quickly as their legs could carry them.

The enemy were routed, leaving their dead on the field, they fled. The victory by three hundred and thirteen men was won against eleven hundred men. Call it a miracle, or chance or fortune of war, the fact is clear that the victory was with those who feared Allah, and who fought to defend themselves and were not the aggressors who had acted upon what The Qur'an had commanded: 'and fight in the cause of Allah against those who fight against you, but commit not the injustice of attacking them first....'

There were fourteen casualties amongst the Muslims. Seventy of the enemy were slain, and as many taken prisoners. The Prophet had even the non-Muslims buried.

After the battle, express orders were given by The Prophet regarding the treatment to be meted out to the prisoners. They were provided with new clothes, the people of Medina were to give them the best available food; not even the advice of such an important personage of Islam as Omar would The Prophet take, when it was suggested that two of the teeth of a war prisoner were to be extracted so that he should not harangue the people so successful against Islam in future. These men in the eyes of the Leader of the Faithful were the guest – uninvited withal, but guests all the same – and where ransom could not be provided for some of them, such men were required to act as teachers for a time 'to pay for their release' so to speak. Many of those nobles of the Quraish who had offered a sturdy opposition to Mohamed were slain in the battle of Badr, Abu Jahl was one of them.

FROM: MOHAMED: THE PROPHET

Battle of Ohud

THE COMPLETE VICTORY of the Muslims at Badr had now consolidated the position of the followers of Islam; but the people of Mecca could not afford to allow to have the news of their defeat percolate into the far corners of the desert, otherwise their prestige as the keepers of the Shrine and above all, their leadership in trade would be irrevocably lost. Also, the idea of revenge in the hearts of the Arabs is keen to a degree; therefore, arrangements for another attack on Medina were immediately started. It was the year 625 of the Christian Era, and only three years after the date when The Prophet had left his native city of Mecca to work his way for Islam amongst his friends in Medina.

Benefiting by the experience of the battle of Badr, the Quraish at Mecca wished to take no chances, but to ensure victory, and so in addition to their own resources they considered it advisable to contract an alliance with the tribes of Tihama and Kinena. The veteran soldier-merchant, Abu Sufyan, now was placed at the command of the combined forces of the Quraish and the desert folk. At Ohud, where walls of hills interspersed with red sandstone and granite roll into deep valleys, about three miles from Medina, the two armies met. Like the battle of Badr, a small body of

Muslims, only seven hundred, faced three thousand of their enemy hosts. One of the interesting features of this battle being that women took an active part on both sides.

With his usual care, The Prophet had planned the position of his men so as to leave no point of vantage through which the enemy could launch a surprise attack. At a cleft in the hills, he specially posted a strong body of archers to guard the opening and remain at their places even when the battle was finished. The battle raged furiously, the clashing of arms was deafening, women were urging their Quraish warriors. 'Courage! Ye sons of Abu Dar; courage', they shouted. 'Courage! Ye defenders of women! Strike home with the edges of your swords!' The Quraish rushed at the Muslims with flashing swords, the Muslims defending hacked their way into the thick of the battle. They slayed, they cursed, they yelled, Hades itself was let loose upon the Muslims. Hamza, the renowned warrior of Islam, cut his way to the heart of the Quraish legions, men fell before Ali like chaff, Omar's sword was showing no mercy. Again and again, the Quraish attacked and were repulsed. Then Talha, the pagan standard bearer, stepped before Ali and, brandishing his sword, defied him, crying: 'You Muslims say that our dead will go to hell, and yours to heaven; let me send you to Paradise.' The young warrior of Islam, accepting the challenge, replied: 'Be it so!' and as they fought, Talha was struck down. 'Mercy, O Son of my uncle', cried the standard-bearer. 'Mercy be it', replied Ali, 'for thou dost not deserve the fire.'

The battle had already showed gain to the Muslims; step by step, the enemy were retreating. 'Glory-be to Habol!'

shouted Abu Sufyan. 'Glory be to God!' shouted back Omar by his stand. The Quraish were now definitely weakening, and the Muslims made one great dash to dislodge them. The main body of the troopers were now seen to be in a demoralised condition, a roar of victory rose from the throats of the Muslims. But it rose too soon. The archers who were commanded by The Prophet to guard the opening of the key position, deserting their posts joined the main body of their compatriots. The cleft was undefended. And Khalid Ibn Walid, the cavalry commander of the Quraish, seeing the opportunity, rushed the opening and attacked the Muslims in the rear, and then a battle royal raged.

Men were falling right and left, clouds of arrows swam into the midst of mingled fighters, everybody was so jammed that often the Muslims fought against Muslims. The Prophet was attacked, the weapon of his enemy fell on the headpiece of his armour, making it cut his face, arrows rained on all from all sides. Muslim women were attending to the wounded; the women of Mecca were fighting like their warriors. Hamza fell, then others, there was confusion amongst the Muslims, more confusion occurred, because someone shouted that even The Prophet is slain. But before the vicious report was corrected, the Muslims losing hearts threw themselves upon the enemy with such recklessness that many were slain, the carnage was appalling.

A grey pall began to float over the battlefield, both parties were exhausted, the Muslims still held the heights of Ohud, and the Quraish could not even then force the issue and take advantage of their superior position. After mutilating the slain enemies, the Quraish retreated. 'On returning to Medina 'says Amir Ali, 'The Prophet directed a small body of the disciples to pursue the retreating enemy, and to impress on them that, though worsted in battle, they were yet unbroken in spirit and too strong to be attacked again with impunity. Abu Sufyan, hearing of the pursuit, hastened back to Mecca with his tattered army, having first murdered two Medinites whom he met on the way. He, however, sent a message to The Prophet, saying that he could soon return to exterminate him and his people. The reply, as before, was full of trust and faith: 'God is enough for us, a good guardian is He.'

Although the battle of Ohud did not decide any issue for the contending parties – as battles go – yet it was certain that the serious loss of life, which had been sustained by the Muslims, had not added to their prestige in the eyes of the wild Bedouins, who were anxiously watching the trend of events. The men of Quraish, however, hastened to announce that the power of the Muslims was no match to their warlike clans, which incited the sons of the desert to try conclusions with Mohamed's followers on their own and, of course, enrich themselves with such depredation as are the means of livelihood of the desert born. These resolves were, for obvious reasons, applauded by the Quraish; even active support was promised to the tribes against the Muslims of Medina.

Emboldened and encouraged in this manner, on the first of Moharram in the fourth year of Islamic era, Talha and Khowalid, the two chieftains of the tribe that dwelt in the uplands of Faid, Qutan threw their men in the field against the Medinites. The matter did not even reach the extent of a skirmish, for the attackers, seeing a hundred and fifty men of Islam under Abu Sulma marching out of Medina to face the marauders, took to their heels.

Shortly afterwards, from the uplands of Ghurta, Sufyan Bin Khalid led his men against Medina, his followers were also dispersed by the Muslims under Abdullah Bin Anees. The leader of the recalcitrant tribesmen fell in the battle. But perhaps, the worse treachery of these lawless clans was manifested during the month of Safor. Hijrah, when Abu Bara Kalabi, the chief of the Kalab clan presenting himself before The Prophet, averred that the time was ripe for his clan to adopt Islam. The ground was already paved, all it needed was some religious teachers, who could speak to the people about the tenets of Islam and to invite them to partake of the blessing of Allah.

The Prophet felt reluctant to send any of his missionaries to hostile people, especially when no one could protect them, should the tribesmen themselves prove unfriendly. But Abul Bara guaranteed their safety. Seventy picked men, well versed in the law of Islam, were consequently ordered by The Prophet to go. When they reached near the territory of the Kalab tribe, a messenger was despatched to the head chief of that clan to announce the arrival of the Muslim Missionaries.

The messenger was forthwith put to death, and before these Muslims could realise the peril of their position, they found themselves surrounded by hostile clansmen. Sixty-nine of the Muslim missionaries out of seventy were butchered in cold blood. Amru Omayeh was the only man who escaped out of that whole group which was invited to preach in Nejd by the Najdi clans themselves. Similar treachery is shown by the two other clans, namely Adal and Qarah, to whom ten missionaries were deputed at the request of the tribes. Eight of these Muslim teachers were killed in an ambush by the very same people who had invited them, and the two Khabeeb and Zaid were captured and taken to Mecca as slaves. The sons of Harres bought the former at the slave-market in order to slay him in blood revenge, and Zaid was executed by the order of Sufyan.

The tragedy of these executions is not greater than other cruelties of the Quraish upon the Muslims, but in the scene which proceeded the slaying of Khabeeb, a thinker feels a thrill of religious spirit. Before the executioner severed the Muslim's head, the culprit requested to offer a short prayer, which being granted, Khabeeb stood in prayer for the last time. A crowd had gathered to see the gruesome spectacle: there was a man with bared sabre in hand, the Muslims stood reciting 'O Allah thanks to Thee, the Lord of Mercy and Compassion', he paused. 'To Thee we pray and from Thee only do we seek help', he continued, 'lead us to Thine own way...'

Then he bent low, and touched the ground with his forehead, calm and resigned and even cheerful, death staring into his face; and he thanked Allah, sent blessings to Mohamed; yes, to a God who even then did not lift His Mighty Hand to save His slave, and a Mohamed who could do nothing for a man whose life sap was to be spilt: a materialistic mind might turn away in despair: had he said that he no longer loved Allah and His Prophet, the pagans would have spared him, but that was not, and shall never be, the spirit of Islam. The man rose from his prayer, walked to the block of wood, placed his head on it quietly; the executioner's sword trembled for an instant in the sun, and Khabeeb was no more. There is a lesson in steadfastness for one's conviction in such prayer-of-death, so to speak; there is music in their words as they pray. Yes, music which still resounded in the ears of those who care to listen, who have an entered into the Temple of Spirituality:

'Where music dwells
Lingering, and wandering on as loth to die;
Like thoughts whose very sweetness yieldeth proof
That they were born for immortality.'

And though small engagements in themselves, these skirmishes were indicative, as shadow ripples show the sinister movement of darker waters below. The entire desert area was now bestirred against The Prophet. That these stirrings were engineered by the Quraish requires no proving: it was necessary, as a war measure, to weaken the resistance of the Muslims, by these smaller conflicts, so that when a Quraish attack of greater magnitude was launched, the Meccan troops may find it all the more easy to conquer Medina, and extirpate The Prophet and his preaching from their midst.

FROM: MOHAMED: THE PROPHET

The Expansion of Islam

THE TIME THAT followed the reduction of the Jewish insurrection was one of peaceful penetration of Islam into various corners of the world. The terms of the Hudaiy-ba truce, which stipulated that no Muslims shall be allowed to leave Mecca, had to be struck off at the request of the Meccans themselves.

A general interchange of visits between the Quraish and the Muslims of Medina now ensued. People began to come and go freely between Mecca and Medina. The Quraish caravans passed through Medina on their northward journey; and beyond the fact that Islam, as a religion, was still frowned down upon by the pagans, the intermixing of the population of the two cities assumed its normal aspect.

During this period Khalid, the great cavalry commander of the Quraish, who had so materially changed the aspect of battle at Ohud and was rightly considered the greatest warrior of his time, now embraced Islam on his own accord: with him came Amra Bin Aas, equally renowned in battle and placing his hand between those of The Prophet attested to his belief in the faith of Allah. The former, as we shall see, led the Muslim legions to victory against the Greeks, and the latter brought Egypt within the Islamic fold.

Many other notables bowed allegiance to The Prophet during the time when the Muslims were not implicated in any war, which goes a long way to prove that the expansion of the faith was effected not by dint of sword, but in virtue of what people had seen and experienced of it in times of peace and goodwill at Medina: else it would have been quite easy for the Muslims to impose their religion on the defeated Jews at Khaiber, but The Qur'an had commanded 'there is no compulsion in religion – 'an order which was scrupulously obeyed throughout the time of the men who proclaimed the law of Islam to the world.

With the consolidation of the Commonwealth at Medina, various sections of the Muslims, who were scattered by the atrocities of the Quraish, arrived at the recognised seat of Islam, and the government of The Prophet had now taken a definite shape. It was during this 'recess', too, that frequent attempts were made on Mohamed's life: the most notable amongst them being the case of a Jewish woman who served up poisoned meat to him. One of his followers, upon eating the food, never rose alive from the table; and The Prophet, although he had spat out the morsel, is said never to have recovered from the ill effects of the poison he had swallowed.

Another feature of this period was the Muslim invitation to various kings and state dignitaries of neighbouring kingdoms. Envoys were, therefore, sent to the courts of Heraclius, the Emperor of Greece, to Negus of Abyssinia, to Khusra Parviz, the King of Persia, to the ruler of Egypt, and the chieftains of many Arab principalities. When the Muslim envoy, Wahiyah Kulbi, reached Palestine, he was informed that the Emperor was celebrating his victory over the Persians by paying a visit to Jerusalem – the cradle of his faith, and thus it was here that The Prophet's Letter was given to him.

With great pomp and show the durbar of Heraclius was prepared to receive the Muslim envoy. Surrounded by the high officials of the Church, the emperor, his crown sitting awry on his brow, strode to the dais, where he first summoned Abu Sufyan, the pagan anti-Muslim Merchant prince of Mecca. The testimony which even this avowed enemy of The Prophet gave regarding the personal excellence of Mohamed, and the good which Islam was doing to Arabia amazed Heraclius.

Abu Sufyan stated that the ancestry of Mohamed was very high placed, that in the family of the Quraish to which The Prophet belonged no one had ever before proclaimed himself as the Messenger of God, that the people who first were fascinated by his religion were poor, that according to his religious principles Mohamed did not enjoin upon his followers to rebel against the law and order of a state, that he is very faithful to his engagements, that in battle as in peace his attitude is found to be strictly correct; and – added Abu Sufyan, the enemy of Islam himself – that Mohamed required all to obey God, Only One God, to be truthful, to pray, and to lead an honourable and chaste life.

The Emperor observed that prophets are, as a rule, men of high birth, that according to what Abu Sufyan had said if Mohamed's clan had been the bearer of Kings, one might presume that Mohamed wished to revive the old traditions of rulership, but that clearly did not seem to be the craving in The Prophet's heart. In all other attributes of good conduct – that is of worship, prayer, honesty, truthfulness – these and many others which characterised Mohamed, remarked the Emperor, were just the sort of qualities which distinguish a Messenger of God from the dross of humanity to whom he is sent as a beacon light of virtue. 'If that is so', predicted Heraclius, 'then his domain will stretch far beyond my Kingdoms. I have known that such a Prophet shall rise', he added, 'But naught did I think of such an advent in Arabia. O! I wish that I could wash his feet if I could only go there!' 'The report of this declaration of the mighty Emperor cannot be believed by those who have taken undue pains to call Mohamed an imposter; because their knowledge 'surpasses the wisdom of the greatest philosophers and scholars and kings: for the rest it will suffice to draw the attention to the facts of history to show how the vaticination of Heraclius was fulfilled by the march of events, because the Muslim legions had reached provinces even further than entered the mind of that Great Greek Conqueror.

Then The Prophet's letter was read aloud, which rendered into English is as follows:

With the name of Allah, the Compassionate, the Merciful. This letter is being sent by Mohamed, the slave of Allah and His Messenger, to Harqoul, the Emperor of Roum. I invite you to embrace Islam. If you will become one of the faithful then God shall give you a double reward, but if you do not adopt Islam then the sins of your people will be upon your shoulders. You that are a believer in A Sacred Book, (that is the Bible, therefore, believing in one of Sacred books of Islam) and between us there is common ground of worship, come to that form of devotion we both may worship a unity – a One God – and that neither of us should recognise any other deity than One God. But if you do not agree to this then we make you a witness that we worship One God.

Abu Sufyan's statement, then the observations of the Emperor and finally the definite and clear-cut exposition of the Islamic invitation could not but create a tense atmosphere amongst the Clergy present at the Durbar. The King did not embrace Islam – it was differently ordained – but the Muslim Envoy was returned to Medina bearing the felicitations of the Emperor.

In direct contrast to this reception was the wrath inflicted upon Abdul Lah-bin-Hazafa who was sent from Medina to the court of the Persian King. Gallant soldiers of Chosroes held their swords aloft when their monarch, enraged by the language of The Prophet's letter, paced the hall of audience. Holding it in his hands, 'this letter, this mere application of an uncouth Arab', he shouted, 'begins not with my name – The King of Kings', he tore the epistle into shreds. 'Who is this Mohamed, of what account is he?' he roared: forthwith he dictated a command to his viceroy at Yemen to send a couple of troopers to Medina to arrest Mohamed and bring him in chains to the city of the Persian King of Kings.

The incident is not without its humorous situation: for two soldiers obedient to the order of the Persians did actually ride into Medina; they did approach The Prophet; yes, they had the audacity of conveying their orders to that man, to whose preaching nearly one seventh of the human race was to bow allegiance. 'Like unto the shreds of mine letter', calmly replied The Prophet, 'the Kingdom of thy king be.' And within a short time, pagan Persia had crumbled to dust: for hardly had the Yemenite soldiers reached home, than proud Chosroes had been assassinated by his own son.

Regarding the message to the King of Abyssinia, Tibri records that the Negus had embraced Islam at the hands of Jafar, and had sent a reply to say that he attested to The Prophet being the Messenger of God, and the same authority mentions that the Abyssinian Emperor had sent his son with delegates to The Prophet, but the boat in which the delegation sailed was sunk in the Red Sea.

Presents accompanied a very courteous reply from Egypt; but varied in tone and results were the replies received by the Arab chieftains. One of them, from Hozah Bin Ali, was of interest because he showed his approval of Islam provided he was given a share in the government, which naturally could not be given at a price of the support of anybody. The acceptance of Islam on its own merit was the Summum Bonum of life.

As the origin of the battle of Mutah is linked up with the despatching of these Islamic invitations, its details are pertinent here. Mutah is situated in Syria, where Hauris Bin Amir was sent as The Prophet's Envoy to Busra. The ruler of the province, Sharjeel Bin Umru, was a Christian Arab, who, being a vassal of the Romans, dared not envisage a cause so decidedly different from the faith of his Christian Emperor. But he went a step further by having the Muslim envoy slain and returning a 'reply of war to a peaceful approach.'

This gross breach of peace necessitated an expedition. The Medina Commonwealth could not possibly brook an affront of this description, and so an army, composed of only three thousand Muslim warriors, marched northwards to avenge the death of their peaceful negotiator. A hundred thousand strong were mustered against these men of Medina, who trusted only in Allah; for reposing trust in God is the expression, because this insignificant force of the Muslims was ill-equipped, insufficiently armed, and naturally enough had no great reassurance of reinforcements or imperial resources, such as the Syrians could command.

An undecided battle was fought. The Muslims lost many lives, amongst them Jafar, the uncle of The Prophet; and beyond the fact that the Emperor of the Romans realised that his vassal could not commit atrocities with impunity little else was gained. But to a student of history, most remarkable evidence of equality and impartiality of Islam is shown by the fact that the Command of the Muslim expedition was placed in the hands of one Zaid, the liberated slave of The Prophet. Let me examine the point here, for without we are apt to lose sight of the real significance of Mohamed's preaching.

At that early period of Arabian history, as indeed even The Qur'an in many regions of Asia, blue blood counted above every other distinction in men's lives. People counted their ancestry to forty generations and more, the exclusiveness of bloodstock was something over which people prided themselves. The 'purity' of their blood was the one criterion to judge between the 'salt of the earth' and the common masses. The Quraish of Mecca were the men who were the 'best of men' – the purest of Arabs. They held the trade, the guardianship of the Temple and the prestige of race. The oligarchy of these factors none dare dispute.

THE EXPANSION OF ISLAM

Now, amongst the Muslims at Medina, there were all sorts and descriptions of people: the Quraish of Mecca, the desert tent-dwellers, the tradesmen of the town, those who did nothing better than to mind the camels or graze sheep. Whosoever embraced Islam had to forfeit his haughty attitude of race, colour and tradition. He was merely one of the Muslims: 'All Muslims are brothers', is the injunction. The darkest of all, Bilal, called the faithful to prayer, the sallow complexioned Persian philosopher Sulman, an ordinary work-a-day helper towards the cause, the rich and proud Quraish and the humble tradesman of Medina were on equal footing. Brothers all, with no distinction of colour or race or social distinction: so in this battle of Mutah, whom did you find leading the men proud of race and traditions, the men of Quraish, but Zaid, the liberated slave of Mohamed – a slave as the standard-bearer of freemen with such mighty warriors as Khalid, the Cavalry Commander of Quraish, and even Jafar the uncle of The Prophet under him.

If we value this incident as an index of what equality meant to early Islam, it is because prior to that time equality did not exist; and certainly, equality between the slave and the freemen was inconceivable. The above example stands as a monument of worthy endeavour in the annals of man, to show how one has 'to lose one's caste' upon entering within the pale of Islam, for rank, ancestry, wealth were nullified before the searching test of the law of The Qur'an. Thenceforth they ceased to be Persians, Arabs, Syrians, wealthy or poor, tradesmen or warriors of haughty grace, but simply Muslims – workers in the cause of Allah, whichever way it may lead them. For this alone, if for nothing else, I, as a Muslim, shall always consider Mohamed the first and the foremost man of all times. History has shown its value, nor can it ever show a nobler disciple of Allah to humanity than Mohamed.

FROM: MOHAMED: THE PROPHET

Journey To Mecca

ACCORDING TO THE terms of the truce of Hudaibiyya towards the close of his seventh year of the Flight of Hijra, The Prophet started for Mecca in order to perform the pilgrimage, from which he was turned away on the previous year. Before we go any further into the details of this journey, the discerning eye sees a contrast. Mohamed, it will be remembered, had reached the confines of Mecca during the last pilgrimage season.

A large armed following he had, and in view of the fact that he was being denied the offering of prayers at the cradle of his religion, a right which was not withheld even from the pagan Arabs of the desert, would he have not been justified in having entered Mecca and fought his way to the shrine? 'War in the name of Allah...' is a clear injunction, and is this command not pertinent in a situation when the faithful are not allowed to perform one of the five principle religious duties?

But Mohamed abhorred war, hated to shed blood, so he turned back to Medina, turned back even when his entire following thirsted for the sight of the holy shrine; no, The Prophet cared not to fight unless goaded into it. First, he tried all other means, even to the extent of signing a treaty which some of his disciples considered humiliating. He did this to secure peace and to avoid war.

And yet men blinded with prejudice will stigmatise him as a man of the sword, deliberately suppressing facts of the life with a parallel: but there is more in this entry of The Prophet into Mecca for the purpose of a pilgrimage than the mere recording of the fact that with a large number of the Muslims accompanying him, and after a three days' stay in the city, they left it as peacefully as they had entered it. We must look closely into this visit.

This pilgrimage was being performed according to the treaty of Hudaibiyya, in which it was stipulated that no armed man should enter Mecca; consequently, the Muslims left all their arms at a place some eight miles from Mecca with a party of two hundred men to guard them. The city was deserted, the Quraish had left the place and retired in their tents on the adjoining hills. But a few real admirers and sympathisers of The Prophet had gathered in Nadwa, the Council Hall overlooking the Temple of the Kaaba.

Some light-hearted youths sauntered along the streets, mockingly remarking that the soft air of Medina had rendered the Muslims less able to retain the vigour of the desert born, that those of the Meccans who having adopted Islam had joined issues with The Prophet would rather be in the sheltered life of leafy Medina than face the heat and the fatigue of pilgrimage ceremonies, especially after a long journey. A point small in itself, and yet of deep significance, for in those days, as indeed ever in the history of man a tired-out foe, physically weak, who drags his feet, as it were, has a decidedly encouraging value to an adversary; so The

Prophet ordered his men to show to these men of Mecca that the Muslims did not suffer from any such weaknesses.

For days they would march, thirsty and on short rations, and yet retain a strength equal to the greatest warrior of the day. The faithful were commanded, therefore, to run or to encircle the temple with quick paces, holding their heads erect, showing no fatigue or exhaustion, calling the name of Allah; and then during the last circumambulations slow down to their normal gait. This practice is still carried out by the pilgrims at Mecca.

Ibn Abi Shayba, following Isa Ibn Talha, describes the various scenes of the time very graphically: 'addressing the Black Stone', he says, 'The Prophet declared: verily, I know that thou art nothing more than a stone, powerless to do harm, or be of any use. Then he kissed it... Abu Bakr followed, then Omar, and the rest came and kissed the stone, saying: By Allah, I know thou art nothing more than a stone, powerless to do harm or be of any use, and if I had not seen The Prophet kiss thee, I should not have kissed thee!'

Then, they did honour in the usual manner to the memory of Hagar, who 'being too weak to carry Ishmael any further, her child that was succumbing to thirst, Hagar placed him on the ground in the shade of a shrub and ascended a hill, hoping to see from afar a well or spring; but all in vain. Then, fearing that her son must be dying, she ran up another hill for the same purpose, but with no better results, till in anguish she climbed down to where her child lay smitten with heat and thirst.

'Seven times did she run in despair between the two hills, when worn out she was now near her child, who, as she thought, may be dead by that time but lo! A stream lay nearby, and it was the Zam Zam, a well by the mercy of Allah, the Compassionate, the Merciful.' In order to keep the memory of that incident of Hagar running seven times between the two hills of Safa and Marva, a practice called the Saey was performed by the faithful with The Prophet, as it has continued to be performed year by year by thousands of pilgrims at Mecca throughout nearly a century and a half of Islamic history down to this day. Following this, the sacrifice was made, the pilgrim costume of Ahram consisting of only one sheet, with no stitches or attachments was discarded, and the Muslims were again before the shrine of the holy Kaaba with The Prophet.

The Qur'an had enjoined upon its believers to keep their contracts, to be faithful to their treaties, and Mohamed was showing by his actions at Mecca that he was a model of what he preached. During that stay of three days, it would have been quite possible to occupy that 'vacant city', arms were easily accessible: but The Prophet was incapable of such treachery. The Muslim pilgrims went about the streets of Mecca honouring the memories of early days, behaving peacefully like pilgrims in Allah's way, true to the truce which their leader had signed. 'It was surely a strange sight', says even Muir, whose love for Mohamed was never deep, 'which at this time presented itself in the vale of Mecca – a sight unique in the history of the world.

The ancient city is for three days vacated by all its inhabitants, high and low, every house deserted; and they retire, the exiled converts, many years banished from their birthplace, approach in a great body, accompanied by their allies, revisit the empty houses of their childhood, and within the short-allotted space, fulfil the rites of pilgrimage. The inhabitants, climbing the heights around, take refuge under tents, or other shelter among the hills and glens; and clustering on the overhanging peak of Abu Qubay, thence watch the movements of the visitors beneath as, with The Prophet at their head, they make the circuit of the Kaaba, and the rapid procession between Safa and Marwah; and anxiously scan every figure if perchance they may recognise among the worshippers some long-lost friend or relative. It was a scene rendered possible only by the throes which gave birth to Islam.'

On the eve of the third day, the Quraish approached Ali to say that the stipulated time was over, so just as peacefully as they had come, the two thousand Muslim pilgrims left Mecca after the pilgrimage. There is, no doubt, of course, that this visit of The Prophet was of great value to the cause of Islam in Mecca and around. People had the opportunity of witnessing, perhaps for the first time, how devoted the followers were to their leader of Islam; they also saw with their own eyes that the religion of Mohamed had very considerably reformed the personal behaviour and outlook of many whom they had seen before in Mecca.

The safe return of the pilgrims to Medina was an occasion of great rejoicing in the city, and The Prophet set about knitting his system more closely to the requirements of the new commonwealth. What situation, however, obtained now in Medina? The greatest European scholar of his time, A. von Kremer, attests that The Prophet founded a political system of an entirely new and peculiar character – peculiar, of course, in the sense that no such law was given to the world before – it was a system in which the Church and the State worked hand in hand, the one was the integral part of the other. In the beginning, as we have seen, he invited his people to believe in the One God – Allah – but, as Von Kremmer thinks, along with this he brought about the overthrow of the old system of government: that is in place of the tribal aristocracy under which the conduct of public affairs was shared in common by the ruling families, he substituted an absolute theocratic monarchy. We shall have an opportunity a little later of again examining this point.

FROM: MOHAMED: THE PROPHET

A Fight to The Finish

THE SHEIKH HAD been the powerful leader of his clan for over twenty years, and during that time many hazards overtook him; but towards the close of the first Great War the raids into his territory became a little too frequent for his liking.

Again and again, he defeated the rival clansmen till reports reached him of the escapades of a brigand who 'hunted alone', as it is said in Arabic. The adventures of this lone, wild brigand became quite a mystery in the desert. The Sheikh himself resolved to capture, or kill, this brigand, single-handed, and so he started off on his own in that pursuit to the fines of the great desert of Arabia.

'In the rugged passes of the outer desert', said the Sheikh, 'existence is sufficiently exciting, but only, as elsewhere, if you court excitement. On that particular afternoon, I found it humdrum enough. But suddenly my Arab sense of forewarning leaped to my mind, for those hills were strange to me, and I felt that Akbar the Black – as we knew the lone brigand, and for whom I was looking – could not be far away.

'I do not know how and why I felt it, but the feeling was persistent.

'Then I dozed off into a half-sleep. Then excitement! Well, couldn't I have it at once if I wanted? Wasn't it on tap, here at my elbow? I knew he worked alone, and what could be more exciting than a man-to-man struggle in these picturesque wilds?

'And after all, it was Akbar who saw me first.

'I was now squatting under the cover of a rocky defile when something chill and uncomfortable touched me all too familiarly behind the ear.

'"Just sit quite still", said a voice in perfect Arabic. That's a jezail rifle you feel, not an earring. No, don't reach for your gun... throw your shooters and knife as far from you as possible."

I obeyed promptly.

'"But who are you?" I asked. "Surely there's some mistake?"

'"None, I assure you. You wanted to meet me."

'"So you're Akbar, are you?" I twisted round and had a good look at him. Gracious Allah!" I cried, "you're no man of the desert. You're certainly tanned enough, and your clothes are just the thing for a brigand, but what does it mean, in the name of Satan who rides on black goats?"

'"You're right", he said. "I am a foreigner, but I'm Akbar all the same."

'"And what are you doing this for?"

'"My idea of sport, just as yours seems to be the opposite. They don't want me in my native land. Perhaps they had good reasons, but that's another story. The question is, what am I going to do now that I've got you?"

"'If you think I'm good for a ransom, you're greatly mistaken", I assured him.

"'In that case", he said, "I've no option but to…"

'What his intentions were – I shall never know; just then I lunged at him with my knee. It struck him heavily amidships. His jezail went off harmlessly, and so did I. In a minute, I had collected my guns and was in the saddle. At about fifty yards, he fired again. I responded. Then I got to the other side of the hill, for I knew what I was in for – a long and stern duel with a man to whom life was as nothing, and who would track me till one or other was out of action.

'Getting my horse to lie down, I took up a position behind some bushes, which I thought commanded both sides of approach. I waited in this cramped state for perhaps half an hour before anything happened. Then a bullet from the rear sent my headgear flying from my head.

'I cursed but crouched low. Then I fired three times rapidly, fanwise, so that I might discover where Akbar was hidden. But from the long stretch of dwarf bush which had lain behind me came not a movement.

'Again, I fired, and this time a bullet whizzed not an inch from my ear. Was the fellow trying to scare me, or merely playing with me?

'Time passed, hours of it, and not a flutter or movement could I see. The strain was beginning to tell. The rain came down in torrents, the clouds massed.

'It grew dark as ink.

'At last, I could stand it no longer and, mounting my horse, set off gingerly through the gloom by the way I had come, as I thought.

'Presently there was a slipping, squashing sound, and before I could stop him my animal was floundering girth-deep in a bog-and sinking, too! I had reached the neighbourhood of the twin rivers.

'I leapt from my saddle and tried to pull him out, but he was stuck fast. Worse, too, I found that I could not extricate myself. I was put up to the thighs in mud. I floundered and struggled, but with each movement felt myself sinking still farther down. With a mighty effort, I raised one leg from the sticky mass sufficiently to enable me to place a foot in the stirrup, and so I drew myself up on to the beast's neck. Then, standing on the saddle of the floundering brute as best I could, I made a desperate leap and landed on comparatively dry soil.

'But I had lost my rifle, which had fallen into the quagmire, and had now only a revolver. Bang! The darkness was lit up by a flash, and I heard my horse scream in the death agony. I fired where I had seen the flash come from, and drew another bullet, which glanced off my boot.

'Throwing myself on the ground, I crawled and wriggled towards the point where I had seen the flash as quietly as I could. Sidling on, up the slope, I suddenly came to the top, and before I could stop myself, I was rolling down the other side at a tremendous pace. With a terrific bump, I cannoned into someone at the bottom of the little hill.

'So, I had located Akbar all right. We closed in a savage struggle like two wild beasts. "You wanted sport", he growled. "Well, you'll get it, my wild wolf!" and with these words, he punched me so hard in the mouth that he cut through both lips at a blow.

'But I had him by the throat with both hands. I wrenched his head backwards. Blood was flowing from both of us. My mouth and loose teeth pained me horribly, but I groped for my knife and drew it. Setting the point behind his shoulder, I pushed. I did not want to give him the typical Arab stab, but only to disable him. With a last effort, he lifted himself and brought something heavy down on my head.

'The blood gushed down over my eyes, and I fainted.

'When I came to, it was daylight, and scrambling into a sitting posture, dazed and stupefied with the pain in my head, I saw Akbar lying in a pool of half-dried blood.

'"You win", he groaned. "No, it isn't fatal, but I've lost every ounce of blood I can spare and can't move for sheer weakness. What are you going to do about it? You're no pretty picture yourself, you know."

'Well, to cut a long story short, I remained there four days with Akbar, tending him as best I could, and feeding him out of my provisions. I managed to make a fire and some supper. On the fifth day I helped him on to his horse. Why? Well, we had come to know and like each other. From what he told to me, I fancy, any man would have 'gone native'.

'He would not take service with my clan, nor would I join his calling. For twenty miles, I rode behind him and conveyed him safely to a hillside hut where he told me he would receive attention. Then I staggered the rest of the way to my native oasis, more dead than alive.'

'Yes, I heard from Akbar.

'He was a sportsman, for he promised off his own bat that he would leave the country of my beat and seek adventure somewhere else. Like many of his kind, that was all he wanted. Well, he will get it there! Perhaps we may meet again – not in a desert encampment nor in a London drawing-room, however, for he loved and yet hated both the places; and after hearing his story I can well appreciate it.'

Then the Sheikh fell mute.

He could not divulge the secret. The warriors take their secrets to their graves when given in the name of the unwritten law of the desert. Such is life and adventure in Arabia.

FROM: TWENTY ADVENTURE STORIES

The Conquest of Mecca

ACCORDING TO THE terms of the treaty of Hudaibiyya, the Arab tribesmen of Khizaah had been allied to the Muslims of Medina, and thus were more or less immune from the raids of their old enemies, the people of Banu Bukr, but soon the latter attacked the Muslim allies, in which the Quraish of Mecca openly helped the aggressors. Pressed by their enemies, the tribesmen of Khizaah sought the sanctuary of the Temple, but here, too, their lives were not respected, and contrary to all accepted traditions, Noful, the chief of Banu Bukr, chasing them into the sanctified area – where no blood should be shed – massacred his adversaries.

When the aggrieved party sought justice from their Muslim allies, The Prophet, as the leader, demanded an immediate redress for not only violating the treaty but also slaying people in the sanctified area. Three demands were made, the acceptance of any one of them was claimed: firstly, that blood-money should be paid, secondly, the Quraish should terminate their alliance with the Bani Bakr who had so ruthlessly disavowed the truce, and, or finally, the truce should be considered as null and void. The Quraish, proud of their strength, agreed to the third condition: that is, no truce of Hudaibiyya was binding upon them. The Quraish could give neither in spirit nor in deed a clearer ultimatum to the Muslims and their Allies.

Providentially, in such tragic circumstances, the promise of Allah was now to be fulfilled, and The Prophet was destined to claim the House which his greatsire Abraham dedicated to the sacred name of Allah at Mecca. But Abu Sufyan, the leader of the Quraish, was sent later to Medina in order to reopen the negotiations. He, however, met with no success.

On the tenth day of Ramadan, the Muslim month of Fasting, The Prophet led his ten thousand warriors Meccaward. Many more tribesmen, throwing in their lot, joined the expedition on the way. A large army thus encamped outside Mecca. Again, Abu Sufyan was sent to stave off the attack, but the time had come when mediation of this description only showed the more how the Quraish wished to launch fresh treachery. This great enemy of Islam, Abu Sufyan, who had been instrumental in inciting the tribesmen against the Muslims, who had plotted the assassination of The Prophet more than once, who had led his men again and again against the believers, was arrested, but having regard to the merciful behaviour of The Prophet, he was not beheaded.

In the morning, the Muslims surged over the hills and vales of Mecca, but The Prophet had ordered that no one must attack first; there should be neither looting nor plunder, no one who took refuge with Abu Sufyan was to be molested, nor any one harmed who may shut himself in his own house. Company after company of the Muslim warriors entered Mecca unopposed; not a stone was thrown, not a single battle cry raised, not an arrow discharged. The might of Islam had chilled the courage of the men of Quraish: but, anon, a party of the Meccans rose from behind the boulders on the height occupied by the cavalry under Khalid, and before the Muslim commander could realise his position, two of his men lay dead, arrows piercing their vitals. It was that solitary occasion when resistance was offered, when Khalid pursued his assailants, inflicting thirteen casualties upon the Quraish. The rest was quiet, and Mecca was occupied practically without any opposition.

And now notice the situation: the government of Medina was in the hands of one man. All tribal recalcitrancy was reduced to submission, an army of ten thousand strong and more enters in a town where men can offer no resistance, where the treasury of the Temple is overflowing with the accumulated wealth of generations, where merchandise is at the mercy of the conquering army, where in the temple men who had persecuted him stand before Mohamed who exiled him, where Muslims were tortured. What would be the first impulse of a conqueror? Should he not have all his enemies slaughtered now as they were in his grasp, should he not appropriate the treasury, should he not give up the city to plunder? Has it not ever been done in the annals of man, and has the world not condoned such actions, for the defeated must suffer for their sins?

What did Mohamed do in his hour of triumph? He ascended the steps of the idol-infested Kaaba, knocked down the idols, saying, 'the truth has arrived, sin is removed, for infidelity is a thing which perishes!' One by one, the stone-gods dismantled, pictures and effigies deleted, the black slave Bilal was commanded to ascend to the roof of the Kaaba, and call the men to prayer, to the prayer of One God, the One God Who has no partner in His realm, Who was not begotten by any one, and begets none as human beings do. To the men and women of Mecca he gave a general amnesty: only four, and strictly speaking only two men were to be executed for murder, the rest was peace and goodwill; nor were the vanquished compelled to adopt Islam if they did not want to, and then completed the promise that one day a descendant of Abraham shall clean up the sacred House of Allah. The truth of Islam was made absolute: for, indeed, it has been justly remarked that in the story of men there has been no triumphant entry like unto this one of Mohamed's entry into Mecca.

To Mohamed, the conquest of Mecca meant only one thing: the preaching of Islam, and not in any way a desire of megalomania; so, true to his mission, he started his work without delay. On the height of Safa, near the shrine of Kaaba, sat The Prophet. Batches after batches of men came up to him, placing their hands in his, they embraced Islam. The women dipped their hands in a bowl of water after him to take the oath of fidelity, and thus he sat long carrying on with the work for which his heart had hungered so long.

They came from far and near, in pairs, singly, in hordes, to pledge the oath of Islam by saying: 'We shall not adore any but the One God, we shall not commit larceny, adultery, or infanticide, nor utter falsehood, nor speak evil of women.'

Once again, he emphasised the equality amongst the Muslims: 'O! You men of Quraish', he addressed them, 'the pride with which you carried yourselves before during the period when you were in darkness is gone, gone never to return: for God willed it so.

All men are the sons of Adam, and Adam was built of clay.... In the sight of God, those only are nobles, whose actions are pious and free from evil....'

Leaving Maghaz in Mecca to continue the preaching of Islam, The Prophet left the city for Medina after fifteen days.

FROM: MOHAMED: THE PROPHET

The Battle of Hunain & Beyond

HUNAIN IS THE valley which lies between Mecca and the uplands of Taif.

In its neighbourhood also is the region of Zulmajaz, the famous market and a meeting-place of caravans; this valley was chosen by the combined forces of the tribes of Hawazin and their allies to attack Mecca before the Muslim power grew too strong for any effective opposition. In self-defence, an army of ten thousand Muslim soldiers proceeded to check the advancing desert warriors: and this was scarcely after one month of the reduction of Mecca by the Muslim arms, when the faithful thought that the time for a rest had arrived.

In the beginning when the two armies met, the Muslims charged with the fury of battle surpassing any hitherto undertaken by them. The enemy fell back, but it was only a passing phase: the archers of the desert played havoc amongst the Muslim ranks, men fell like leaves in autumn, the warriors of Islam were in confusion. A section retreated, then another, and a third till at one time it appeared that a general rout had taken place.

The knoll on which The Prophet stood was now isolated; the archers concentrated their attack upon it, the enemy was making straight for that spot. 'I am The Prophet', shouted Mohamed, 'I am the true Messenger of Allah', he called to his followers. Abas, his companion, shouted too; gradually, the fleeing soldiers tarried, and forming and reforming, closed their ranks. Throwing themselves upon the enemy with the frenzy of religious devotion, they stemmed the tide and fought to kill or be killed.

The defeat was changed in a trice into victory, the pagan Arabs were completely defeated; six thousand prisoners were taken, whilst a section took refuge in the walled fortress of Taif. The booty which fell in the hands of the Muslims was colossal, judging from the standard of those times, for the defeated foe left behind forty thousand sheep, four thousand ounces of silver, twenty-four thousand camels. These were divided amongst the soldiers, the fifth portion going to the State Treasury and for the poor.

Returning to Jarana, where the captured Hawazin were kept, The Prophet found a deputation awaiting him, says Amir Ali, which solicited the release of their relatives who had been taken as prisoners at the battle of Hunain. Aware of the sensitiveness of the Arab nature regarding their rights, he adds: The Prophet replied to the Bedouin deputies that he could not force his people to abandon all the fruits of their victory, and that they must at least forfeit their effects if they would regain their relatives. To this they consented and, according to Tibri, the next day after the prayer of the dawn, Mohamed had the deputation repeat their requests before the gathering of the faithful. The Prophet replied:

'My own share of the captives, and that of the descendants of Abdul Muttalib, I give you back at once'. His disciples, catching his spirit, immediately followed the example, and six thousand prisoners of war, attests Ibn Hisham, were set free without any further difficulty. I do not need to draw any conclusions here; an impartial judge will readily see what hold The Prophet had upon his people, as also what real magnitude of mercy he could show.

Mention might now be made to the Muslim expedition to Tabak in Syria, where the Christian vassals of Imperial Rome, notably the Arab chieftains of Ghassan, Lagham and Jazam, had persuaded their overlord to help them in attacking the Muslims at Medina. A force of forty thousand men was being gathered, but the Muslims marched to defend themselves with their usual deficiency in numbers and resources under the leadership of The Prophet.

Many Muslims perished with thirst and lack of provisions before they reached Tabuk, between Medina and Damascus, where a halt was called. But what was the surprise of the Medinites upon hearing that the muster of Roman troops could not take place, and that the emperor had his hands full at home. For twenty days, the Muslims waited at Tabuk for a foe that never came, and that in the heat of the desert during the month of Fasting too, the Muslims returned to Medina.

Soon after the return of The Prophet to his headquarters, a deputation of the refractory tribesmen of Taif waited on him. The leader of the delegates, one Otwa, embracing Islam, hurried back to his people, carrying with him the glad tidings of his conversion, but his people were of a different mind: they literally stoned him to death. The martyr's blood, says Amir Ali, soon blossomed into faith in the hearts of his murderers. Seized with sudden compunction, the men of Taif sent another deputation asking for Mohamed's forgiveness and requesting to be allowed to embrace Islam.

They begged, however, a brief respite for their idols: for two years, they could not destroy their stone gods till their people could be persuaded to detach their attention gradually from their objects of worship. The Prophet could not allow it, then a very short period of three months was asked for, but it was refused, for Islam and stone gods could not exist together, and lastly, the people of Taif requested that in the beginning they may be exempted from the five daily prayers. And Ibnul Athir records that The Prophet was emphatic on this point, for he replied that without devotion, religion was of little account. The Taifite then had to accept all the principles of Islam, prayer and worship, destruction of idols and the practice of the Muslim code of morals. But as the worship of idols was born in their bones, they sought the good offices of The Prophet to excuse them from destroying the idols with their own hands, and whom do you think was deputed to perform the duty of breaking these false gods of stone and clay, but Abu Sufyan himself – the selfsame Abu Sufyan, the archdeacon of the great shrine of Kaaba, who had led his men in the name of idol-infested Kaaba against the Muslims on many occasions, and now was a faithful follower of Allah's Messenger.

Many more deputations of Arab clans now came to Medina and embraced Islam: the chiefs of Yemen, Mahra,

Uman, Bahrain and other regions swelled the ranks of the faithful, till to all intents and purposes the entire Arabian Peninsula from the Persian Gulf to the Red Sea, from the southern uplands of Yemen to the northern confines of Medina was Muslim. And be it known that the expansion, the real expansion of Islam took place after the period of warfare. Practically, the nine years which followed Mohamed's flight from Medina was a time of constant defensive wars and expedition; none of the battles proved the fact that Islam made any but incidental and almost insignificant progress as the results thereof.

The Quraish were beaten, the Jews reduced. To the Romans it was made known that their northern legions would find hard adversaries in the Muslims, a few tribal forays were repulsed, but when one examines the net results of these campaigns, it is surprising to note that during the eight or nine years of incessant fighting, Islam as a religion progressed but slowly. But so soon as a centralised system of the Muslim commonwealth was definitely established at Medina, the zenith of which may be said to have been reached only after the Muslim expedition of Syria, the various tribes and clans came to Medina on their own accord and embraced Islam.

This is perhaps one of the most peculiar facets of Islam's progress, and explodes the myth that the preaching of Islam was affected by the sword. The sword, to all intents and purposes, was sheathed at Medina at the close of the eighth year of Hijra, so that there was no militant compulsion upon those who sent their deputations to The Prophet.

Nor indeed, can it be due to the fact that these warlike sons of Arabia, still strong and proud of their racial traditions, were suddenly seized by the fear that the Muslims will throw themselves upon them for the propagation of the faith. In the first place, these tribes were always able to hold their own against the Muslims in battle, or again might very easily form a federation against the growing power of Medina. Furthermore, in case of war, they could always contract treaties with the Muslims of good neighbourliness, and retain the right of worship in their own way, such as the terms accorded to the Jews: indeed, even to those Jews who were defeated at Khaiber.

What possible excuse is there then for not believing that these Arabs did come within the Islamic fold of their own accord; and what facts defend the theory that Mohamed spread his doctrines by a flaming sword; and finally, if you are at war, does it necessarily mean that you have been an aggressor? But you must pass judgment only when in possession of the full facts, facts without prejudice, and those that are not 'based on inferences', such as in Muir's writings, though truth sometimes escapes even through his lips, for instance, when he wrote: 'Never, since the days when primitive Christianity startled the world from its sleep, and waged a mortal conflict with heathenism, had men seen the like arousing of spiritual life, – the like that suffered sacrifices, and took joyfully the spoiling of goods for conscience' sake.'

Although Mecca had fallen during the eighth year of the Hijra, yet the full injunctions of Islamic pilgrimage were postponed till a later date: so after the expedition of Tabuk, when the time of the pilgrimage drew near, in the ninth year of Hijra, The Prophet commanded that it should be performed in complete obedience of Islamic canons; consequently three hundred pilgrims under the leadership of Abu Bakr, with Ali as standard bearer, and preachers were sent to Mecca from Medina.

This being the first pilgrimage on lines of the original pattern of Abraham, Abu Bakr read the sermon proclaiming that various ceremonies were to be performed strictly according to Islamic practices on that occasion and ever after, detailing the method of performing the several rites and prayers. This concluded, Ali rose and recited some verses of Surah Barat from The Qur'an, and announced on behalf of The Prophet of Allah that thenceforth no non-Muslim shall enter the Holy Precincts of the Kaaba, and no one shall encircle the shrine unless properly clothed; and that all engagements and treaties with the heathens after a lapse of four months should be considered null and void. The last item of the announcement is significant to show that at a time when truth had been acknowledged on all hands and the government of One God was an established fact, there was no room for idol-worship.

Even in this instance, the Muslims were advised to carry through their engagements up to date of their termination which was then only four months. It quite definitely meant that the belief in One God was the only idea on which the Established Church of The Prophet could have dealings with other people: otherwise, how could the heathens be bound to their commitments in a treaty with those who were not heathens? The underlying fact being that paganism is devoid of all religious conception, and therefore of honour on which the foundation of solemn pledges between two peoples are founded: hence with such people peaceful negotiations would ultimately dwindle down to war, and wars above all the Muslims did not want.

FROM: MOHAMED: THE PROPHET

The Life of The Prophet

AFTER GIVING A detailed narrative of what The Prophet Mohamed did as a public man, it is pertinent to examine his attitude towards his friends and relatives, his wives and children: and this facet of his character is of utmost value, because in essence it is not detached from his public virtues, for he had no dual personality. He married Khadija, a widow of forty years of age, when he himself was fifteen years her junior.

During the lifetime of Khadija, he had no other wife, but upon her death he married a virgin, Ayesha, the daughter of Abu Bakr, his age then being fifty-two; others he took in marriage were the relative of Omar and other ladies. Towards his daughter Fatima, the wife of Ali, and his grandchildren Zainub, Hasan and Husain, his love was great, for he had seen no grandchildren from the male side of her descendants.

On closer examination, we find that he practised polygamy. He acted in circumstances which best suited the condition of life obtaining then; practically all of his wives were women of an advanced age, and such widows as had been rendered destitute by the after-war results, in which their husbands had given up their lives for Islam.

There can be no question of sensuality here, no question of any considerable wealth which might have come to The Prophet by contracting such marriages, in not a few cases, as historical instances show, it was a political necessity, and a gracious act for protecting the honour and liberty of Muslim womenhood, also due to giving support to those who needed support, and deserved it. The life of such women in the harem of The Prophet was not enviable from the point of worldly goods, for without exception, all of them lived from hand to mouth: indeed, when some of them hoped for a measure of comfort, they were told frankly that Mohamed had no power and right over the state treasury beyond that of an ordinary member of the faith. A distinct example of this is furnished by the report of Omar, who visited the private apartment of The Prophet, and found him sitting on a bare cot. The various other items in the room were a mat, a bowl, a skin for keeping the drinking water, and the name of this man was in the mouths of monarchs and kings and chiefs of Arabia from north to south.

But what is this law about the plurality of wives according to which Mohamed acted; The Qur'an says: '... then marry such woman as seem good to you, two or three or four; but if you fear that you will not do justice (between them) then (marry) only one...' By this injunction no obligation to marry four women is made, only permission is granted, and a limit imposed. It is strictly speaking both a negative and an affirmative command, for it is conditional upon one bestowing the equal love and to doing justice between one's several wives. This condition is the crux of the situation, if that equal justice cannot be done, then polygamy is strictly banned. Now for a man to be equal in his devotion and just treatment towards his several wives at one and the same time is a task much beyond any average man; whosoever succeeds in this is decidedly not an ordinary man.

The review comes to the point when one may ask, was Mohamed such a husband who could treat his wives with equal justice, and facts prove it to be so. He treated them with kindness and courtesy, their maintenance allowances, though meagre, were the same, they all behaved towards him with equal kindness. Judging from the state of common society, one will be inclined to think that, if these ladies were not perfectly satisfied, they would have showed it only too readily because, even at the time when the power of Mohamed was at its zenith, the society of the desert was not free from evil tongues, and how great would have been the delight of the enemies of Islam to give wings to the reports of a discord in The Prophet's family.

We have no record of such evil reports; indeed, so great was the love between the wives of The Prophet towards each other that when evil was spoken of Ayesha, her rival bore testimony to her virtue. This is probably the most extraordinary proof, clear and undisputed, how the wives of Mohamed agreed amongst themselves, which indirectly supports the belief that The Prophet's treatment was that of justice towards his womenfolk. And so, if there be a man like unto him who could dispense equal justice amongst his wives, ordinary laws which frail man has made for himself are not valid, he is a man apart, a model to strive after. In this regard we should not, of course, forget that monogamy was made a matter of legislation in Europe by the Emperor Justinian, a Roman and a Pagan jurist.

In his manner of speech, he spoke very slowly and deliberately with a firm and clear voice, never hurried over his words. When speaking, his gaze was often lifted towards the sky. He never spoke without reason, when he gesticulated his arm rose from his side; he scarcely ever laughed aloud, but always had a smile on his lips. He walked very quickly, and his eyes did not roam as he paced in the market.

His dress was always simple, often patched and of coarse cloth. A long shirt covered the upper part of his body, the lower by a sheet, and he never used trousers. On his feet, one never saw anything but sandals; and, of course, he tied a turban upon his long flowing hair. On account of poverty – for even in the days of his greatest glory, he continued to be poor on account of giving away everything in charity – he neither cared nor generally found good food, but he liked honey, olive oil and vegetables whenever procured. He was neither very fond nor was often able to buy meat. When on his deathbed, he asked Ayesha, his wife, to give away the last remaining gold coins in the house to the poor so that when he died, his personal belonging consisted only of an armour – which was also in mortgage with a Jew – a mattress of dried palm leaves, and a water skin.

His daily routine, when in Medina, was a curious blending of work of the Church and the State. After the prayer of the dawn, he held an open court; rich and poor alike assembled to tell him of their public and private matters. Cases were heard, and justice given, envoys received and despatches dictated, and then after a brief sermon, he used to rise to pray. The public function now over, he used to go to one of his wives, make his bed, fill the water receptacles, sweep the floors, mend his sandals, or saddle, or do any other odd job which his good wife wanted him to do, even go to the market for her shopping. Then another short prayer was performed, after which he visited the sick and the poor, calling at the houses of his friends, seeking news of their welfare. Mohamed was an ideal citizen.

In the afternoons, before a large gathering of men and women, the various religious items were explained by him. Any man could come and have his doubts removed or his wrong redressed; the prayer of the late afternoon terminated this sitting, when Mohamed made a round of his harem, a few minutes with each wife, for an hour or so, till children claimed his time, with whom he played, and now the black liberated slave Bilal was calling the Faithful to the prayer of the sunset when The Prophet was again leading the Faithful in prayer.

This done, a short sermon was then given, a brief court held, and Mohamed went to any one of the houses of his harem where all women folk were assembled and talked to them till the last prayer of the night, when he retired to solitary prayer and rest. He slept for only a few hours, then rose and prayed and meditated, and used to go to bed again for a brief time, rising again to pray and to bed till dawn when the day's work began. The energy of the man was extraordinary; he never complained of fatigue, never asked for food till it was brought, never lost his temper: 'for anger is thy greatest enemy', he used to say.

Reverting to his durbars and meetings, it is significant that he destroyed the emphasis of dignity and rank and instilled equality amongst the Muslims, that when strangers used to come to the durbar they had to ask as to which was Mohamed. But despite this, there was a distinct etiquette of the meeting. No one could ask anything while he was standing: no interruptions were permitted. On one occasion, an uncouth Badu of the desert barged in and in a loud voice asked The Prophet as to when will be the Last Day of the world.

The Prophet was engaged in answering the question of someone else, he did not reply. The son of the desert insisted, and called out more loudly than before for an answer, again The Prophet ignored him, for he had not completed his reply to the other man. Eventually he turned to the Badu: 'The Last Day of the world shall be', said The Prophet, 'when the custodians will not respect their trust!' The man of the tent-dwellers did not understand as to what that meant: 'it means', enlightened The Prophet, 'a time when the government of the people will go into incompetent hands, and justice has left the world.'

It was on a particularly hot day when the government of the Muslims gathered in the quadrangle of the Mosque at Medina, awaiting The Prophet. In the meantime, the gathering of the Faithful was split up into two sections: one section deliberated on the pure ethical questions of the creed, and the other sitting under another tree were grappling with some practical points. 'I am a practical man', said The Prophet upon entering, as he joined the latter section: 'for I have been sent to show to the people how to live as God wishes them to live.'

The courtesy of Mohamed, of course, has become a proverb; or Ikhlaqay Mohamedi, the courtliness of The Prophet is still an expression common amongst the races of the East. He is never reported to have said Nay to anyone. He never contradicted anybody unless it was opposed to The Qur'anic laws, never did he get wroth with any man because of a personal affront; he paid equal regard to the humblest and the richest, he would turn away his face when anyone spoke ought but good of a person.

And above all, his pertinacity was par excellence, and this has been proved over and again in every walk of his life both in peace and war, in matters of state or in his family life. He was slow to arrive at a decision, but once whatever was resolved he meant to carry through in the face of all opposition and even persecution, as we have noted in his career. He had a charming way in giving practical lessons to people; as for instance, someone came to him complaining of extreme poverty and sought alms.

The Prophet asked him whether he had any belongings at all: 'Belongings, forsooth', replied the man, 'I have only a bowl and a cot, and that is all I possess.' He was commanded to bring the cot and the bowl, which Mohamed auctioned for a small sum. 'Take half of this money to thy children, and with the other half buy a rope and an axe, go into the country and gather wood and sell it'. After a time, the man presented himself before The Prophet, and showed his good earning. 'Verily', said Mohamed, 'thou art blessed, for thou hast worked and earned by the sweat of thy brow: for

Allah does not love begging'. Here is a practical lesson for you if you want any. Regarding his strong sense of justice, we have instances to show that once, when laying the law against theft, a woman of Arab aristocracy was charged; he said that even if his own daughter committed the crime she would be punished like a common criminal. In the eyes of Allah all are equal, and none so pleasing as he who abides by the law.

Another point about Mohamed which is apt to be forgotten is that he has left an indelible mark upon the history of mankind for one particular reason, that alone distinguishes him from others. Quite apart from the fact that he is acknowledged as a Prophet, even as a personality, as a general, a statesman, a merchant, a father and a husband he has created a pattern infinitely superior to anything known in the story of man. And that is his personal influence, his personality.

In this particular, Mohamed has no rival, for within his own lifetime people so far apart as Basra and Mecca, Medina and the cities of Yemen were behaving, acting, even thinking in the way Mohamed did. That he transformed a pagan people, and such inveterate warriors as the Quraish into a humble, peace-loving people, and to act according to the injunction of The Prophet is possible only for a man whose claim for the mastery of the world is indisputable. His birth was shrouded in no mystery: from a human father and mother he was born, he lived an ordinary life, and yet lived to deliver his people from the slough and degradation, all within ten years, is a task which staggers imagination.

If that does not mean a personality without a compeer, what else is it; if that did not mean that his message had a more than ordinary potency, how would one account for the progress, such rapid and firm progress, of the law of Allah proclaimed in wondrous language as The Qur'an, regarding which even the pagan poet-laureates declared La Kalamul Bashar – 'these are not the words of a human being?'

Let us also not lose sight of the fact that it is at once the pride and glory of Mohamed's message that his religion is a practical religion, a law consistent with the life of the world, for to withdraw one's hands from worldly activities is strictly forbidden, the progress of Society and participation in it is enjoined upon: 'to be in the world and not of it', is the idea; as therein is unfolded the beauty of the creation, and divine attributes of Allah himself, – for:

> There is a tongue in every leaf
> A voice in every rill,
> A voice that speaketh everywhere,
> In flood and fair, through earth and air,
> A voice that's never still.

And the testament of the guiding of humanity was Revealed to The Prophet: 'The servants of the Merciful are they that walk upon the earth gently, and when the ignorant speak to them, they speak; Peace! they that spend the night in worship... they that spend neither profusely nor niggardly... and slay not a soul that God hath forbidden... and commit not fornication... they that bear not witness to that which is false; and when they pass by vain sport, they pass it by unconcernedly...'this Mohamed left to humanity: and though the candle may have been blown out, the light remains.

FROM: MOHAMED: THE PROPHET

The Prophet: The Last Phase

THE LAST YEAR of The Prophet's life and Ministry had now dawned, it was A.D. 632 of the Christian Calendar, for the Revelation came to him in The Qur'an: 'When there comes the help of Allah and the victory (of Mecca), and you see men entering the religion of Allah in companies; then celebrate the praise of your Lord, and ask His forgiveness, surely He is oft-returning (to mercy).' North and south, east and west, Allah's message had been conveyed, and the whole of Arabia was now at the feet of The Prophet.

His original work was finished, his mission fulfilled, and Mohamed now so forewarned about his journey to a different world made preparations to perform the pilgrimage to Mecca as the undisputed head of the Muslim Church, the only Church that mattered in Arabia. It was necessary to perform this pilgrimage, the last pilgrimage as it turned out to be of Mohamed's life, for the various ceremonies which the master performed, the faithful should learn by first-hand knowledge, the several injunctions and practices of the pilgrimage, a pattern which remains intact up to this day, nearly fifteen hundred years after him.

With him, now more than a hundred thousand pilgrims performed the devolutions, and rites at Mecca and the regions encompassing it. In the sun-smitten plains and hills at Arafa a concourse of humanity awaited his final sermon. From his camel, he called the faithful to hear him: 'All the practices of paganism are now trampled under my feet', he lifted his voice, 'the Arab and non-Arab are equal, Adam was the father of all, and Adam was built of earth. The Muslims are brothers, equal in status, give the same food and dress to your slaves as you yourself use.

'None shall remember, and carry on the blood feuds of yore, all that sum which was charged as interest on loans is condemned and unlawful, fear God in your treatment towards women; for the right of women is just as great upon you as your right upon women. I leave the Book, The Qur'an for you; hold fast to it, or you shall so astray, give the due to whom due is to be given in heritage, adultery should be punished by stoning the person, a son who disavows his father is accursed, pay your debts, a loaned article to be returned, the guarantor is to be held responsible for what he guarantees'. Then he paused and asked what would they say to God about him if that enquiry were made: all replied that they shall attest that Mohamed had conveyed Allah's commands to them; The Prophet held up his finger: 'O! Allah, be a witness to what they have said', he concluded.

After this long sermon, other shorter addresses were given by The Prophet during this his last pilgrimage; as, for instance, when saying goodbye to the faithful, he said: 'learn all you require regarding the pilgrimage from me, for this is probably my last pilgrimage. Do not adopt your pre-Islamic habits and begin to strike at each other's necks after I go; for you will have to face Allah one day who shall require you to answer for your sins. The man who commits a sin, he alone is responsible for it, not the son for his father, and a father for the deeds of his son.

'Regarding the government, let me emphasise', added The Prophet, intending to kill the demon of colour and race prejudice, 'let me say, that even if blackest of all slaves is your officer or ruler and he conducts your affairs according to the Book of God, then obey him. Five times daily you should pray, keep fast during the month of fasting and obey the Commandments so that you may be the accepted ones.' Then again, he asked whether he had conveyed God's message and, receiving a reply in the affirmative, called to Allah to be a witness to it: after that, he enjoined upon those present to convey his words to those who were not present there at the moment, so the farewell pilgrimage ended and The Prophet was once again in Medina.

After the pilgrimage, in the eleventh year of Hijra, A.D. 632, physical frailty of Mohamed was making itself felt. The poison given to him at Khaiber was again distressing The Prophet; and yet even within a few days of his death, he continued to lead the faithful in prayer. Having said goodbye to his flock at Mecca, it was always a great thought to him that he had not prayed for the dead who had fallen at the battle of Uhad; and to that grave he now bent his steps. There, standing beside the grave of his brave and faithful servants, he prayed, and with such earnestness that although they were now buried for eight long years, one would have believed that he was in mourning for someone who had just died.

On the eighteenth or nineteenth of the Muslim month of Safar, nth Hijra, The Prophet went to the graveyards of the Muslims and felt somewhat indisposed upon his return. For five days, his illness was hardly noticed, but on the sixth day, he was decidedly worse and stayed in the house of his wife Ayesha; indeed, he had become so weak that he could hardly walk, for Ali and Abas had to help him to the harem. Repeatedly now, he endeavoured to go to the mosque in order to lead the prayer, and just as frequently fainted, till Abu Bakr was commanded to take his place at the head of the faithful at worship.

The illness took a serious turn, and he asked for paper and a pen to have his wishes recorded, the first being that no pagans should be allowed quarter in Arabia, the other that the envoy of foreign nations should be received with the same respect and should be given the same hospitality as was accorded to them during his time, the third wish could not be recorded, but over and over again he repeated 'hold to The Qur'an, consider it your way to righteousness, goodwill and peace...' Again and again, he said that those are accursed who worshipped the graves of their prophets, as the last injunction that in the religion of Islam nothing is worthy of worship save the One God, and that The Prophet was just one like unto them, a mere man, a son of Adam, made of clay and no part of divinity; though a messenger of Allah's commandments. He was anxious that men should not fall to the error of grave worship.

The morning on which Mohamed was to die, he pulled aside the curtain of his apartment and watched the worshippers at the prayer of the dawn, bending and swaying to the Allah Whose words he had come to announce; and The Prophet felt satisfied: his life work had been fulfilled, what more does any man wish for, what more can any man have? Thenceforward, he began to sink rapidly, in the afternoon any moment appeared to be his last, he recited 'there is now none so great a friend as He', and with this on his lips, The Prophet of Allah died.

Men could not believe that such a personality was just as frail as any man in the face of death, none thought him really dead: a man with such a power over the hearts of men could not, would not bow to death, but death in Islam is considered a call, a command of One who has made all, and His call when it comes is to be obeyed. To this call, who would the more readily respond than the Messenger of God himself. To a bewildered people, Abu Bakr announced the sad news and emphasised the fact that The Prophet was a human being subject to the laws of life and death like any earthborn and that he had considered himself as such, a Prophet though he undoubtedly was.

The dead body was washed by Ali and others; in the small room where he died in Ayesha's house they lowered him in his grave: thus the spirit of the great Prophet took flight to the 'blessed companionship on high 'on the first of Rabi I, about the 28th May, 632 of the Christian era. Abu Bakr, one of four of his great Companions was elected as the leader of the Faithful: the other three Khulafar Rashidin, or the Commander of the Faithful after Abu Bakr were Omar, Osman, and Ali.

'From Him we Come and to Him we Return.'

FROM: MOHAMED: THE PROPHET

The Cardinal Practices of Islam

THE FOUR CARDINAL practices of the Muslim religion are Prayer, Charity, Pilgrimage and Fasting. Whereas the Semitic precursors of Islam possessed no definite formulae for intercession, Mohamed was the first of the race to demonstrate the value of prayer as a means of moral elevation and purification of heart. As The Qur'an has it: 'Rehearse that which hath been revealed unto thee of the Book, and be constant at prayer, for prayer preserveth from crimes and from that which is blameable; and the remembering of God is surely a most sacred duty.'

As even a non-Muslim scholar has said, the temples of Islam are not made with hands and its ceremonies can be performed anywhere upon God's earth. At home or abroad, the Muslim, at the prescribed hour, approaches his Maker in brief supplication. Prayer is not a matter for the intervention of priests, but for each individual human spirit. The Islamic concept of prayer embraces supplication five times a day and, without understanding, is held to be of no avail.

Certain rites and ceremonies accompany the due observance of prayer, yet these are all regarded as subsidiary to piety and contriteness of heart. Cleanliness is a necessary preliminary to communing with Allah, hence the rites of lustration, yet mere physical purity is not held as implying true devotion. He who prays turns his face toward Mecca as being the Centre where the Faith had its birth.

Still, Muslim prayer possesses its own peculiar symbolism. Among the various gesticulations, motions and signs which a Muslim makes when praying several of the more outstanding may be noted. In the first place, he raises the hands and touches the lobes of the ears, then folds the hands across the abdomen or lets them drop by the sides. This implies that the worshipper raises his hands from worldly affairs, and presents himself as a slave of Allah, the folding of the hands representing a slave's attitude. Even The Qur'an in Oriental Court circles, ministers and envoys adopt this attitude before the ruler, and at durbars the highest officials fold their arms in the presence of Kings.

In the second phase of prayer, the Muslim worshipper stands and directs his gaze on the ground, to signify that he has been moulded from the earth to which he shall return. He recites the prayer of thanksgiving to Allah. Whilst reciting this, the attitude of mind prescribed is one of humility before one's Creator.

The supplicant then bends at right angles from the waist and recites the praises of Allah. Then he prostrates himself and touches the ground with his forehead and recites the formula praising God. The whole physical intention is opposite to that displayed by a man who stands erect, throwing back his body, his chest thrust forward, which is the attitude of defiance, the other being the idea to bend so definitely that the impression of humility is conveyed.

Charity is a marked feature of the Islamic faith. By Muslim law, everyone who can afford it is bound to contribute part of his possessions for the upkeep of the poor of the community. This was usually one part in forty, or two and a half per cent of all goods or profits on trade or business. But alms are due only when the property amounts to a certain value and has been in the possession of the owner for at least a year, nor, it is noticeable, are any alms due from cattle.

At the end of the month of Ramadan, the month of fasting, and on the day of Id-ul-Fitr, which celebrates the conclusion of the Muslim period of fasting, the head of the family has to give away in alms a measure of wheat, barley, dates, raisins, rice, or any other grain, or the value of the same, for himself and for every member of his family and for each guest who breaks his fast or sleeps in his dwelling during the month.

Those who receive the alms are specially indicated by the practice of The Prophet himself. They are the indigent, or beggars, those who help in the collection and distribution of the alms, slaves desirous of buying their freedom who have not the wherewithal to do so, debtors who cannot pay their debts, a particularly merciful dispensation. Pilgrims and strangers were also included among those in receipt of alms. General charity is also inculcated by The Qur'an in terms the most pressing.

Whereas fasting among most of the nations of antiquity was a matter more of penitence than abstinence or mortification, the institution of fasting in Islam has the definite object of encouraging spirituality through self-denial. Useless and unnecessary asceticism or mortification of the flesh is severely forbidden, the general intention being rather a chastening of the spirit by imposing a restraint upon the body. Fasting is not permitted to the sick, the weakly, the pilgrim, the student or the soldier, or to women in poor health.

The rule as to fasting, given in The Qur'an, is as follows: 'O ye that have believed, a fast is ordained to you, that ye may practise piety, a fast of a computed number of days. But he among you who shall be ailing, or on a journey shall fast an equal number of other days. And they that are able to keep it and do not shall make atonement by maintaining a poor man. But if ye fast, it will be better for you if ye comprehend. God willeth that which is easy for you'.

It may perhaps be said that the idea of pilgrimage was incorporated in the Muslim religion with the very particular object of bringing together Muslims from all parts of the world at one definite centre. The Prophet recognised that were some annual reunion not prescribed that the more distant Muslim communities might readily fall into sectarianism and schismatic tendencies, and as this was to be avoided at all costs, The Qur'an emphasised and instituted the yearly pilgrimage to the shrine of the Kaaba.

This wise provision has done more than any other to cultivate among the various Muslim sects and nationalities a spirit of general brotherhood. At Mecca, men foregather from all the ends of the Muslim earth and in a spirit of the utmost piety behold those scenes where were enacted the drama of The Prophet's early struggles and his latter triumph and consider among these sacred surroundings the institutions which he gave to humanity in his inspired words. Each year in the religious capital of Islam is rekindled the spark of that perfervid piety which glows in the hearts of the Muslims.

Even now, after more than a thousand years of Islamic history, many caravans from Jeddah journey Meccaward. With head shaven and wearing only one white sheet as the pilgrim's costume, the pilgrim nestles down in his mat-covered litter, which is tied on the back of his camel. The rocking movement to and fro of the litter, keeping time with the recitation of the names of Allah. 'I am in Thy Presence, O, the Mighty', one prays and the tongue seems to cling to the roof of one's mouth with thirst, but imbued with an intense feeling of religious fervour, the pilgrim continues, 'lead me in Thine own way, O, Allah, as I approach Thy Throne'. And the ship of the desert moves on with his fellows, munching all the time, quite oblivious of the scorching heat that beats upon the brown rocks, painting everything now violet, now red, now grey.

An indescribable feeling came upon the pilgrim on seeing the two whitewashed pillars which stand some three miles outside the city of Mecca, to mark the inviolable sanctuary of Islam, within which no blood must be shed; and all of a sudden, in the lap of encircling brown-grey hills appears Mecca.

Its buildings stand in the midst of a distant violet haze, and a huge cry of prayer from the thousands of the faithful lifts to the skies. Then they plunge into silence, a silence of reverence; some prostrating, others kneeling and lifting their tear-dimmed eyes to the city towards which they had prayed five times a day all their lives, as their ancestors had done for over a thousand years of Islamic history.

Wearing the regulation costume, they wait in the sullen heat while the sun beats down on their shaven head till room is found to approach the holy precincts. Thousands of pilgrims pace the Harem-Sharief, or the Great Mosque, waiting to kiss the mystic Black Stone, which, set in silver, is built in a wall of a small room covered by the Carpet. Around this structure, wide marble floor is laid, on which the faithful walk as they encircle the Kaaba seven times on entering the Mosque.

In the midst of this vast quadrangle of some 280 paces long and eighty paces broad, surrounded as it is by the double arches of the colonnades, stands Kaaba, where the bending and swaying of the worshippers, the loud recitations of the faithful as they face the heart of the Mosque, or clung to the curtains of the mystic Kaaba, appears to the pilgrim a world of its own.

For ten days or so, our world congregation is engaged in prayer in Mecca. From early morning till late at night there is nothing but one round of prayer and meditation. There is no lighter side to the life in Mecca. From the point of view of strict Islamic injunction, there should be nothing but that spirit in the city, because this exclusiveness of the atmosphere is considered to bring out the real essence of the faith, the more so to its follower in contrast to what he might have used in other countries prior to his coming to the pilgrimage.

Only in the evenings, when the heat of the sun abates a little, yet the rocks are warm with the day's heat, could one walk in the many covered bazaars, and examine those wonderful silks and beads that are made in and around Mecca, or climb up the adjoining hills, particularly when the moon rises, then one sees Mecca lying in the hollow as a fairyland of silver, solemn, still, mysterious, glowing with no electric lights but tallow candles paling away in the distance. The scene robs one of the fatigue of that stiff climb. Then many more religious ceremonies claim the attention of the faithful to the termination of the pilgrimage.

And in the gloaming, which quickly is swallowed up by the darkness of the desert, the pilgrim caravan moves back to the shore. Men and women, all pilgrims, appear to be dazed; they seem to drop suddenly into a vacuum completely cut off from all life of moving humanity. A joy fills their hearts for having performed the holiest action of Islamic religion. New feelings thrill their minds, and as the moon hangs like a scimitar over the brow of the rocky defiles, a thin streak on the pale face of the limitless sands is the pilgrim caravan, as that moving thread of life treks in and out of the desert hills to the shores of the Red Sea at the close of the pilgrimage.

It must not be imagined, as unhappily it too often is, that the pilgrimage to Mecca is undertaken by Muslims because of their own personal desire to gain reflected glory from a journey to the sacred precincts, for before he is deemed worthy of pilgrimage, a Muslim must have proved to his co-religionists that he is fitted for such an honour. Several conditions are laid down which are well recognised throughout Islam as being essential to the character of a pilgrim. He must be a man of ripe judgment and intelligence; he must undertake the journey of his own free will. He should possess sufficient means to carry him in comfort to Mecca and to pay for his subsistence there, and he must leave sufficient wherewithal to support his family during his absence. Again, the journey must be practicable, which means that he may be placed in some part of the world whence he may find it most difficult to make his way to the Holy City.

From these considerations, the wise and spiritual character of Islamic religious law may readily be gathered, as will the wonderful adaptability of its precepts to all ages and nations, its reasonable and logical nature, and its unfriendliness to anything that savours of the mysterious or of sentimental ignorance. It is, indeed, a most coherent body of doctrine dealing with primal truth – a corpus of religious law drawn from the natural instinct of humanity toward belief in the Divine. Thus, it is in accordance not only with the earliest faith of Man, but with his strivings for enlightenment, it is, indeed, not only a link between the Old world religion and the New, but, through its natural qualities, it constitutes a basic indication of true and unadulterated faith throughout the ages. It may indeed be said to be the world's most characteristic effort towards the formation of a religion in which all men may find agreement. In its straightforward teachings there is nothing of dubiety. Its tenets are capable of expansion in the light of modern development, its Charity is unstrained, it cannot be perverted unless by ignorance or bigotry.

The fundamental nature of Islam is well illustrated by its agreement with those doctrines which have at different periods of the world's history governed human conduct. It lays down the belief that men will be judged by their works alone, that omnipotent Providence is loving and merciful and that patience and resignation are essential to the loyal man. It inspires meticulous reference to conscience, a scrupulous study of motive and a strict reliance upon the assistance of God in all human affairs. No religion has so well gauged human character or is so practically designed to instruct its weakness and this is in itself perhaps the best criterion of the Muslim faith in that it supplies a certain guide to conduct in the affairs of everyday life, inculcating a large Charity, self-denial and a spirit of mercifulness. Nor, although rational in the extreme, is it lacking in the most lofty idealism. Nevertheless, it deals with the real and the actual, its strict intention being the elevation of humanity to the ideals of perfection. In so doing, it realises that the nature of man is frail and it seeks to refine him from his imperfection by the inculcation of brotherliness, forgiveness and benevolence.

Particularly does the doctrine of Islam trend to a state of human benevolence apart from false sentiment. It must be an active principle of life. The Muslim is taught to pardon his enemies and to refrain from strife, to deal with all men justly, to glory in right-doing, right-thinking, and right-speaking, and to regard all men as equal in the sight of God. Islam is indeed a path to be trodden, a life to be lived, and however its ancient ideals may have become shadowed or occluded by unworthy ones, like those of other religions, by the mists of time and controversy, they still remain a clear and inspired digest and commandment as to the manner in which man should deal with his fellow man.

It has been well said that an approach to the All-Perfect is the essential principle of Islam. The charge so often brought against Islam that it is narrow in its prohibitions and commandments might be brought against any of the higher types of Religion, and such a charge fails miserably when it is recalled that unless a definite and well-defined path be followed, and too wide an interpretation be eschewed, the entire spirit of religion is stultified and rendered nugatory.

Moral ideas, unless expressed in positive form, rendered precise, and of definite sanction, are obviously useless to men in any state of society, barbarous or civilised. It is not the higher ethics of a faith which appeals so much to human sentiment, when all is said, as those provisions which affect the daily lives of individuals. And indeed, it is only in virtue of the strictest accordance of the laws and rules of a faith with common morality that it can hope, through its professors, to rise to the heights of spiritual excellence. That the seed of spirituality must be implanted in soil of pious everyday duty was perceived by The Prophet more keenly than by any great religious teacher in the history of man.

FROM: MOHAMED: THE PROPHET

The Qur'an

For the benefit of those readers who cannot peruse the Qur'an in Arabic in which it was originally inspired, and who are not familiar with its subject matter and traditions, it is necessary to preface this collection of extracts from it by a brief explanatory statement.

The Qur'an is the scriptural book of Islam and was revealed to The Prophet Mohamed for mankind by divine authority. The language in which it is written is the purest form of Arabic known to scholarship, so just and eloquent in its idiom and quality that, although frequently challenged to produce even a few verses to equal its beauty of expression, the non-Muslim poets of The Prophet's era found themselves unequal to the task, and were compelled to admit that it impressed them as being a work more divine than human.

'The Book', as devout Muslims call it, was not revealed at one time to The Prophet Mohamed, but at different periods throughout his prophetic career. He was inspired to receive it in the first instance on the heights of Mecca, during a night of prayer in the year A.D. 610, when he was forty years of age. On that occasion the following verse was vouchsafed to him:

'Read, in the name of your Lord, who created, He created man from a clot, Read, and your Lord is Most Honourable, Who taught (to write) with pen, Taught man what he knew not. Nay, man is most surely inordinate.'

This verse is known as 'the Clot' because of the outstanding word of the verse. From the date in question, more or less continuously for the next twenty-three years – that is until the death of The Prophet – the work of revelation proceeded, until by degrees the whole of the Qur'an was unveiled.

The manner of revelation was thus:

When The Prophet felt himself inspired as the medium of divine utterance, he called for Zaid, his secretary or, failing him, for some available scribe or amanuensis, to whom he dictated a number of verses, sometimes of considerable length, sometimes comparatively brief. The order in which the verses were to stand was arranged by The Prophet Mohamed himself, so that at the time of his demise, the entire Qur'an was in complete written form.

At that date, its contents were widely known, and thousands of people had either read or heard it read so frequently that they could recite it word for word without the slightest error. By this means, the tenets of the Muslim faith were easily and quickly disseminated throughout the several Islamic countries, and even today public reading or reciting of the Qur'an is one of the most usual methods of spreading the faith.

Some six months after the death of The Prophet, the first Khalifa, Abu Bakr, at the behest of the second Khalifa, Omar, caused the pages of the Qur'an to be collected, and arranged its material into book form. The volume thus compiled came into the possession of Omar, who bequeathed it to his sister. The third Khalifa, Usman, had a number of accurate copies made from the original text for the use of the faithful throughout Arabia.

It is the proud boast of the Muslim worshipper that the book he cherishes has not been altered by a single letter or even by a diacritical point since it was reduced to writing from the utterance of The Prophet thirteen centuries ago. This is, indeed, quite the most remarkable claim of its kind in the history of sacred literature. When one recalls how the sacred books of other creeds have been altered and tampered with until scholars have hesitated to credit them with any authority whatever, the unimpeachable authenticity of the Qur'an must be regarded as among the phenomena of the world's inspired revelations.

The Qur'an in its essence is descriptive of a code, or system of morality, ethics and life-conduct of the most comprehensive character. It lays down a rule or 'way' of life for the faithful Muslim of the fullest and most meticulous kind. He believes that there is nothing outside its scope.

The Qur'an, according to the Muslim code, supplies sound direction for all the affairs and perplexities of life. The pious Muslim, when in doubt as to his line of conduct, searches his memory for the text appropriate to the situation, and never fails to find it. Thus, besides being an ethical guide and a handbook of morality, the Qur'an is also a book of good manners and an authority on the humanities.

No Muslim is permitted in any way to alter the text of the Qur'an, and in translating it, the most extraordinary care has to be exercised. Millions of people commit it to memory every year and recite it during the month of fasting in its entirety.

It is not to be implied that the extracts from the Qur'an which appear in the following pages are in any way representative or embracive of the spirit of the Qur'an as a whole, or that they have been selected as the choicest passages of that immortal work. My selection has, indeed, been dictated almost entirely by considerations of modern utility, that is, I have tried to confine it to excerpts which seemed to me to supply guidance on the problems of modern life.

I hope, however, that the reader will not remain content with mere excerpts but will be encouraged by their perusal to read the Qur'an as a whole for the sake of the nobility and beauty of its grave philosophy and its wise and courageous humanity, as well as for the emanation of the divine spirit of which it is eloquent.

The religion inculcated by The Prophet Mohamed is a purely monotheistic one, that is, it recognizes one God alone, and is, indeed, the only religion in the world which separates the identity of God from all other relationships. In so doing, it makes a very clear and cogent appeal to the natural instinct in mankind to believe in one almighty Father and Creator, perfect and unparalleled. The way of life set forth in the Qur'an is that of virtue unalloyed. In no other religion, perhaps, is virtue so plainly shown to be its own reward.

Sin carries with it the germs of future punishment, which cannot be avoided. To sin against the law of God as revealed in the Qur'an is assuredly to invite consequences of chastisement if the misdemeanour be petty, or disaster to soul and body if it be serious. Thus, man makes his own fate; he is not inexorably led by destiny, as so many non-Muslim writers on the Islamic religion would have us believe, but has perfect free-will inasmuch as, although 'the scheme of things entire 'has been planned by the Almighty from the beginning', a large margin of absolute freedom has been left to individual conduct.

The Prophet Mohamed found the religion of his people a low form of tribal fetishism and superstition, incorporating the worship of stones and similar objects. The feeble sanction this belief retained among them was insufficient to check irregularities of the grossest kind. Immorality and dishonesty were rife among the Arabs of his youth and the law, both religious and civil, was more honoured in the breach than in the observance.

These abuses The Prophet set himself to abolish. He recognized that under such a degrading paganism as then obtained in Arabia the race was bound to deteriorate and finally disintegrate and disappear unless a higher form of faith were adopted. In seeking for this, he was guided by an instinct, to cast himself on the compassion of that unknown God who, he felt rather than knew, must govern the Universe.

After making an exhaustive study of other religions, he discovered in them some things that were of excellence, and this he freely acknowledged in a manner of such frankness as has never been equalled in the course of religious controversy. But in these systems, he was repelled by the invasion of the idea of strict monotheism by tenets which in one way or another detracted from the supremacy of the personality of God, to which he adhered with an inspired insistence of faith.

Imitating the ancient patriarchs of his race, he sought to walk with God. Much of his mystical methods and philosophy is indeed due to the influence of patriarchal tradition, and in this he was surely and soundly guided, as it was in consonance with the whole ancient practice and higher thought of the Semitic peoples.

Seeking diligently for God, steeping himself in the essence of the emanation of the Absolute, he at length became conscious of his worthiness and ability to act as the medium of divine revelation. Then, the heavenly afflatus descended upon him, and he did not shrink from the public utterance of what had been revealed to him. At first his fellow countrymen were inclined to scoff at what they believed to be his pretensions to inspiration, for in his case, as in that of others, credence for prophets in their own country is far to seek.

But eventually, they could not fail to be impressed by an earnestness and a conviction so intense and so manifestly unselfish. The best elements among his people recognized that if the world is to be saved from comparative ruin, it must embrace the teaching and system of this man who spoke out of divine authority, and who pointed to them the way out of shame and confusion to the path of honour and order.

In time, the native goodness that is in all peoples responded to The Prophet's appeal, and gradually grew daily and burgeoned into a passionate enthusiasm for righteousness which swept the dregs of the old paganism and immorality before it into oblivion. But The Prophet Mohamed, even in the height of success, maintained a singleness of purpose which revealed the genuineness of his intention. A man of less faith or righteousness, carried away by the success of his plan, might have made pretensions to divine origin or supernatural character.

But it is to the everlasting glory of The Prophet that he not only disdained and discredited all assumptions of the kind, but sternly discouraged them. That he, a human man, had been made the mouthpiece of the living God was, he maintained, a circumstance of more value to mankind than if he had possessed any association with divinity, as it proved the ability of man, would he worthily and humbly approach the Creator, to achieve direct communication with God.

If the legal code of secular conduct laid down by The Prophet is strict, it was so dictated by the social looseness which preceded his season of authority. But this notwithstanding, it is agreed by all sound critics that it is capable of expansion and adaptation to modern uses and necessities.

It contains the germ of all worldly politics and moral and behaviourist codes and systems. It is so constructed that its application to the larger issues and problems of modern existence is not only perfectly feasible, but capable of any rational extension by persons of honest purpose, and its value from this point of view has long been recognized not by the jurists and doctors of Islam alone, but by those of other faiths and codes.

FROM: EXTRACTS FROM THE QUR'AN

The Spirit of Islamic Ideals

PERHAPS NO PART of the Islamic ideal is so greatly misunderstood as the particular spirit which underlies and goes to inspire it. Broadly speaking, it may be asserted that the cardinal truth regarding the spirit of Islamic thought is the sense of unity which it emphasises. This, of course, arises out of the idea of the oneness of Allah, His essential unity, the integral nature of His being. Allah, according to Muslim belief, was not begotten, was not united in marriage, nor had He any progeny. He is unique, nor does anything stand between Him and that humanity which is His creation.

This conception of unity is found as a natural sequence in every department of the Islamic religion and polity. If, for example, we seek for it in the idea of worship we discover it in full measure. Five times a day the world of Islam, wherever it may be situated, addresses itself in prayer to its Creator. Thus, when one Muslim is praying at dawn at afternoon, at late afternoon, at sunset or at night, he is aware that every Muslim is doing precisely the same, whether it be in China, in India, in Afghanistan, in Arabia or in England. Moreover, he is observing the same particular motions and is reciting his devotions in Arabic, whatever his mother tongue.

There is thus a universal language in use among Muslims, and by praying at one and the same hour they establish a universality of time. A unity of worship is also respected, and this is associated with a consensus of spiritual thought and impulse. At the hour of prayer, too, each and every Muslim faces Mecca, so that all the circumstances of prayer embrace that ideal of totality which springs from the belief in one God.

The centralisation of the Muslim world in Mecca, where all races of whatever colour and language trend in pilgrimage, brings about, furthermore, a universality of social thought. From Mecca, men return to practically every part of the world, carrying with them those ideals of brotherhood which transcend race and language and which compose a tremendous force for the quickening of the belief in social equality. Five times a day, master and servant stand side by side in prayer, and this alone suffices to quicken a sense of fraternity unknown in Western society.

These considerations are jointly and severally indicative of two express ideals: the oneness of God and the oneness of humanity, for God is one and so are His creatures. What other system of thought has so definitely established an ideal so expressive of unity?

It is often rashly stated that the nature of the Islamic religion is highly dogmatic, that its institutes are hedged round by hard and fast laws almost of the nature of taboos. The folly of such a statement is extreme opinions as to the utilisation of natural forces wherever they were to be encountered. It was the destruction by The Prophet of the fear of elemental force, of the superstitions that lay behind the belief in the potency of inanimate things, that in the first place made is possible for men to explore the potentialities of nature. Before his time, the mere fact that they worshipped these forces and were thus afraid to examine or harness them for the behoof of humanity, had made a scientific attitude impossible.

Within the following generation, not one but many schools of scientific effort in thought, in chemistry and in early engineering, arose in various parts of the Islamic world. One has only to point to the extraordinary genius of the Arab and Moorish schools of Chemistry upon which all modern chemical endeavour has been founded, to prove that this was so. Indeed, it is not too much to say that had it not been for the liberal and modern outlook of The Prophet, the position of Science, The Qur'an would certainly be many generations behind. The false taboo broken, men at once addressed themselves to the study of the physical nature of those elements they had previously adored, and in so doing unloosed possibilities and marvels beside which the ancient magics supposed to be resident in the subjects of their studies, paled into insignificance. If nothing else suffices to prove the finality of Mohamed's prophethood, the inspiration which he thus set free would demonstrate its divine quality, nor is this of which we speak in any way related to dogma, justified as it is by science.

It is, however, still more irrational to regard The Prophet's belief in the life hereafter as of the nature of a dogma. More than ever does man now believe in a continuance of life beyond the grave. Man is the outcome of a long and special development, and it is scarcely conceivable that the brief period of his existence on this earth should be other than a preparation for another and fuller life.

The separate existence of spirit is generally acquiesced in The Qur'an by men of all faiths, and these will readily agree with The Prophet's attitude to this great question. But it is not so generally understood that Mohamed, more than any other teacher, laid particular stress on the more precise character of the afterlife, especially with regard to its atmosphere and conditions. The idea that he regarded it as a mere sensuous Paradise has, of course, arisen out of the exaggerated notions of later non-Muslim scholiasts and commentators, from whom Islam has suffered, as have other religions. But an examination of his inspired revelation will provide a very different picture of the afterlife from that which is entertained by popular supposition. If the antagonist of Islam condemns it because it necessitates a belief in Eternity, then he must at the same time condemn the belief of millions of non-Muslims.

A point worthy of note regarding The Prophet is the veiled character of his personality. This extraordinary man who changed the course of human history, how much is actually known about him? He was not divine; no divine birth was claimed for him. But he certainly possessed the divine right of personality in the worldly sense of the term. The phrase 'Divine Right of Kings' describes the significance of the term in this respect.

Kingship has usually rested upon three bases: armed force, wealth and segregation from the public. The army always established the power of the king, money supported it and rendered him popular, but undoubtedly the most potent instrument for creating an atmosphere of divine right is personality. Legends were woven around the name of king until, to the minds of the people, he appeared almost as a god. He was unapproachable, he did not mix with the people, the mass-mind conjured up legends regarding him until he appeared remote and dwelling in an almost non-human sphere.

But when The Prophet began his mission, he was destitute of any of those advantages. He had no armed forces behind him, the people were hostile to him, he was without means and so far from being remote from the public they could have access to him at any time, for Mohamed had practically no private life. In this, he was unlike most Oriental kings and potentates, who at that period were seldom seen in public. It was, indeed, the open book of his personality which made him so popular as a ruler and which permitted him to alter the relationships between monarch and subject.

Mohamed indulged in no supernatural manifestations; he lived a plain and simple life, a poor man's life indeed, he never flinched from practical work, he fought like a common soldier in the ranks, bought and sold goods like an ordinary tradesman, mixed with people of every kind and made no difference between persons as regards condition of birth, or wealth. At length, by this means the whole of Arabia lay at his feet and gave allegiance to one God. The old idea of the peculiar sanctity of prophets and leaders was broken forever so far as the Islamic religion was concerned, for Mohamed showed that it is the part of the true leader to identify himself with those he leads, and not to appear as on a different plane from them.

If this liberal attitude was not carried out by later Islamic rulers, it was certainly not the fault of The Prophet, nor was it due to the weakness of the lesson which he had bequeathed to them – a lesson which might well be taken to heart by all governors of men wherever their lot may be cast.

On his deathbed, and when too feeble to join his followers in the worship of Allah in the Mosque at Medina, he faced his end cheerfully. 'My mission is fulfilled, praise be to Allah', he said, lowering the curtain of his cell that looked toward the mosque. Pagan Arabia had been redeemed to the eternal glory of this wondrous man, who, single-handed, approached the gigantic task of changing a world, and succeeded in changing it to his own virtuous desire.

The great triumph of Mohamed was that he brought the idea of the unity of God back to a world which had practically forgotten it, and in a certain sense had never realised it. As is well known to the students of Comparative Religion, the modern researches have established the truth of the hypothesis that primitive man, wherever he is to be found The Qur'an, naturally believes in the existence of a great God who looms behind the dark superstitions which form the religion of the savage. Doubtless, behind the fantastic beliefs of the pagan Arabians, this ideal of a single great deity was to be found obscured by broken mythologies and gross fancies and, indeed, we are assured that their Semitic brethren in Palestine and elsewhere had long entertained a similar doctrine.

But the struggle for the supremacy of that belief was a prolonged one, covering nearly 2,500 years of time. The Jahvists of Palestine certainly made the earliest essays in monotheism, but the deity whom they placed above all others was simply a form of a rather localised wind-god, and not even the most strict among Jewish or Christian doctrinists would now agree that this early form in any way resembles the later conceptions of deity recognised by their faiths. It was, indeed, reserved for Mohamed to give to the world the first conception of God as a being of justice and mercy, not associated with any particular mythology, race or nation, not favouring any particular people.

This, indeed, had been the curse of the older religions, but when they conceived the idea of a great God, he was usually regarded in the light of a national leader, a god of battles, whose chief desire was the triumph of his worshippers over their neighbours. This tribal idea of God, Mohamed discarded entirely, substituting for it a belief in the idea of a world deity, a god to whom the peoples of all the earth were equal.

Out of this conception of godhead, there could not but emerge a much more liberal spirit of tolerance.

When the people of Islam conquered a province, and that province accepted their faith, its inhabitants at once became their equals. This is, indeed, the secret of the ready acceptance of the Islamic faith even The Qur'an, by millions of people in Africa and Asia. Christian missionaries and other observers frequently express great surprise at the manner in which mere Mohamedan merchants succeed in converting pagan peoples in these continents, where they, with all their experience and equipment, have failed; but the reason for their success is to be discovered in the circumstance that the son of Islam adopts an attitude of fraternalism which the European Christian is loath to affect. While his religion may dictate to the Christian the necessity for brotherhood, his racial inhibitions and traditions make it almost impossible for him to carry it out, but this in no wise restrains the Muslim.

Unity is, therefore, both the nucleus and the aim of the Islamic faith and polity. A unity which springs from a belief in the oneness of the Creator, and which spreads out to and inspires everything in creation. From this idea of oneness, every belief in the Islamic faith has its rise and sanction; there is one God, one Prophet, one faith, one law, one status for mankind. The beautiful and simple perfectness of the scheme is the best proof that it emanated from a divine source, and directed by a personality, who has changed human history.

FROM: MOHAMED: THE PROPHET

Mecca Revisited

I AM WRITING this in Mecca – a new Mecca.

It is twenty-five years ago, almost to the day, since I visited and studied the then new Kingdom of Saudi Arabia and its Dependencies. In this time, almost unbelievable changes have occurred in the improvement of economic, educations, and hygienic conditions. The port of Jeddah has a new quarantine, capable of handling four thousand Muslim pilgrims at a time.

In the pilgrimage season, on average, one aircraft lands at Jeddah's modern airport every five minutes. Each traveller must pass the health control. No longer is condensed sea water consumed: water piped through the mains from the abundant spring of Wadi Fatma provides the rapidly growing city with two million gallons of fresh water daily.

Modern shopfronts and towering buildings line the main thoroughfare four thousand of the newest motor-vehicles ply each day between the pilgrim port. And Mecca along the newly asphalted road to the Holy City.

As we sped along this motor road, passed the ribbon-development of air-conditioned villas, it was evident that even the road itself had changed. Beyond the control point, past which non-Muslims must not travel, the road builders have quite literally carved their way with bulldozers through the bleak igneous hillsides. The stark turrets of guardian forts built by Turks perch deserted on the hilltops.

His Majesty King Abdulaziz Ibn Saud's vigorous campaign long since broke the power of marauding bandit gangs to whom so many exhausted pilgrims once fell victim. At regular intervals along the road, concrete shelters and tapped water provide welcome breaks for the Hajis – many of whom still journey on foot in the blazing heat – to rest and drink.

On either side of the forty-five-mile road, the former brackish wells which provided the only refreshment before are falling into unregretted disrepair.

At Kilometre 10 out of Jeddah, a flourishing government-established agricultural centre produces fruit and vegetables. Here, seedlings for new tree plantations are reared, and new crops suited to the arid soil are tested. At off-peak periods, when Jeddah's water consumption drops, Wadi Fatima water, piped from forty-five miles away, is diverted through the irrigation channels to this site. Within five feet of the desiccated desert soil, I saw melons, auberges, tomatoes, and many other plants flourishing here under a competent Saudi agronomist.

The Arabian-American Oil Company's concession at Dharan has poured life-blood into the Saudi Arabian economy, masking His Majesty King Abdulaziz Ibn Saud not only independent of pilgrim revenues, but also able to embark on ambitious projects for opening up the country's potentialities.

Even in Mecca, the market shops are piled high with goods from America – including radios and other electrical goods, and even tinned foods from the American heartland. I never saw an old car during my visit and, seemingly, only the latest models are in demand and use.

Education and hygiene have greatly improved living conditions in the city, though the traditional devoutness and charm of the Meccans have not altered since my first trip to visit the 1926 World Conference.

Here, in the Holy Sanctuary, the essentials of the Shrine naturally remain unchanged. Under the blazing heat of the sun, the circumambulation of the towering black-draped Kaaba continues ceaselessly.

At the time, great improvements have vastly contributed to the comfort of the pilgrims. In the enormous quadrangles arched colonnades, electric fans mitigate the heat of the day. Devout worshippers may read their holy books at night under electric lighting, while the Call to Prayer is now made through amplifiers.

Sheikh Mohamed Shatta, the director of Saudi Arabian Broadcasting, who controls an enthusiastic band of Arab workers – many of them are Palestinian refugees – plans to let the Muslim world hear within a few months the voice of Mecca five times a day on the shortwave. Maintenance and rigid policing continue ceaselessly within the sanctuary.

The former unhygienic and fly-ridden roadway between the hallowed points of Safa and Marwa (associated with Hagar's running in search of water), has been roofed over, cleaned up and paved, to transform what was once an unpleasant scene into a delightful experience.

Within the Sanctuary, folding sun blinds shield the worshippers from the fierce Arabian sun. Where one bought water at two-and-a-half riyals (five shillings) a glass twenty-five years ago, it is now available in abundance.

Effective quarantine measures, pest control and efficient use of modern germicides have entirely eliminated epidemics, in spite of the fact that there are at times as many as five hundred thousand pilgrims taking part in ceremonies.

In Mecca's most important hospital, the Director General of Public Health explained that water was the keynote of local hygiene. Old insanitary wells are being displaced by a supply from the uncontaminated spring at Ain Honain, about twelve miles from the city. Even at the Holy Well of Zam Zam, within the precincts of the Shrine, a motor-pump is being installed to do away with manual drawing.

As soon as piped water became available in Mecca and Jeddah, there was a seventy percent drop in the incidents of water-borne disease. Typhoid, once endemic, has virtually disappeared.

The most recent testing time for Saudi Arabian health services came three months ago, with a serious outbreak of Gambia Malaria. From an initial incidence of three hundred cases daily, the epidemic was stamped out within the brief period of two months.

Although there is still a regrettable lack of domestic sanitation in the houses of Old Mecca, I was assured that modern flush systems will be installed as the shortly expected increase in the water supply is achieved.

Flying from Jeddah in the Saudi Airlines machine northeastwards to see the King at Riyadh, one noted the long, tortuous ribbon of the Riyadh road. The former five-day motor journey has been telescoped into a three-and-a-half-hour flight over tactless desert and wind-eroded mountain peaks. As we neared the Saudi capital, the green cultivated desert settlements of the Wahabi Brethren created by the King for the roving tribes indicated that the nomad settling scheme was bearing fruit.

Within ten minutes of landing, I was lodged in the Royal Guesthouse –a palace built in three weeks for the recent visit of King Zahir Shah of Afghanistan. An unusual honour was granted to me, for the King, who looks robust for his seventy-odd years – granted me an audience the same afternoon, though reception audiences are usually in the morning.

Now the world's fourth greatest oil producing nation, Saudi Arabia's collaboration with the American enterprise is cordial and close. The Dhahran instillations are of a magnitude beyond belief, considering their age to be just over twelve years.

In addition to oil, American interests and engineers are actively working on problems of the country's water, agriculture, technical education – and even on railway-building.

Four thousand Americans reside in the oil-producing area alone, producing a monthly average of two million tons of oil. Experts of President Truman's Point Four Plan are also working here; and I met an engineer in charge of water in the south.

While there is every indication of increasing Arab-American cooperation in the Saudi Peninsula, British activities here also exist, though naturally on a much smaller scale. Among those worthy of note is the building by a the British of the Jeddah-Medina road, of which nearly fifty miles have already been laid.

A British military mission is helping to train units of the Saudi Army, while reel pioneering work in the anti-locust campaign is being carried out by an enterprising British group whom I visited, and whose cheerful spirit and hard work is to be admired.

His Majesty King Abdulaziz's sons have been most efficiently trained in the difficult art of government. They include the Crown Prince Emir Saud, the Viceroy of the Hejaz, and the Foreign Minister, Emir Faisel, and Emir Mansur, the Minister of Defence.

To British well-wishers of the Saudi regime, Emir Faisel's name is an abiding memory of cordiality and wise statesmanship. It is no less so to the controlling minds of the Muslims who I have met. The sons of the King are loyally served by such men as Sheikh Abdullah Sulaiman and Sheikh Mohamed Surur in the realms of nationally economy; and Sheikh Fuad hamza and Sheikh Yussuf Yasin in International Affairs.

Finis

www.ingramcontent.com/pod-product-compliance
Lightning Source LLC
Chambersburg PA
CBHW022057090426
42743CB00008B/639